CRIMINOLOGY

Over 1,300

QUESTIONS AND ANSWERS

UK, EU AND INTERNATIONAL CRIME/LAWS

BY

James Safo

LLM (Master of Laws o/g), BA(Hons), Dip criminology, Dip. Business Law, legal researcher. Cert Ed, Cert Acct. Microsoft specialist

Content | From Approx. page

Disclaimer (Exclusive clause)

The author and all employees disclaim any incorrect interpretation wrong answers to questions or text, harm include emotional, psychological, and physical or any form of harm to the reader/listener or being given information by third parties. Furthermore, this disclaimer protects all contributory people, directors, employees, 3rd party, and author and will not be liable for any injury caused.

First edition June 2020

Dedication

I dedicate firstly to the Trinity: Almighty God, Jesus Christ and the Holy spirit.

And by God commandment,

Secondly, To all my hypocrite friends and those who gain as a result of my miscarriage of justice

As a believer in Almighty God, I forgive you all, but you must pray to God for forgiveness

.

Preface

This publication is about 600 pages divided into 44 chapters and sub chapters contain more than 1,300 questions and answers. Is specially written as reference for everyone to benefit include police, probation officers, prosecutors and lawyers. College, undergraduate and postgraduates up to Master of law level. in most cases people appear reluctant to read the whole book or even chapters to gain the knowledge. As a legal researcher, I found people are more likely to glance through the questions, chose their interest, then refer to the page for the answers which this book provide. The answers are straight to the point and most of the terminology have been defined and explain to help both lawyers and non-lawyers to refer to

This publication covers many frequently asked questions which include; both national and international crimes, statistic, law enforcement agencies who combat them. some sensitive crimes. countries of high criminal, safe countries, The sources of international criminal laws, How some countries use their military power against weaker nations and then they claim self-defence

I have gone in depth some of the potent crime include, drugs, sex, alcohol, tobacco, Hi-tech computer oil, fuel, weapons, human parts and sale, trafficking, types of fraud. I have also look at the psychology of the criminals, youth antisocial/ delinquency, violence, types of properties crime, terrorism, 419, Aggression, Genocide, War crimes,Torture, Drug offenses, Bribery of foreign public officials, Human trafficking, Cybercrime, Organ trade, Wildlife trade, Blood diamond, Counterfeiting, Illegal mining, Money laundering, Illegal gambling, Arms trafficking, Illegal unregulated and unreported fishing, Illegal logging and much more. Have covered terrorism, genocide, war crime. Establishment of different international bodies to deal with both national and international crime. Immunity of head of state from criminal activities,. The Biggest challenge facing enforcement of international law, some key legal terms in criminology and lot more

As result of most of my readers request who have read many of my books, this publication is similar format as some of my academic questions and answers books example The Law" over 1,160 questions and answers which covers most of United

Kingdom, Europe, human right and international laws. Financial accounting (over 1,142 questions) on most areas of financial accounting, and “Love all faiths” about 1,200 questions and answers on about 15 different religious faiths

I hope this publication gives invaluable knowledge but as always, laws are always being in transient amended, abolished etc. but hope this might lead to research more of one’s interest.

Acknowledgement

This book is totally devoted to our creator who I serve as his slave,
I cannot compare myself to Jesus Christ, or God's prophets up to prophet Muhamad who was believed to be the last prophet who God revealed his Holy words the Quran.
But I can say to the whole world that the journey God has taken me through is equivalent to prophets Job and Joseph as reported in the Bible and Quran and shortly to be published my autobiography.
I also accept the philosophy books on Buddhism Hinduism, Sikhism and any book which highlight God's ten commandments in full to be practiced by their followers as way of life. God accept and gave human being the choice of how, when, where they wish to worship, praise and Glorify Him. We must all forgive and love each other irrespective of faith, creed, gender so that we can be strong and united. In other to give us a chance to be selected to go to heaven on the judgement day.
On judgement day, it will take less than "15" fifteen minutes for all human in the universe, dead and alive from when the first human Adam was created, and the decision cannot be appealed.
I predicted in 2014 that only about 1% people may go to heaven, which might even include people who

practice the ten commandments but do not go to church.

Who is God

I regard" God \ Allah " as the Greatest architect, Geometrician and the Greatest, overseer of the universe, omnipotent, just, holy, independent, spirit, one, personal. God can hear, see, speak to, feel, smell , control actions of human , animals and plant at the same time.

He is Almighty, everlasting and Sovereign God.

he is the only one who can penetrate into the secret recesses of the heart of human because. He is the head king, eternal, and immortal, invincible the only wise god be the kingdom, the power and the glory for ever and ever.

About the Author

I was an abandon child at the age of about four. As an adult I became a high-profile international entrepreneur based in England for over twenty-five years I was arguably one of the most successful black people in Europe at the time, I have six children and five grandchildren by 2020. On two occasion over 30 years I lost everything but bounced back stronger than before. I then faced miscarriage of justice after 40 years in in United Kingdome, But I bounced back stronger despite conspirators attempt to kill me. I understand, I am leading author publisher of religious books in the world which include on all the major faiths and most of them translated to Arabic, Chinese, English French, and Spanish. Also one of few authors in Europe who have written academics books for colleges universities in different subjects include Law, accounting, business, healthcare, counselling, psychology, criminology poems etc (list of books just before reference page of this book) , (over 30 books paper backs and 35 eBook). My qualifications include four degrees and fifteen diplomas/certificate LLM(Master of Laws o/g) (to complete 2021), BA(Hons) law and accounting, cert, Ed, RMN, GN, cert ACCT, Dip. Business law, computer, writing-films, radio biography, Microsoft specialist certified professional certificate in financial and management accountant and more etc (See list just after reference page). Three times I was strip of my wealth, and three times I came back stronger but this time I feel more closer to Almighty God than before. My message to universe; Forgiveness and love everyone, believe, trust and have faith in God, is key to heaven. Although faith in God is invincible, it makes impossible possible.

CONTENT Approx. page.

Criminology question and Answers

Chapter 2

Definition (Q 1-12)

1. Q: Why do crime happen
2. Q; Define criminology
3. Q: How will you define criminology simply?
4. Q: Defend crime in another perspective.
5. Q: What need to be considered when defining criminology
6. Q: How did William and Me define criminology theory
7. Q: How did the House of Lords in United Kingdom define crime
8. Q: How did Blackstone defines crime
9. Q: How did sociology derived their definition
10. Q: What other ways can crime be define?
11. Q; Why is criminology sometimes called "criminal justice theory"
12. Q: Define criminology in broader view?

Chapter 3

Crimes (13-40)

13. Q; Name examples of crimes
14. Q Define theft
15. Q: Name one type of theft and give reason
16. Q: What could be the effect of stealing.

17. Q: give example of stealing you have witnessed or heard of
18. Q: How do some people steal
19. Q; Give example of opportunity stealing?
20. Q; Who gives chance for stealing?
21. Q; How do the thieves behave?
22. Q: Give another opportunity stealing
23. Q: How does opportunity stealing from vulnerable people.
24. Q: name one thing opportunity thieves use?
25. Q: What do this usually steal when they break into properties and when does it take place?
26. **Q:** Give serious crime you have heard?
27. Q: Describe another incident
28. Q: Describe shop lifting?

Petty thief

29. Q:Describe example of petty thief
30. Q: Give example of violent crime?
31. Q: Give another example of crime

Racial abuse

32. Q: Who are the victim of racial abuse?
33. Q: Give an example of racial crime?
34. Q: What is police reaction in racial and violent areas

Sexual assault

35. Q: public place does sexual assault takes place?

Drugs

36. Q: who are target in drugs
37. Q: What happens when the buyers do not have money.
38. Q: Name few other crimes
39. Q: What result from unemployment?
40. Q: What other crime globally

Chapter 4

Perceiving these criminals (Q 41-56)

41. Q: are available to detect these criminals.
42. Q: Explain where and how CCTC use to detect crime?
43. Q: Explain where and how Alarm is used to detect crime?
44. Q: Explain where and how car alarm is used to detect crime?
45. Q: Explain where and how Police is used to detect crime?

46. Q: Explain where and how CCTC used to detect crime?
47. Q: Explain where and how Lie detector been uses to detect crime?
48. Q: Explain where and how communication been uses to detect crime?
49. Q: Explain where and how citizen arrest been uses to detect crime?
50. Q: Explain where and how community policing been uses to detect crime?
51. Q: Explain where and how reward has been uses to detect crime?
52. Q: Explain where and how identity parade been used to detect crime?
53. Q: Explain where and how identity parade been used to detect crime?
54. Q: Explain where and how football authority been used to detect crime?
55. Q: Explain where and how security and protection been used to detect crime?

56. Q: Explain where and how Whistle blowers been used to detect crime?

Chapter 5

Theory (57- 93)

57. Q: Do human needs “theory” and why?
58. Q Give examples of generalisation theory?
59. Q: What is the problem of theory of generalisation?
60. Q: When do people turn to over generalise and why?
61. Q: In what areas can over generalisation be harmful?
62. Q: Define acceptable behaviour and how it could unfairly lead to suspect of crime.
63. Q: What are the main types of theories?
64. What is concrete theory?
65. Q: What is Abstract theories?

Common Sense Theory v. Scientific Theory

66. Q: What is common sense theory
67. Q: Give example of some believe which is not true?
68. Q: What is the problem of common-sense theory?
69. Q: What is the way we think?
70. Q: What did Fred Kerlinger view about common sense and scientific theory in relation to the current trend in criminal justice research

71. Q: According to Fred Kerlinger, what is common sense theory based on?
72. Q: According to Fred Kerlinger, what is scientist theory based on?
73. Q: According to Fred Kerlinger, how is control in science, explain control in this context?
74. Q: According to Fred Kerlinger, what is the reaction of non- scientist.
75. **Q**: According to Fred Kerlinger, what do people think of metaphysical explanation?
76. Q: What does metaphysical explanation mean and give example?
77. Q: While it is true that scientists reject metaphysical arguments as unscientific?
78. Q: why scientists do not attempt to answer many important questions, such as “what is justice?” especially in criminal cases?
79. Q: If scientist cannot give metaphysical explanation, which areas of study can?
80. Q: Why do scientist disagree about theory?

81. Q: What non-scientific method of knowing that cause problems in criminal justice system
82. Q: Explain "method of tenacity"?
88. Q: What is "method of authority"
83. Q: Give an example of why authority sometimes needs to be challenged?
84. Q:Explain the method of intuition.
85. Q: Explain different meaning of "theory" between scientist and non-scientist?
86. Q: Why is it that scientist reluctant to use the word proven?

What Makes a Good Theory?

87. Q: From scientific point of view, what is good theory?
88. Q: What is the difference between social science and natural science
89. Q: Name two method of measuring and test theory of not knowing?
90. Q Explain Quantitative *research*?
91. Q: What is qualitative research
92. Q: How do we regard good theory?
93. **Q:** What is parsimonious?

Chapter 6

Crime problem solving (94-125)

94. **Q:** What are the two-problem solving method use in solving in crime?
95. **Q:** What does PROCTOR stand for?
96. Q: What does SARA stand for

97. Q: SARA, if the problem Accidental drug related death involving methadone , what will be the Analyse cause
98. Q: : SARA, if the problem Accidental drug related death involving methadone , what will be Response for tactic or treatment
99. Q: SARA, if the problem Accidental drug related death involving methadone, what will be the assessment output
100. Q: SARA, if the problem Accidental drug related death involving methadone, what will be the expected result
101. Q: SARA, if the problem is Disorder late at night at pizza parlours What will be analyse cause?
102. Q: SARA, if the problem is Disorder late at night at pizza parlours What will be Response Tactic/Treatment

103. Q: SARA, if the problem is Disorder late at night at pizza parlours What will be assessment output?
104. Q: SARA, if the problem is Disorder late at night at pizza parlours What will be expected result.
105. Q: What does PAT stand for
106. Q: What does PAT element use for and what does it focus.?
107. Q:Using PAT, if there had been a crime, what will be the response regarding “Place”
108. Q: Q:Using PAT, if there had been a crime, what will be the response regarding “Offenders”
109. Q:Using PAT, if there had been a crime, what will be the response regarding “Victim”
110. Q; What other measures can be done?
111. Q How can the community reputation improve?
112. Q Using SARA, what do the investigators do?
113. Q: Give three major reasons why the assessment stage in SARA is very important
114. **Q;** What is assessment of how a crime been dealt with
115. Q: Do investigator get rid of successfully assessment?
116. Q; List about four different types of success investigation by police.
117. Q: Describe good assessment
118. Q: Why must investigators be careful when using SARA for problem solving.

119. Q: Give examples of poor use of SARA within problem solving include:
120. Q: What are criminology theories:

A; theories must be grouped in some way before they can be systematically studied.

121. Q: Describe how Akers (2000), how many theories divide
122. Q; What is the first group of theories?

A: The first group consists of theories of making and enforcing criminal law,

123. Q; What is the second group of theories?
124. **Q:** Describe Classical criminology?
125. Q: Describe Positive criminology,

Chapter 7

STATISTIC on crime (126-139)

126. Q Why are statistics taken and who takes them?
127. Q; What was crime in 1995
128. Q: What was police statistic of crime in 1997?

129. Q: What was the crime rate in Wakefield, United Kingdom

130. Q; Why are some crimes not detected especially computers?

131. Q: Name other crimes that statistic is carried out?

132. Q: What was statistic of crime in 2013

133. Q: What was statistics in 2018

134. Q: Crime in England and Wales in 2019/20

135. Q:global What is the crime statistic in Northern Ireland?

136. Q: In a table form give List of Top Ten developed nations/ Countries with Highest Crime Rates

137. Q:How is international crime classified?

138. Q: Name top ten countries with highest crime

139. Q: Name top ten safe countries in the world?

Chapter 8

Courts (140-164)

140. Q: name some courts in united Kingdom?

141. Q which of these deals with crime

Magistrate court

142. Q Who are the decision makers in Magistrate court.?

143. Q what is another name for magistrate court and why.?

144. Q: What cases are heard in magistrate court?

145. Q: What restriction on magistrate court?

146. Q: What happens if accuser is found guilty?
147. Q: How do magistrate deals with juvenile cases.
148. Q: How can magistrate deal with under nine years old?

Crown court

149. Q: name some crimes heard in crown court?
150. Q: What cases are heard in crown court?
151. Q: Give brief description of drugs cases heard in crown court.
152. Q: Give brief description of INDECENT ASSAULT.
153. Q: Give brief description/example of Sexual Assault heard in crown court.
154. Q: Give brief description of RECKLESS DRIVING heard in crown court.
155. Q: Give brief description of HANDLING; heard in crown court.
156. Q: Give brief description of FRAUD;

heard in crown court.

157. Q: Give brief description of Give brief description of BURGLARY;
158. Q: Give brief PUBLIC ORDER;
159. Q: Give brief description of Violence
160. Q: Give brief description of Give brief description of Children
161. Q: Name other crimes?
162. Q: who act for the state or the prosecutor in crown court?
163. Q; What is the first stage in hearing?
164. Q: Who are involved in crown court prosecution?

Chapter 9

Jury service (Q;165-172)

165. Q: Which court uses Jury services?
166. Q How are Jury selected?
167. Q; who are excluded to serve Jury service?
168. Q; What obligation do the Jury undertake?
169. Q: How do jury come to decision?
170. Q: Who can stop crown court proceeding?
171. Q: What sentence can crown court deliver and give example?
172. Q: What rule is used in crown court?

Chapter 10;

Appeal systemin United Kingdom. (Q;173—185)

173. 172; Q: where does the convicted person start appeal?

174. Q: Who is involved in crown court appeal?
175. Q: What is meaning of “A TRIAL DE NOVO”
176. Q: What happen if the appeal failed.?
177. Q Who can appeal to the High court?
178. Q: What happen if the appeal is unsuccessful in High court?
179. Q: what condition can one appeal to supreme court?
180. Q: What next if appeal failed in supreme court?.
181. Q: If one is found guilty in Crown court, what is option?
182. Q: In High court who hears the case.
183. Q: What happened if the single judge refuse the appeal?
184. Q: What happened if the full court refuse the appeal?
185. Q: What happened if the full court and CCRC refused the appeal?

Chapter 11

ECHR EUROPEAN COURT OF HUMAN RIGHT

1998 (Q;186- 197)

186. **Q;** What is rule 2.4?
187. Q: What is rule 4.1
188. Q:What is rule 5.1
189. Q; What is rule 5.7
190. Q: What is rule 5.6
191. Q: What is rule 5.4e?
192. Q; What is ECHR ARTICLE 6.2
193. Q; When was Brexit referendum?
194. Q; When was the schedule for Brexit to happen
195. Q; when was Brexit extended to?
196. Q: When did Britain actually left the European union
197. Q: What is the likely consequence of Brexit

61

Chapter 12

Criminal Agencies (Q; 198- 216)

198. Q:Name few criminal agencies
199. Q: How many police forces in England and Wales?
200. Q: When did the number increased?
201. Q: Who heard each force and when did the law passed?
202. Q Briefly describe Police duty?

203. Q: Can police use force on suspect?
204. Q: Name some powers that Act 1996 gave to police.
205. Q: Can one obstruct police arrest?
206. Q: Why should police keep community consent?
207. Q: What did Lord Scareman say in 1981 about the police force?
208. Q; When did the United Kingdom introduce measures to help police?
209. Q: What is the function of the DPP?
210. Q: Who advice the police?
211. Q: When was probation service form?
212. Q: What was the initial duties of probation services?
213. Q: What is the probation service now?
214. Q: Elaborate brief details of probation service?
215. Q: Which act deals with prison service?
216. Q: Give summary of prison officers job?

Chapter 13

International crimes (Q;217- 293)

217. 216; Q: Name some international crime and countries involved?
218. Q: Define Aggression
219. Q: Is there international proviso on aggression?
220. Q: Give an example of aggression?
221. Q: Is there limit in ICC

Genocide

222. Q: What is the definition of Genocide?
223. Q: Is there any conditions on states
224. Q: Give an example of Genocide?.
225. Q: How can genocide be control
226. Q: Briefly explain genocide convention?

War crimes

227. Q; Why do countries have defence department?
228. Q what has contributed more hostility among states
229. Q: What do you consider foreign
230. Q: Give an example of war crime?
231. Q: Why was the Roman empire criticized on the trial of Peter Von Hagen Bach.?
232. Q: How did the definition of international crime derived?.

233. Q: who normally act as mediator in international wars?

Crimes against humanity

234. Q; Initially who is responsible to define and implement humanity that is how citizens are treated?
235. Q: Name a case of concern regarding humanity?
236. Q: Who has intervene on humanitarian grounds?
237. Q: Briefly explain Nuremberg charter?
238. Q: Who drafted codes for international law.
239. Q: Why was 1998 ICC statute enacted?
240. Q: Who accepted to end torture?
241. Q: When was agreement to end domestic torture?
242. Q: Give an example of domestic torture?
243. Q: Why is the convention definition of torture too narrow?

244. Q: what do you think of international crime on torture?
245. Q: what has the international community done on drug abused?
246. Q: when was action taken on narcotic and chemical drugs?
247. Q: what action has been taken on psychotropic substance?
248. Q: What action has been taken to combat drug trafficking?

Terrorism and threats to civil aviation

249. Q: How is terrorism been defined
250. Q: How did Principal Treaties define terrorism?
251. Q: Give an example for international terrorism?
252. Q: Is hostage a form of terrorism?
253. Q: How is bribery defined as a crime?
254. Q: How many countries agreed to combat bribery
255. Q; Give example of the bribery?
256. Q: What measures taken to avoid bribery?
257. Q: why did the bribery agreement failed?

Human trafficking

258. Q: Define and give example of human trafficking?
259. Q: Give example of human trafficking
260. Q; What convention deals with human trafficking

Cybercrime

261. Q: Briefly explain cybercrime?

262. Q:Give example of cybercrime?
263. Q: How do United Nation fight Cybercrime?

Organ trade

264. Q: Define red market (organ trade)
265. Q:Which country legalized organ trade
266. Q: Which agenda dealt with prevention of organ trafficking?

Wildlife trade

267. Q: Is trade of wildlife a crime?
268. Q: How is wildlife trade protected?
269. Q: Give one country as wildlife crime?

Blood diamond

270. Q: What is blood diamond?
271. Q: Give example of blood diamond countries?
272. Q; How was blood diamond outlaw?

Counterfeiting

273. Q: Define and give example of counterfeiting crime?
274. Q: What measures are in place to fight counterfeiting?

275. Q: How do forgery classified?

276. Q: Give example of counterfeit crime?

Illegal mining

277. Q why is mining illegal?

278. Q: Who carried out illegal mining?

279. Q: Why and Where do illegal mining take place?

280. Q: Define money laundering?

281. Q: How is money laundering organism?

282. Q: What is affiliated to money laundering and who prosecute?

Illegal gambling

283. Q: Define gambling?

284. Q: Give an example of illegal gambling

Arms trafficking

285. Q:Define Gunrunning?

286. Q: Who keep records of illegal arms?

287. Q: Give an example of illegal arms?

Illegal unregulated and unreported fishing

288. Q: When do fishing become illegal?

289. Q:What effect is such crime?

290. Q:Give an example of illegal fishing

Illegal logging

291. Q:Define illegal logging?

292. Q: Give an example of illegal logging?

293. Q: What laws prevent illegal logging?

Chapter 14

International Gang Crimes (countries)(294-310)

Mexico

294. Q; Why is there organized gang crime in Mexico?
295. Q: What does Mexico gang trade in?
296. Q: Give an example of Mexico gang?
297. Q: What action has the Mexico government taken to combat gang crime?
298. Q: What organize crime is EL Salvador involved?
299. Q: When did EL Salvador gang started?.
300. Q:Give example of organize gang in El Salvador

Italy

301. Q; Name one gang group in Italy and where it originated?
302. Q: What do Italy gang deals with?
303. Q; What action has the Italian
304. Q: What is Mozambique gang associate to?
305. Q: What do Mozambique gang trade in?

Japan

306. Q: Briefly describe Japan gang crime?
307. Q: Why is the gang activities appears to be accepted by the local people?
308. Q: What do Japan gang trade in?
309. Q: why there is no control of the gangs in Japan?
310. Q: why are some states crimes are regarded as international?

Chapter 15

Sources of International laws (Q;311-365)

A critical evaluation of the Sources of International Law;

311. Q: What is international laws
312. Q: Where is the source of international laws?
313. Q:what has been the aim of Article 38 of ICJ
314. Q: How is the Article 38 of ICJ described?
315. Q: What does article 38 of ICJ direct international courts?
316. Q: Does Article 38 of ICJ helps judgement to be made in courts?

Treaties and Conventions

317. Q: Briefly explain treaties and conventions?
318. Q: What is the significance of treaties and conventions?
319. Q: Where was the concept of Article 38 found?
320. Q: What other ways can treaties be perceived?
321. Q: what is “soft law” treaty
322. Q: What do some treaties provide?

323. Q: Who have to abide by treaty?
324. Q: Give example of treaty deal with specific agenda.?
325. Q: What treaty can be source of law?
326. Q: Can treaties create organisation?
327. Q: What happens if decision under treaty not binding?
328. Q; What is Bilateral treaties?.
329. Q: How is treaty form?
330. Q: how can treaties be policed?
331. Q: What influence effectiveness of treaties?

International Customs

332. Q: Describe international custom?
333. Q: How can custom be accepted as international law?
334. Q: Give an example of international custom?
335. Q: Explain Opinio juris?
336. Q: What is regarded as international customary law?

337. Q: Where can practice of international practice law be found.?

338. Q: Give some examples of customary international law

339. Q: How is customary law used

340. Q: Give example of customary laws used in criminal case?.

341. Q; Can customary law be used by ICC(international criminal court?

342. Q: What is the weakness in customary law?

343. Q: Is it easy to prove state practice and customary law if no treaty exit?

General Principles

344. Q: What is General principal of Law?

345. Q: How is the General principal applied?

346. Q: What are the sources of General principal of law?

347. Q: Why can they be used in any develop country?

348. Q: How can General principal be regarded as independence?.

349. Q: In what other areas can general principals be applied?

350. Q: How can General principal be used to assist judges?

351. Q: What areas of law has judges applied municipal principles?

352. Q: How is criminal law treated on international platform?
353. Q: how has the international economic law benefited?
354. Q: Name one of the principles of general principles?
355. Q: What do member states share in general principle?
356. Q: How can general principle be cumbersome?

Judicial Decisions and Teachings of highly qualified publicists

357. Q: What do we mean by Judicial decision?
358. Q: Why does judicial decision rely on considered Article 59 of ICJ?
359. Q: How is the decision of the permanent court of justice valued?
360. Q: What does Article 38(1) (d) says
361. Q: How does domestic legal system compare with judicial decision?

362. Q: What is used to determine legal rules?
363. Q: What has influenced the scope of international law?
364. Q: What has the teachings been used?
365. Q: Give summary of Article

Chapter 16

Drug; (366-450)

definition

366. Q What is the definition of Drugs
367. Q:What is the WHO(World health organisation) definition of drug addiction
368. Q: How does criminal law define an addict?
369. Q: Who is regarded as Drug abuse or misuse?
370. Q: who is classified as Utilitarian drug user.
371. Q:who is classified as Recreational

drug user

372. Q: Who is casual drug user?

Route

373. Q: How can drug be taken?
374. Q ; Under which section of the 1983 act will judge disregard drugs intake
375. Q: What has the accuser to proof?
376. Q: What does the medicine act. 1968 covers?
377. Q: what does Custom and excise management act 1979 deals with?
378. Q; what does Drug trafficking act 1986?
379. Q: what does Control drugs act 1985 covers

380. Q: what does Intoxicating substances act 1985covers?
381. Q: what does Road traffic act 1972
382. Q: what does Health and Safety at work act 1974
383. Q:what does Section 7 of Health and Safety
384. Q: When was drug offence Act?
385. Q: Give summary of the control drugs
386. Q: What does section 4 of 1971 Act?
387. Q: What and why did Act introduce during the first world war on drugs?
388. Q: What was the prohibition Act?
389. Q: When was poison Act?
390. Q: Can accuser use intoxication as defence?
391. Q: What does symptoms of drugs depends on?
392. Q: Can drugs cause mental disorder
393. Q: Give an example of Class “A” drugs
394. Q: What is the reaction of class A
395. Q: what is court sentence for possession of class A

396. Q; What is the street name of Hallucinogens

397. Q: Give some example of class B drugs

398. .Q: What are some signs and symptoms of class B

399. Q: what is punishment for possession class B drugs.

400. Q; What is punishment for supplying class B drugs?

401. Q: Give the name of class c and street name?

402. Q: Give some example of Class C

403. Q: What are some of the signs and symptoms

404. Q: What is punishment for possession?

405. Q: What is the punishment to supply class C drugs

406. Q; How is investigation carried out?

407. Q: What are some signs and symptoms of class A illegal drugs?

Cocaine class A

408. Q:What is the street name for cocaine?

409. Q:What is the appearance of cocaine

410. Q; How is Cocaine administered?

411. Q: How is Crack classified?

412. Q: What is the street name for Crack?

413. Q: What is the appearance of Crack?

414. Q: How is Crack administered

Ecstasy

415. Q What class of drug is Ecstasy

416. Q: What is the street name?

417. Q: What does Ecstasy look like?

418. Q: How is Ecstasy administered?
419. Q What is the side effect of Ecstasy
420. Q: What class is heroin drug?
421. Q: What is the street name for heroin?
422. Q: How does heroin look like?
423. Q: How is it administered?
424. Q:What class is LSD?
425. Q what is the street name?
426. Q: What is the appearance of LSD?
427. Q How is LSD administered?
428. Q: What is the side effect of LSD
429. Q Is LSD addictive

Mushroom

430. Q: What is mushroom classification
431. Q: what is the street name of mushroom?
432. Q: what does mushroom look like
433. Q: How is mushroom taken?

Amphetamines

434. Q; What classification is Amphetamines?
435. Q:What drug and colour is

436. Q What is the street name of Amphetamines?

437. Q: What is the appearance of Amphetamine?

438. Q: How are Amphetamines administered/

439. Q; What is the side effect of Mushroom?

Cannabis

440. : What class is cannabis?

441. Q: What are the street names for cannabis

442. Q: What does cannabis look like?

443. Q how is cannabis taken?

444. Q: What is the side effect of cannabis?

445. Q: Give example of Stimulant drugs

446. Q: What is general side effect of stimulant drugs?

447. Q: name some Depressant drugs

448. Q List some side effect of Depressant drugs?

449. Q; What is the consequence to possess solvent class c drugs?

450. Q; What are the side effect of Solvent Class C drugs?

Chapter; 17

Drug Trafficking (Q;451-476)

451. Q: Give some specific international fraud?

452. Q: What is the effect of drug trafficking?

453. Q: What effect on mental health?

454. Q: What happen if individual travel to meet criminals?

455. Q; Give example of drug trafficking countries?

456. Q: Who handle drug trafficking?

457. Q: Give example of how drug trafficking take place.
458. Q: Give example of the carrier route
459. Q: What happens to the drug carrier on arriving at the destination example U.K airport?
460. Q: What happens to the drugs?
461. Q: How can WEAPONS undergo trafficking?
462. Q: How can the stock market be frauded?
463. Q: How can investment be affected?
464. Q: Explain what BOILER is?
465. Q How is the effect on United Kingdom economic?
466. Q; Where do the trial of drug trafficking start?
467. Q: What measure has the United Kingdom government put in place to prevent illicit drugs?
468. Q: What is another way for community to help each other
469. Q How can drug trafficking be solved?
470. Q: What measure needs to be put in place to prevent drug trafficking?

471. Q: How did Russia defence comment on criminals?
472. Q: How do fraud affect individual:
473. Q: What has United Nation warn countries?
474. Q: What favours the criminals?
475. Q: Does crime be transferred across countries boarders
476. Q: Why is Belgium considered the main smuggling country in Europe for hand rolled tobacco?

Chapter 18

Statistic (Q;477-498)

477. Q; Give the statistic on drugs by British crime survey in 2006/7?
478. Q: In 2017 how many people died in United states of America from drug overdose
479. Q; In 2017 how many people died in United states of America with substance abuse disorder
480. Q: In 2017 how many people died in United states of America who had illicit drugs
481. Q: What is the most used illicit drug I America in 2017
482. Q: According to CDC (Centre for Disease control) in America, give statistic of death from drugs misuse?
483. Q: How many people had mental health problem as result of drugs

484. Q: How many in 2018 hospitalised with drug poison?
485. Q: How many deaths related to drug misuse (England and Wales) in 2016
486. Q; What percentage of adults took illicit drugs in2016/17 in (England and Wales)
487. Q: In 2016, what percentage of children use illicit drugs drug use among children (England)
488. Q: Name the top five counties with worst or severe drug problem?
489. Q: Which country is first free illegal drug use
490. Q: Which country is second free illegal drug use
491. Q; Which country is third free illegal drug use
492. Q: Which country is fourth free illegal drug use
493. Q: Which country is fifth free illegal drug use
494. Q: Which country is sixth free illegal drug use.
495. Q: Which country is seventh free illegal drug use

496. Q: Which country is the eighth free illegal drug use

497. Q: Which country is ninth free illegal drug use

498. Q: Which country is tenth free illegal drug use

Chapter 19

Court Orders (Q; 499-507)

499. Q: Summarise ways to solve crime?

500. Q: What can the court do?

501. Q: What is injunction?

502. Q: Name few types of injunction?

503. Q: What is Prohibition?

504. Q: What is mandatory?

505. Q: What is interlocutory?

506. Q: What is Perpetual?

507. Q; What is interim?

Chapter; 20

Violence (508-518)

508. Q: Define violence?

509. Q: What are violent conduct?

510. Q: Name types of violent?

511. Q: Define domestic violence?

512. Q: define Battered women?

513. Q: How does violence end up?

514. Q: Name other types of violence?

515. Q: Is battering women acceptable in some culture?

516. Q: When did control of women started?

517. Q: What did the Bible say about women?
518. Q; Who are violence towards?

Chapter 21

Property crime (Q:519—571)

519. Q: Define property?
520. Q; What does property come under?
521. . Q: What is tings in action?
522. Q: Describe property from criminology point?
523. Q: How does the law define property?
524. Q; How does the theft Act define property?
525. Q: Is Anatomic specimen property?
526. Q; Name other property?
527. Q: What is export Quotas?
528. Q; Give example of General property?
529. Q:What is criminal damage as per case law?
530. Q: What is criminal damage as per case Division court
531. Q: What is criminal damage as per case Concise dictionary?

532. Q: What is criminal damage as per case Lord Lane?

533. Q: How do one regard dishonest in relation to Actus Reus?

534. Q: Based on the definitions of damage, give example of property not damage?

535. Q: Give example of intangible property that qualified as property damage?

536. Q: Define Destruction?

537. Q: What does the law say about Property mis-description

538. Q: Under actus Reus, is death or water flowing regard as stolen

539. Q:Is cheque or cash property?

540. Q: What do the court say about one partner cash a cheque with only his or her signature?

541. Q: what happen if the cashing of the cheque with one signature result the account being overdrawn?

542. Q: explain the implication of transferring money from one country to another?

543. Q; What happen if someone steal a cheque?

544. Q: When can land be regarded as stolen?

545. Q; What offence if a tenant pick fruit from tree?

546. Q: What happen if the tenant visitor or partner pick fruit from the tree of the tenant?

547. Q: What happen if someone pick flowers etc from somebody land?

548. Q; What happen if someone pick fruit to use and then decide to sell it later?
549. Q: What happened if someone purchase and unpaid goods, but no invoice issued.
550. Q: When do property burglaries occurs?
551. Q: What happen in warm seasons?
552. Q: What time do property burglary occurs?
553. Q: Do victims able to give time to police?
554. Q: In united Kingdom what time do property burglary?
555. Q; What preparation thieves make before stealing?
556. Q: What element burglar consider?
557. Q: what do some criminal do with information?
558. Q; Where do burglars occurs?
559. Q: Why are some houses burgle few times?
560. Q: What about unoccupied property?
561. Q: What about property near heavy traffic?
562. Q: What other houses prone to bugle?
563. Q: What property are concessionary burgle?

564. Q: What property could be bugle?

565. Q: What can deter thieves?

566. Q; How can light affect thieves?

567. Q: What about the situation of property?

568. Q: How does accessibility affect bugler?

569. Q: How do security affect beglaring?

570. Q: Explain presentation of cheque and situation of the account in which the cheque is presented?

571. Q: when does a cheque becomes recipients property?

Chapter 22;

Computer crime (Q;572-620)

572. Q: What is Hi-Tech crime?

573. Q: What is Botnets?

574. Q: What Act deals with computer fraud?

575. Q: What is Website spoofing?

576. Q: Name some method the are used to attack computer?

577. Q: Give example of hackers?

578. Q; What means do criminal use to communication?.

579. Q: How do the fraudsters use the media?

580. Q: How do the fraudster protect themselves?

581. Q: In computer fraud, what is VIRUS?

582. Q: how does the VIRUS operate?

583. Q: How can the VIRUS affect the data on the computer?

584. Q; Are there more than one type of virus and which one is more dangerous
585. Q:Explain EXTORTION in computer fraud?
586. Q: What does DOS means?
587. Q: Explain how DOS is used to defraud on computer?
588. Q: What does DDOS Mean?
589. Q: Describe how DDOS is used to commit fraud?
590. Q: What is PING OF DEATH?
591. Q: What is the E-MAIL BOMB use in computers?
592. Q: Describe INTELLECTUAL PROPERTY crime?
593. Q Describe STEALTH VIRUS?
594. Q; Describe WORM for computer fraud:
595. Q: Describe the activities of TROJANS.?
596. Q: What is ADWARE?
597. Q: How does POP-UP ACT?
598. Q: What is ADWARE activity on computer?

599. Q: Describe SPYWARE?
600. Q: How can SPYWARE affect the computer?
601. Q: What is MALWARE?
602. Q: What is MALWARE activity?
603. Q; How can SPYWARE be installed?
604. Q: What other use is MALWARE?
605. Q: What is PHISHING?
606. Q: How does PHISHING act?
607. Q: What is SPAM?
608. Q; What is spam use for?
609. Q: Who is SOCIAL ENGINEERING in computer fraud?
610. Q: What is TCT/IP Attack?
611. Q: What is SYN FLOOD?.
612. Q: What is "MAN IN THE MIDDLE" computer fraud?
613. Q: What is SPOOFING?
614. Q: What is REPLAY
615. Q: What is WIRELESS
616. Q: what is the motive of website attack?
617. Q: What is the main motives of the fraudsters?
618. Q: Why do some criminal hack computers?
619. Q: What does inexperience criminals do?
620. Q: What is the effect on global business by the computer fraud??

Chapter 23

Statistic on computer fraud Q;621- 626)

621. Q: Give brief information of Home net providers survey?
622. Q: Give brief information of BBC survey?
623. Q: What damage did DoS and DDoS cause in 2002
624. Can spam be sent to mobile phone?
625. Q: What is VARIANT OF ZEUS and what they can do?
626. Q: What is police survey on computer attack?

Chapter 24

prevention of computer fraud (Q:627-673)

627. Q; Has the law enforcement has the technical skills?
628. Q: Why is it difficult to deal with some crime?
629. Q: Why is it difficult with Intellectual property crime?
630. Q:How must business or organisations protect themselves from computer fraud;?

631. Q: What recommendation should be in the organisation security policy?
632. Q: What must be aims of hard and soft ware protection?
633. Q: With regard to hard and soft ware, what do the criminals target?
634. Q: What do they use to target banks?
635. Q: How do some companies protect their website?
636. Q; what do you regard as the efficient prevention policy/
637. computer virus?
638. Q: What can be used to prevent Spyware?
639. Q: What can be used to prevent Adware?
640. Q:What can be used to prevent Phishing?
641. Q:What can be used to prevent Firewall?
642. Q: What can be used to prevent fire ware?
643. Q: what can be used to protect hardware.
644. Q: How do one provide protection\prevention of wireless security?
645. Q: What does WEP (wireless encryptment privacy do?
646. Q: What does Wi-Fi protected access (WPA) do?
647. Q: What does Mac Address filtering function?
648. Q: What is function of SSID (SERVICE SET IDENTIFIER)
649. Q:What is function of WIRELESS ANTENA;
650. Q:how do you protect DATA SECURITY

651. Q: What is function of SMART CARD?
652. Q:What is function of SECURITY KEY FOB?.
653. Q:What is function of BIOMETRIC DEVICE;
654. Q: What do we mean by a ENCRRYPTED PASSWORD?
655. Q; What is EVENT LOGGING AND AUDITING;
656. Q: What does Encryption use for?
657. Q: What is the function of HASH ENCODING?
658. Q: What is the function of SYNMETRIC ENCRYTION.
659. Q: What is the function of asymmetric encryption
660. Q: What is (VPN) VIRTUAL PRIVATE NETWORK
661. Q: What is the best way to physical protect/secure Hardware.
662. Q: Name few devices to secure hardware?
663. Q: What can BIOS use for?
664. Q: Which of those attackers is most dangerous

665. Q Give reason of your choice

666. Q: Why didn't you choose Intellectual?

667. Q: Why didn't choose Extortion?

668. Q: Why in my opinion Dos and DDos are more dangerous?

669. Q: How does Dos and DDos affect network?

670. Q: How does Dos and DDos affect access?

671. Q: How does Dos and DDos affect servers

672. Q: How does Dos and DDos ability to use Trojan cause havoc

673. Q: What is the effect of Dos and DDos using Trojans

Chapter 25

Computer Hackers (Q: 674-681)

674. Q: How do you define Computer hacker?

675. Q: What is the Aim of the Hackers?

676. Q: Name two date of United Kingdom Act on computer misuse?

677. Q: Give case law in which the Act was used?

678. Q: give another case law?

679. Q: What was the appeal grounds?

680. Q: What did Lord Lane say on the appeal?

681. Q: What does the criminal damage Act 1971 say about computer?

Chapter ; 26

Youth Crime (Q: 682—720)

682. Q: Define Youth crime

683. Q: Legally what does youth refer?
684. Q; Which court deals with youth and who preside?
685. Q: How is proceeding in Juvenile court?
686. Q: what sort of sentence for juvenile offenders?
687. Q: What other sentence available in juvenile court?
688. Q: What consist young offenders team and under what Act.?
689. Q: What age group are immune from prosecution?
690. Q: what Act provide such immunity?
691. Q What happen if adult persuade youth under 9 to commit crime?
692. Q: What debate had been for children 10 and 13
693. Q: what did Lord Jauncy say about a 12-13 age group
694. Q: What did Lord Lowry say about a child?

695. Q; What is are some of the factors that contribute to youth crime?

696. Q: how does youth unemployment contribute to youth crime?

697. Q: how does identity contribute to youth crime

698. Q: how does media contribute to youth crime?

699. Q: how does communication contribute to youth crime?

700. Q: how does parental discipline contribute to youth crime?

701. Q: how does education contribute to youth crime?

702. Q: how does domestic violence contribute to youth crime?

703. Q: how does lack of resources contribute to youth crime?

704. Q: how does lack of support contribute to youth crime?

705. Q: how does lack of activities contribute to youth crime?

706. Q: how does material world contribute to youth crime?

707. Q: how does opportunity crime contribute to youth crime?

708. Q: how does technology contribute to youth crime?

709. Q: How does not being warn contribute to youth crime?

710. Q: How does low punishment contribute to youth crime?
711. Q: How does low school attendance or drop out from school contribute to youth crime?
712. Q: How does abuse contribute to youth crime?
713. Q: How does lack of support contribute to youth crime?
714. Q: How does Pressure contribute to youth crime?
715. Q: How does low self-esteem contribute to youth crime?
716. Q; How does lack of guidance contribute to youth crime?
717. Q: How does the lack of CCTC in the area contribute to youth crime
718. Q:Name as many as possible anti-social problems that can cause youth crime?
719. Q: How could anti - social behaviour could be transferred to the public?

720. Q: Give example of how group of people express their emotion of violence threat, messages to the owner or to the public and is common

Chapter 27;

Anti-social/Delinquency (Q 721- 741)

721. Q: What did Socrates, the Athenian philosopher describe young people BC
722. Q: How did Daily post paper described some children?
723. Q: How did Daily Graphic describe some young people
724. Q:How did Cohen describe anti-social people?
725. Q: How did the media describe youth disorder?
726. Q: Who acknowledge anti-social behaviour?
727. Q: Who developed Farrington et al 2006 on delinquency
728. Q: List the six categories of delinquency by Farrington et al 2006?
729. Q: How was Farrington et al carried out?
730. Q; How did study by Cambridge university carried out
731. Q: Give about thirteen anti-social behaviour and the effect of anti-social on some people

732. Q: Name three ways to create safer and sustainable environment?
733. Q; What will you suggest for social control?
734. Q; What must be the strategy for saver environment?
735. Q: What is expected outcome?
736. Q: Name some ways to avoid anti-social behaviour through education?
737. Q: What can intervention program include?
738. Q: What are some factors to prevent reoffending
739. Q: What is STATUS OFFENDING?
740. Q: what characteristic result from short term anti-social?
741. Q: How does low income affect crime?

Chapter28

Statistic on youth crime (Q:742-749)

742. Q: What is the 2005 British crime survey?
743. Q: Which areas in UK are safer?

744. Q: Which areas in United Kingdom suffers more antisocial?

745. Q: What is the cost of vandalism of anti-social.

746. Q: What is the Characteristic of antisocial?

747. Q: In a graph, explain graph

748. Q: In a graph explain antisocial potential?

749. Q: How will parent behaviour affect youth?

Chapter 29

Criminal Psychology (750—769)

750. Q: What is psychology?

751. Q: What is Forensic?

752. Q: What is Forensic psychology?

753. Q: who also use forensic psychology?

754. Q: Name one psychological tools for investigation?

755. Q: Can psychology be bias?

756. Q: Who was the first forensic psychologist?

757. Q: Name some other known psychologist

758. Q: Describe Psychological economic?

759. Q: Describe Psychologist Herbert Simon argument about people

760. Q: Describe Thaler and Sinstein opinion on status Qua

761. Q:What does Thaler and Sinstein think of over confidence people?

762. Q: What is BOUNDED RATIONALITY?

763. Q: what can prevent people offending?

764. Q Why did psychologist Eysenck say about why people commit crime?
765. Q: What is ICAP theory?
766. Q: How could personality be detected?
767. Q: What is criminal behaviour?
768. Q; What is white collar crime?
769. Q: What is Deviance/deviant behaviour?

Chapter 30

Offender profilin (Q;770- 781)

770. Q: what is definition profiling?
771. Q: How is profile of criminal?
772. Q: What sort of description the police might need?
773. Q: How does Brent Turvey, M.S.San Diago describe deflation of criminal profiling?
774. Q: What other waves can be used in criminal profile
775. Q: How is profile of criminal?
776. Q: Name few Aims of collecting criminal profile?

777. Q: How many concepts for assessing behaviour
778. Q What main goals that Holms and Holmes (200) considered When investigate a criminal
779. Q: What are the six steps by Holms and Holms to identify offender?
780. Q: Explain the Ainsworth (2001) used four approaches to identify the offender?
781. Q: Why is profiling of a criminal difficult?

Chapter 31

procedure for criminal life (Q; 782- 799)

782. Q:Described briefly the five main procedure in gathering information for criminal profile
783. Q: Why do police take DNA from suspect.
784. Q: What sort of investigation police do on break in or theft
785. Q : How do police get knowledge of suspect?
786. Q: What about the suspect behaviour?
787. Q:What happen if the victim think he/she saw the accuser
788. Q: What happen in difficult and serious cases?
789. Q: What other means have other people used to identify suspect?
790. Q: Briefly describe the six steps of the Scientific Method Of Crime Reconstruction?
791. Q: What is the first step in the reconstruction of crime using scientific method?

792. Q: What is the second step in the reconstruction of crime using scientific method?
793. crime using scientific method.
794. Q: What is the fourth step in the reconstruction of crime using scientific method?
795. Q: What is the fifth step in the reconstruction of crime using scientific method?
796. Q: What is the sixth step in the reconstruction of crime using scientific method?
797. Q: What should the conclusion of crime reconstruction highlight
798. Q; What is status quo bias?
799. Q What are some factors for some do and others don't commit crime

Chapter 32

psychological autopsy (Q:800-816)

800. Q; Name few reasons why Psychological autopsy carried out?

801. Q; what must be done when one discover the body?

802. Q; What will the police do in their investigation.?

803. Q; what happen to the victim body when the police finish their investigation?

804. Q: When will the body be released to the family?

805. Q: Why is study of the victim important?.

806. Q: Describe three areas using Turvey theory?

807. Q: What items do police investigate near the victim?

808. Q: What is the first thing police might consider?

809. Q: Why do police check the victim records?

810. Q: Give an example of an actor who committed suicide?

811. Q; Why is it necessary to interview people after unexpected death?

812. Q; why do police need to check deceased victim medical records?

813. Q: Why do police interview other people after the unexpected death

814. Q: What can be used to trace a murderer?

815. Q: What do police consider in case of murder

816. Q: What else do the police investigate?

Chapter 33

Terrorism (817---838)

817. Q: What is United Nation definition of terrorism

818. Q: What is United Kingdom definition of terrorism?
819. Q: What does Act 1989 s. 18 says?
820. Q: What does the terrorism Act 1996 s. 58 say?
821. Q: Use a case law to define terrorism?
822. Q: What is United States of America definition of terrorism
823. Q: Give as many examples of terrorism attack in the world?
824. Q: What are some of the reasons for terrorist attack?

Type of terrorism

825. Q: Give example of nationalist terrorism?
826. Q: Give reason and example of religious terrorism
827. Q: what is State sponsored terrorism
828. Q: What is Narcho terrorism.
829. Q: What is cyber terrorism?.
830. Q: Explain computer Hackling?

831. Q: How does computer use to steal classified files etc?
832. Q: What is the funding for terrorist?
833. Q: What do they use the money for?
834. Q: Give example of money earned or country spend on terrorism?
835. Q: What must we do to do to prevent terrorism
836. Q: Must we have discussion with terrorism?.
837. Q: what biblical evidence to support given chance to enemy?
838. Q:How can agencies help to prevent terrorism?

Chapter 34

FRAUD (Q;839—921)

839. Q; what percentage of illicit tobacco smuggle in freight?
840. Q: What success UK had in the 2000s.
841. Q: Why do people carry out cigarette fraud?
842. Q: How organised is cigarette smugglers?
843. Q: Where in 2015,United Kingdom (HMRC) found illegal tobacco?
844. Q: Which town in UK involve in UK's largest illegal tobacco factory
845. Q: How much does it cost United Kingdom in alcohol fraud in 2000s
846. Q:What did the losses consist of?
847. Q: What is targeted in diversion fraud?
848. Q: How is illegal alcohol sold?

849. Q: What measures are there to combat alcohol fraud?
850. Q: Apart from alcohol, what other fraud criminal do at the same time?
851. Q: which countries are targeted in alcohol fraud?
852. Q: how many people died in United State of America of alcohol misuse in 2012
853. Q: In 2010, what was the cost of alcohol misuse for USA
854. Q How do criminal carry out alcohol fraud in UK and Europe?
855. Q; what does oil include?
856. Q: Are fraud of fuel the same in every part of UK. And give loss of revenue by various UK government.?
857. Q: What is oil fraud?
858. Q: Name some oil fraud types?
859. Q; Explain laundering in oil fraud
860. Q; Explain Mixing in oil fraud

861. Q: Q; Explain Misuse in oil fraud
862. Q; Explain Smuggling in oil fraud
863. Q; Explain Decanting in oil fraud
864. Q; Explain Biofuel/vegetable oils in oil
865. Q; How do criminals in oil operate in Northern Ireland (UK)?
866. Q: In other parts of UK, what does oil fraud involves?
867. Q: What is tied oils?.
868. Q: What and why did the government introduce strategy on oil?

VAT FRAUD

869. Q: Name the three types of VAT fraud?
870. Q: What method do they use to defraud?
871. Q: Explain Registered and unregistered evader fraud
872. Q: Who are these people and why do they defraud the system?
873. Q: Who are not requested to register for VAT?
874. Q: How does unregistered evaders fraud occur?
875. Q: Briefly explain VAT theft fraud?
876. Q: Name the types of VAT thief fraud
877. Q: what type of business do commit vat theft
878. Q; Explain and give example of country export fraud?
879. Q: What is country export diversion fraud?.
880. Q: When can Repayment fraud occurs?

881. Q: Explain and give example of Repayment fraud?
882. Q: How has advance technology helped VAT criminals?
883. Q: What is Missing trader intra-community (MTIC)
884. Q: What is another name for MTIC and involve what?
885. Q: What does carousel fraud involves?
886. Q: Who is involved in MTIC and Carousel
887. Q: What sort of Goods attract MTIC fraudsters
888. Q: Give history of MTIC VAT fraud?
889. Q: How many types of benefit fraud and which department in United Kingdom is being defrauded?
890. Q; Give an example of the magnitude of the fraud and which areas of the DWP.
891. Q; How does the fraud occurs?
892. Q: Who and how investigate the fraud for DWP?

893. Q: how much is estimated loss from benefit order books alone?

894. Q; How do the criminal get away with their identities criminals steal ?

895. Q: How do some criminals obtain records of victim?

896. Q: What measure was implemented to reduce benefit fraud?

897. Q: Who is responsible for investigating Inland Revenue fraud?

898. Q: Who is more likely to defraud the inland revenue and how?

899. Q:Name other areas of Inland Revenue fraud?

900. Q: What is another way that the Inland Revenue recover some of the tax evaded?

901. Q: How does paying employee cash defraud inland revenue?

902. Q: How is benefit administered by Inland revenue could be used to defraud the inland Revenue?

903. Q: How is the inland revenue dealing with fraud from 2017

904. Q: Who might be involved in private sector fraud?

905. Q: Name some private sector fraud?

906. Q: Which country are notorious of 419 fraud?

907. Q: Briefly explain 419 fraud

908. Q: Why do people become involve in the 419 fraud?

909. Q: How were people deceived?
910. Q: Give an example of victim losses
911. Q: Why do some people fall victim to 419 fraud?
912. Q: Explain how are the 419 fraudsters using improved technology?
913. Q: Have the people aware of technologist?
914. ; What are some of the qualities other people?
915. Q: What sometimes affect or influence people to get them into 419 Fraud
916. Q: Why do the fraudster create false account?
917. Q: Briefly explain lottery prize fraud and give an example.
918. Q: Briefly explain data protection fraud?
919. Q: Briefly explain commercial and financial fraud?
920. Q: how do the fraudsters within the company account for their fraud?
921. Q: How can senior company employee use their accounts to commit fraud?

Chapter 35

Summary of crime (Q;922- 957)

922. Q:How can the United Kingdom crime and disorder help to prevent crime
923. Q: What is the aims and objective of CPS (Crown Prosecution Service)?
924. Q: What is the police involvement in crime prevention?
925. Q: What is the function of the PCC?
926. Q: What is the core role of the crime prevention partnership?
927. Q: Give some example of transnational
928. Q: How has technology affect government action?
929. Q: What is United Kingdom objective in tackling crime?
930. Q: Why do police have to work with other global crime prevention agencies or Interpol to combat terrorism?
931. Q: What is the best way to solve world crime problem?
932. Q: Give few ways of police monitoring (police power)? In crime prevention.?
933. Q: How can the public help the police in crime prevention?
934. Q: What measures has the government of United ?
935. Q:Who might be considered as terrorist

according to the ACT 1996 section 58

936. Q: Name one publication for solving crime problems
937. Q: What is the aim of the check list to reduce crime
938. Q: Give brief analysis of crime prevention?
939. Q: Give brief investigating method of the victim as in a psychological autopsy?
940. Q: with regard to crime reconstruction, summarise measures considered?
941. Q: What is induction in any case of crime?
942. Q; What is Deduction in crime investigation?
943. Q: What is Abduction in crime investigation?
944. Q: What is Typology in crime investigation?
945. Q: What is synthesis in crime investigation
946. Q:What is analysis in crime
947. Q: What is apotheosis in crime investigation
948. Q: What is theories in crime investigation?
949. Q: What is Patterns in crime investigation?
950. Q: What is Leads in crime investigation?.

951. Q: What is Clues in crime investigation?

952. Q: Are all investigation the same?

953. Q: Draw a chart of how a seasoned investigator would probably investigate the Homicide, Rape, robbery, burglary crimes

954. Q: Explain Mode Operandi (MO)?.

955. Q: In a table form explain crime investigation?

956. Q: Explain “A Primer On Logical Reasoning”?

957. Q: Explain the Law Lords in the supreme court of United Kingdom?

Chapter 37

Self-defence (scenario) (Q; 958—1003)

958. Q: What act is right of self-defence?.

959. Q: what did article 51 condition of use as self-defence?

960. Q: What are the variable to use article 51 of UN?

961. Q: Considering the scenario given how is the conflict be assessed?

962. Q: Give The Foundations of the Proposal by the Military in the scenario

963. Q: Who instigate the conflict?

964. Q: What means was used to unite the factions?

965. Q: What has the Odesian propose for self-defence?

966. Q: What is the Legal Implications under the United Nations Charter?

967. Q: What did ICJ (international court of justice ruled in this case?
968. Q: How did the ICJ view the Iran v USA in 2003?
969. Q: Why was the stipulation in the UN articles?
970. Q: What does article 2($) of the UN state?
971. Q: When can "Use of force" as a Preventive Action under the "UN Charter"
972. Q: What is UN view on threat?
973. Q: Explain the Caroline formula on self-defence?
974. Q: What is the legal definition of imminence?
975. Q: What does imminence refer to in UN terminology?
976. Q: Who can stop an attack on another state?
977. Q: What did the UN Security council view on the Iraq v. Israel war as self-defence?
978. Q: How did UK and Sierra Leon used Caroline formula?

979. Q: Explain Principle of Immediacy, Necessity, and Proportionality in relation to ICL international customary law?.
980. Q: Name some of the wars in which ICJ refer to using international customary law?.
981. Q: What did the court said about the Nicaragua case?
982. Q: Comment on the Oil platform case on self-defence?
983. Q: Comment on the arm activated in Congo?
984. Q: How do the court define necessity
985. Q:What other opinion can necessity be understood?
986. Q: What evidence must a nation provide for using force as self-defence?
987. Q: Explain proportionate in relation to international law?
988. Q: what legislation that govern the use of force as self-defence?
989. Q: What measure in place for nations responding to attack?
990. Q: Explain the principle of immediacy?
991. Q: After considering all the aforementioned when can a nation implement self-defence by military means
992. Q: What other option can the nation/Odesian military have?
993. Q: Who make the final decision of using force in self-defence?

994. Q: Why do nations have to take into consideration United Nations guideline before using military as self-defence?
995. Q: Considering the scenario given what is your opinion
996. Q: Can the military action be preventive measures?
997. Q; What do the military have to do to implement " right of self-defence?.
998. Q: In this case, what needs to be addressed?
999. Q: What will be proposer to resolve the conflict supported by resolution?.
1000. Q; Can Leiden policy recommendation be used to justify the use of military in self-defence?
1001. Q: If the military have the right for self-defence, what do they have to consider before taken any action.
1002. Q: What else do the military have to proof before taken any action?

1003. Q; What is my final conclusion on the military action?

Chapter 37

Immunity for head of state (Q:1004-1043)

1004. Q; What is the function of ICC?

1005. Q ; What is article 27 of ICC?

1006. Q; What is the degree immunity might apply?

1007. Q; What was reaction of Al-Bashir case?

1008. Q; How did Mudukuti view the decision by ICC in AL-Bashir case?

1009. Q; How did Nouwen view the decision by ICC in AL-Bashir case?

1010. Q: Give background of the AL-Bashir case

1011. Q; When was the second warrant issued

1012. Q: How did the Arab League reacted to the two Warrants

1013. Q: What action was taken against Jordan for failing to arrest AL- Bashir?

1014. Q: Name some of other cases where the member states ignored ICC.

1015. Q: what was the Appeals chamber decision on the Jordan case?

1016. Q: What does the customary international law views on immunity for head of state

1017. Q: Do head of state have immunity against prosecution?

1018. Q: Briefly explain Article 27 of ICC

1019. Q: What is the concept of immunity from international customary Law perspective?

1020. Q: Explain personal immunity?

1021. Q: give an example of arrest warrant in personal immunity case?

1022. Q:Explain functional immunity

1023. Q: How does the appeal chamber view immunity?

1024. Q: Name some statue that the court relied on?

1025. Q: What is the notion of immunity for head of state?

1026. Q: How can immunity be removed from head of state?

1027. Q; How does customary international law form jurisprudence from ad hoc tribunal.

1028. Q: Briefly explain Article 98?

1029. Q: Explain what one mean by "third state" as per Law of treaties Article 2

1030. Q; Does the immunity relevant with reference to Rome Statute?.

1031. Q: what does the court regard Article 98?

1032. Q; Does the court greatly contradict itself by the above interpretation of article 98 section 131, article 21 and 27 of the ICC statute. statement.

1033. Q:Explain with example of idea of functional and personal immunity?

1034. Q; How does immunity applies?

1035. Q: How can arrest Warrant be executed?

1036. Q: Why was the arrest of al- Bashir

1037. Q: How does the ICC implement its mandate?

1038. Q: What is the implication of the court relying on customary law?

1039. Q: What is the problem could involve inerplitation of Articles

1040. Q: Can a judgement be use as case law for another case?

1041. Q; Can individual be protected from international crime?

1042. Q; How far is head of state protected?

1043. Q; Can head of state escape ICC

Chapter 38

International terrorism (Q;1044—1094)

1044. Q:Why is it difficult to define terrorism?

1045. Q: Why is it important to have international definition of terrorism?

1046. Q: What did Newman E. view on terrorism definition?

1047. Q: How is terrorism interpreted by people?

1048. Q; Which area is lack of terrorism definition useful?

1049. Q: Can state commit terrorism and give example?

1050. Q; Name few examples of how nations can sponsor terrorism group?

1051. Q: How can one interpreted action being condoned by state?

1052. Q: What other terrorist people?

1053. Q: How can terrorism be compare?

1054. Q: What is the size of people or leaders in terrorism?

1055. Q; What weapons do terrorist use?

1056. Q; What are the tactics of terrorist?

1057. Q: Who do terrorist target?

1058. Q: what is the aim of terrorism?

1059. Q: How can terrorism be compare to?

1060. : Name some Terrorist organisation?

1061. Q: What reason the IRA gave for their action?

1062. : What reason ANC gave for their action?

1063. Q What strategy did the ANC used?

1064. Q: Who were ETA and what was their motivation?

1065. Q: What was the duration of ETA?

1066. Q: What did the ETA action?

1067. Q: What is one of reasons for terrorism?

1068. Q: What was used in the French revolution?

1069. Q; What do some terrorism claim reason of their action?

1070. Q: In United Kingdom, how is criminals assessed?.

1071. Q: How do terrorism create terror?

1072. Q: In terrorism targets those who already identify positively with the terrorist group what is their aim?

1073. Q: In terrorism targets those who are their declared opponents, what is their aim?

1074. Q: What is the aim of terrorist in targeting non- committed bystanders?

1075. Q; what is the aim of the terrorist own organization?

1076. Q; What is the terrorism aim in reference to rival groups?

1077. Q: According to Schmid, A. P (2005a) " Root cause of terrorism" name some causes of terrorism?

1078. Q: Name some organisation who have provided definition of terrorism?

1079. Q: In general what does terrorism refers

1080. Q: Which book contains about 260 definitions of terrorism?

1081. Q: From academic viewpoints, what is considered in arriving the definition of terrorism?

1082. Q: What law is used to punish terrorism?

1083. Q: What is the UK definition of terrorism

1084. Q: How does Spain define terrorism?

1085. Q: Where can one find Canada definition of terrorism?

1086. Q: where do one find France definition of terrorism.

1087. Q: where in USA can one find definition of terrorism?

1088. Q: Can terrorism be enforced under international law.

1089. Q: why is it difficult to punish terrorist?

1090. Q: Which bodies do the United Nation use on terrorism.

1091. Q: What does the international Bill f human Right consist of?

1092. Q: Briefly describe the Lockerbie bombing?

1093. Q: What are the Islamic state?

1094. Q: When and where was the greatest terrorist attack in the western countries?

Chapter 39

ICL (international criminal laws)

ICC(international criminal court)

(1095- 1149)

1095. Q: When was the United Nations created?

1096. Q: Who is currently the UN Secretary General?

1097. Q: Who are the five permanent members of the UN Security Council?

1098. Q: Is Eu court of Human Right base in

1099. Q: As of 2017, there is only one country in the world which failed to ratify the UN Convention of the Rights of the Child 1989. Which one?

1100. Q: On which day of the year is International Human Rights Day?

1101. Q: Where are the headquarters of the UN based

1102. Q: Who was the first person convicted by the International Criminal Court?

1103. Q: Which of the following is not a member of the United Nations?

1104. Q: How do state states consent to international law?

1105. Q: Why do states choose to be part of international treaties

1106. Q: What is ICL (international Criminal Law) function?

1107. Q: What condition can person be tried in foreign country?

1108. Q: What must the prosecutor established?

1109. Q: What difficulty exit in such prosecution?

1110. Q; What is the function of the Treaty of Versailles (1919).

1111. Q: What article was used against German emperor?

1112. Q: when was creation of modern international criminal justice?

1113. Q: What are the two-military tribunal?

1114. Q: why were the military tribunal created?

1115. Q: What and when did the Rape of Nanking?

1116. Q Give brief account of Nanjing massacre?

1117. Q: What is the Rape of Nanking now refer to?

1118. Q: name one prominent army general prosecuted after the second world war?.

1119. Q: Name the two-tribunal established by UN

1120. Q: who adopted the Rome statute in 1998?

1121. Q: What is the main reason for international law to act?

1122. Q: Where can we find retribution aspect of law?

1123. Q: Is retribution use as revenge?

1124. Q How does prosecution affect the victims of crime?

1125. Q: What is Principle of legality known in Latin?

1126. Q: What does the principal of legality states?

1127. Q: What is the punishment part in Latin.

1128. Q: What does nullum plena sine ledge mean?

1129. Q: What is Principle of non-retroactivity

1130. Q: What is Presumption of innocence

1131. Q: What can lead to individual to be prosecuted?

1132. Q: What is command responsibility as per ICL recognition?

1133. Q; What is the doctrine of Command responsibility?

1134. Q: What is the doctrine of Universal jurisdiction on crime?

1135. Q: What is the reason why nations prosecuting criminals?

1136. Q; Name one case dealt with under universal jurisdiction?

1137. Q; Summarise the main issue in the Congo v Belgium case?

1138. Q: Why was Belgium involvement?

1139. Q: what grounds did Belgium sought extradition

1140. Q: Give example of how a state fails to prosecute an alleged criminal?

1141. Q: Give brief description of Belgium v Senegal, 2012)

1142. Q: what does ICTs stand for?

1143. Q: What is Ad hoc international tribunal

1144. Q: give example of Ad hoc tribunal?

1145. Q; What is the principle of primacy in international law.

1146. Q: why are some nations hesitant to act against criminals in their own state?

1147. Q; name few circumstances that the ICC might asserts its jurisdiction?

1148. Q: What other reason that a state might be unable to prosecute individual.

1149. Q: What is expected of state by ICC or international tribunal?

Chapter 40

War Crimes (Q: 1150-1172)

Definition

1150. Q: How will you define war crimes

1151. Q; Which article can you find definition of war crime in The Charter of the International Military Tribunal at Nurnberg (IMTN Charter) 1945

1152. Q:Which article can you find definition of war crime Statute of the International Criminal Tribunal for the Former Yugoslavia (ICTY Statute) 2009

1153. Q: Which article can you find definition of war crime Statute of the International Criminal Tribunal for Rwanda (ICTR Statute) 2010

1154. Q:Which article can you find definition of war crime The Rome Statute of the International Criminal Court (ICC Statute) 1998

1155. Q: what is the core doctrine of Geneva Conventions?

1156. Q; what are state require to do under the Geneva convention?

1157. Q: What constitute war crimes?

1158. where do one find the essential elements to prosecute war crimes?

1159. Q: Before a state brings prosecution against individual or group what must be establish first.

1160. Q: What factors must be considered to determine NIAC rule

1161. Q; How does Article 8(1) of ICC says

1162. Q: how can CAH (crime against humanity) view on crime?

1163. Q: give an example of prosecution under article 8(2) of ICC(international criminal court?

1164. Q: Reference to CAH (crime against human) Which Article can definition of CAH be found? The Charter of the International Military Tribunal at Nuremberg (IMTN Charter)

1165. Q: Reference to CAH (crime against human) Which Article can definition of CAH be found? Statute of the International Criminal Tribunal for the Former Yugoslavia (ICTY Statute)

1166. Q: Reference to CAH (crime against human) Which Article can definition of CAH be found? Statute of the International Criminal Tribunal for Rwanda (ICTR Statute)

1167. Q: Reference to CAH (crime against human) Which Article can definition of CAH be found?. The Rome Statute of the International Criminal Court (ICC Statute).

1168. Q: In what circumstance can CAH be committed?

1169. Q: Explain the term systematics in the definition of CAH?

1170. Q: What does definition of systematic focus on?

1171. Q: What are the main element in CAH

1172. Q: What is Mens rea element in CAH

Chapter 41

Genocide 514 (1173-1187)

1173. Q; Where does the word genocide originate and what does it mean?

1174. Q: How did United Nation acknowledged genocide?

1175. Q: When was Genocide convention and name the main architect?

1176. Q: When did United Nation first dealt with Genocide?

1177. Q: What happen in the Armenian genocide?

1178. Q: When did the convention adopted

1179. Q: What were the main reason for Genocide convention in 1948?

1180. Q: Give the United Nation definition of genocide.

1181. Q:What does Article 1 state?

1182. Q: What did the weakness identify in the convention?

1183. Q: What are some of the reason a person can be guilty of genocide?

1184. Q: What is the Mens rea of genocide?

1185. Q: Give a case of genocide?

1186. Q: Briefly explain the media case

1187. Q: Why can one describe ICC to begin to disintegrate and end?

Chapter 42

The biggest problem with international law is how to enforce it (Q1188- 1235)

1188. What is The Biggest Challenges Facing the Enforcement of International Law.

1189. Q: How does politics affect enforcement of international law

1190. Q:How is the 21st century activities affect enforcement of international law?

1191. Q: Why is international law crucial?

1192. Q: What evidence of effort to enforce international law?

1193. Q; Give example of when international law was enforced?

1194. Q: What other ways that enforcement can be implemented?

1195. Q: Why do some nations only adhere to enforcement of international laws?

1196. : Give example and case why nations self-interest lead to agreement?

1197. Q:Give an example of warrant of arrest issued in 2005?

1198. Q: In 2010, who was warrant issue against and what happened?

1199. Q: How does domestic politics affect international law enforcement support with case?

1200. Q: has research been carried out regarding influence of sectarianism?

1201. Q: what does the term sectarianism mean ?

1202. Q: What else can sectarianism signify support the answer with case?

1203. Q: Considering the two definitions of sectarianism how can compliance of international law come to play.

1204. Q: How does authoritative countries influence law enforcement?

1205. Q; Explain the weakness in international law?

1206. Q: How has Sectarianism influence in some nations?

1207. Q: Do religious doctrines affect enforcement of international law?

1208. Q; Which countries might lack democracy due to sectarianism?

1209. Q: Give examples of some states activities that hinder law enforcement?

1210. Q: How does sub-Saharan countries compare with other states?

1211. Q: How does Western countries policies affect international law enforcement give example?

1212. Q: What method can be used for such research of enforcement?

1213. Q: What does review consider?

1214. Q: Where do I get the sources to support my argument of international law enforcement

1215. Q: what were the terms I used for the research?

1216. Q: Are there obligatory law international law enforcement?

1217. Q: How are national interest known?

1218. Q: What other laws highlight problems of international law enforcement?

1219. Q: Has there been any change in enforcing international laws since human right in1998

1220. Q: How can sovereignty of state influence international laws?

1221. Q: What is global agreement amongst state with regard to international laws. Human Right

1222. Q: In emergency what happened to Human Right laws?

1223. Q: Q: How can absolute power make head of state?

1224. Q: Why did the head of state of the in the world war denounce treaty of Versailles

1225. Q: What effect to have international obligation?

1226. Q: When and what reason did human right started to take effect?

1227. Q: What did universal declaration of human right demanded.

1228. Q: What other way can enforcement of international law be achieved?

1229. Q: Q: What must nations do to avoid violation of human rights?

1230. Q: Give some norms of human rights that support law enforcement to prevent abuse?

1231. Q: What has encouraged people to protect each other against abuse?

1232. Q: Name some countries who violate human right and avoid enforcement of international law?

1233. Q: Is it easy to resolve implementation of international laws?

1234. Q; Why do some state refuse to enforce international laws

1235. Q: How should international law be applied?

Chapter 43

Miscellaneous (Q;1236-1246)

1236. Q: Which area of the dating agency do exhibit dishonesty which means theft and crime.?

1237. Q: What about men using female photos/video/punster to trick men on internet for money?.

1238. Q: People pretending to be diplomat to defraud the public?

1239. Q: Can crime enforcement officer be charged with crime?.

1240. Q; Can members of parliament claim immunity to crime.

1241. Q: Do some government policies encourage crime.

1242. Q: Do you think historic crime allegation is fair

1243. Q: Do you think women should be paid to make force or true allegation.

1244. Q: Due to equality law and human right, must men be paid for reporting sexual or violence offence by women?

1245. Q; How must abuse of power and position be punished

1246. Q: What should happen to doctors who breach duty of care?

Chapter 44

Key legal terms used in criminology

1247. Q: What is the function of the UK house of Lords?

1248. Q: What does Advocate mean?

1249. Q: What does accused mean?

1250. Q: What does acknowledgement in law mean?

1251. Q: What does Acquittals of a person mean?

1252. Q: What does the case is adjourned mean?

1253. Q: What does Adoption mean?

1254. Q: What does adultery mean?

1255. Q; What does Affidavit mean?

1256. Q; What is Affirmation?

1257. Q: What is appeal?

1258. Q: What is attachment of earnings

1259. Q: What is award mean?

1260. Q: What is bail?

1261. Q; Who is regarded as bailiff?

1262. Q: What does bankrupt mean?

1263. Q: Who is barrister or counsel?

1264. Q: What is Bench warrant?

1265. Q: what is Indictment?

1266. Q: What is Bind over?

1267. Q: What is Bind over for sentence?

1268. Q: What is Brief?

1269. Q: What is case conference?

1270. Q: what is Caution?

1271. Q: What is Caveat?

1272. Q: what is Cessate Chambers

1273. Q: Who is Circuit Judge Civil?

1274. Q: What is Civil Justice Reform?

1275. Q: what is commissioner of oath

1276. Q; What does Committal means

1277. Q: Concurrent sentence?

1278. Q: What is Consecutive sentence?

1279. Q: What is Contempt of court?

1280. Q: what is Corroboration?

1281. Q; Describe county court?

1282. Q: Describe court of appeal

1283. Q: what is Court of protection?

1284. Q; Describe Crown court?

1285. Q; how is Crown court divided?

1286. Q: Describe first Tier?

1287. Q: Describe second tier

1288. Q: Describe Third tier?

1289. Q: What is decree Nisi

1290. Q: What is decree absolute?

1291. Q: Explain divisional Court?

1292. Q: what is expert witness?

1293. Q: What is Garnishee?

1294. Q: Name some branches of High court?

1295. Q: What is Indictable offence?

1296. Q:What is justice of the peace?

1297. Q: who are Law lords?

1298. Q: Who is the Lord Chancellor?

1299. Q: Who is Public trustee?

1300. Q: Who is regarded as Queens counsel QC?

1301. Q: What is trial window?

1302. Q: Explain tribunal and give example?

1303. Q: What is restitution?

1304. Q: What is Winding up?

Chapter 2

QUESTIONS AND ANSWERS

Definitions of criminology

1. Q: Why do crime happen

A: The gap between the wealth and poverty, urbanisation, religion, government war, trade, technology mass media.

Drugs, lack of discipline by parent at home and in schools, poverty drive people to crime, laziness, greed and alcohol, no effective police force, the media, television and newspapers, films and computer games make people learn to commit crime, large towns and cities make people think they can get away with crimes. Criminal in prison learn more crime from fellow inmate, police corruption get involved with crime.

2. Q; Dafne criminology

A:The term criminology is difficult to define because there are several ways of looking at it, depending on the background of the person defining it, There had been different definition of crime

3. **Q:** How will you define criminology simply?

A: , criminology could be defined as the study of various ways of systematically thinking about the description, prediction, explanation, and control of crime

4. Q: Defend crime in another perspective.

A: a crime is simply a behaviour that persons in power chose to prohibit or command. For this reason, individual criminal acts may have very little in common.

A major issue in criminological theory is the incredible range of human behaviours that can be regarded as criminal Furthermore, the common thread of being illegal does not mean that the behaviours are alike in any other meaningful sense. This is why an increasing number of criminologists advocate limiting criminological theories to specific acts or a range of closely related acts.

5. Q: What need to be considered when defining criminology

A:knowledge concerning the ethology, prevention, control and treatment of crime and delinquency, includes the measurement and detection of crime, legislation and practice of criminal law, as well as the law enforcement, judicial and correctional systems.

6. Q: How did William and Me define criminology theory

A: Williams and Me share (2004), criminology theory , Theory, Aristotle, Plato and Cicero) define crime as what is done by people which the society in the country (local) regards as acceptable or normal and what is abnormal.

7. Q: How did the House of Lords in United Kingdom define crime

A The definition by the House of Lords in a case between Board

of Trade. V. Owen 1957) AC 602 House of Lords; An unlawful act or default which is an offence against the public and renders the person guilty of the liable to legal punishment.

8. **Q:** How did Blackstone define crime

A: Blackstone defines crime as "A violation of the public rights and duties du e the whole community". Crime is a breach of duty imposed by law for the benefit of the community at large.

9. **Q:** How did sociology derived their definition

A: The most common specific definition of criminology comes to us from *sociology.* We can gather the importance (and dominance) of sociology within criminology from the preface of Williams and McShane's (2004) popular text, *Criminological Theory.* While there are other approaches to the study of crime, since the 1920s criminology has been oriented toward sociology.

10. **Q:** What other ways can crime be define?

A: Scientist and sociologist comment on biological and psychological theories of crime.

11. **Q;** Why is criminology sometimes called "criminal justice theory"

A: In broad sense, criminology could also be called *criminal justice theory* because in a narrower sense; several academic disciplines look at it differently usually with a specific focus on the theories and methods of the specific discipline.

12. **Q:** Define criminology in broader view?

A: a broader definition that encompasses more than the view of one specific discipline. The basis of all criminology, regardless of discipline, is the use of a systematic way of thinking. Systematic thinking occurred long before modem sociology, and those early thinkers thought about crime. This means that some very early thinkers (e.g., Aristotle, Plato, Cicero) must be considered if a complete picture is to be drawn.

Chapter 3

Crimes

There are many types of crimes in the world in general and United Kingdom in particular
I will say that stealing, racial abuse including violet attack and drugs had been increase in a lot of local areas

13. Q; Name examples of crimes

A:Thef, These opportunities stealing, Petty Theft, Racial abuse Sexual assault, Drugs, Other Crimes

14. Q Define theft

A: Taken something that does not belong to you without permission is a major crime, not just in my area but in the world. And it started before the Roman Empire

15. Q: Name one type of theft and give reason

A: stealing which occurred due to a lot of reasons including deprivation, greedy, kleptomania, or thief want to be somebody who have work to achieve what he has.

16. Q: What could be the effect of stealing.

A: There are many effects associate with stealing including causing bodily harm, causing distress.

17. Q: give example of stealing you have witnessed or heard of.

A: An arm rumbling where the thieves threaten the bank staff with a gun.

18. Q: How do some people steal

A: Professional thieves always plan in advance; they may go to the anticipate site to survey and to plan.

19. Q; Give example of opportunity stealing?

A; Some of the stealing had been an opportunity mission example pick pocket for purse credit cards

20. Q; Who gives chance for stealing?

A: The vulnerable people are those who are careless such as leaving the front door open, leave the car unlocks expose the purse in one pocket.

21. Q; How do the thieves behave?

A; threaten people to hand over their jewel such as neck lace watches diamond and gold rings

22. Q: Give another opportunity stealing

A; There had been reports of care staff stealing from the old people, the sick especially those patients who do not have next of kin or any advocate. This is opportunity theft. Other form of stealing is forging signature on cheques to withdraw money from the vulnerable people.

23. Q: How does opportunity stealing from vulnerable people.

A; May happen unnoticed and might go on for some considerable time.

24. Q: name one thing opportunistic thieves use?

A: Thieve use credit card pin number to withdraw money from people account.

25. Q: What do this usually steal when they break into properties and when does it take place?

A: There had been a number of thieves breaking into properties to steal televisions, stereo, jewels clothes, money, which has taken place mostly during the day when people have gone to work or night when people asleep.

26. **Q:** Give serious crime you have heard?

A: One day a bugler enter a house during the day, tied the man and his daughter in suppurate chairs, tied their mouth, threaten them with knife for the man to show where all the valuables and money were, the thieves worn, mask and groves, one of them stayed with the man and he daughter whilst the other ransack the valuables. When they finished, they left the house still leaving them tied up in the chair.

27. Q: Describe another incident

A: incident occurred in retailer shop, when gang of thieves went to the shop through the back door when the shop has just closed. The thieves were blindfolded, UN pluck the phone disconnect the CCTV and took the tape, and got away with all the till money, cigarettes other small valuables and some alcohol, they left the shop owner tied up in a chair.

28. Q: Describe shop lifting?

A: crimes reported were shop lifting in major supermarket in Marks and Spencer, involves stealing clothes jewel, cigarettes, and some small items. The thieves carry the goods to the till area and then disappear from the shop without paying, but most of them were identified using on the CCTV and were caught by the security officers.

Petty thief

29. Q:Describe example of petty thief.

A; There had been a lot of Petty thief in the market stalls for clothing, food and money, I have heard of gang go to the market stall, one of them was talking to the owner whilst the other load his bag with fruits and get away without paying, this has been common occurring.

30. Q: Give example of violent crime?

A: Violent crime whereby people on the street had been threaten, took all his jewel and money mobile phone and run away in a car.

31. Q: Give another example of crime One was

forced out of his car being threatened with gun and the thieves took his purse, money, mobile phone car key and drove his car away.

Racial abuse

32. Q: Who are the victims of racial abuse?

A: very common in the area they target the black, Asians, mixed race, the India people calling them all sort of names I dare not repeat, shouting at them on the street "Packy go home" and so on.

33. Q: Give an example of racial crime?

A: There had been occasion when foreigners had been attacked at night, beaten up and left him lying in a pull of blood, taken all his money and mobile phone. Thieves put fear in foreign people that most of them do not go out at night for fear of being attacked

34. Q: What is police reaction in racial and violent areas

A; Police do increase number of on foot police usually in pairs on the street during the day, and police cars patrolling the area increased

Sexual assault

35. Q: public place do sexual assault takes place?

A, sexual assault, harassment attempted rape at night especially when people come out from the pub or night club.

Drugs

36. Q: who are the target in drugs

A: Adult drug dealers target the young who in fact are used to sell the drugs because they knew that they may not be convicted by the Crown Prosecution Service or the police. Because of the age.

37. Q: What happen when the buyers do not have money.

A; In area where drug dealing occurs, there is also increase in stealing for the drug users or the addict to get money to buy drugs.

38. Q: Name few other crimes

A: threat murder assault; robbery, taken without consent, manslaughter, intoxication, wounding bodily harm, blackmail, deception, juvenile crime drug fighting, football hooligans

39. Q: What result from unemployment?

A: Due to the high unemployment in the area, there had been a lot of benefit crime and people who had been working and claim benefit. In addition some women give false accusation on men so that they could get victim support benefit from the state.

40. Q: What other crime globally

A: Some religious faiths, whereby the Muslim and the Christians have taken the law in their hand to fight back the constant abuse.

Chapter 4

Perceiving these criminals

There had been different ways of detecting the crimes as recorded in the local and national and international papers and police communication seculars

41. Q: are available to detect these criminals.

A: C CTV; alarm; car theft. police; DNA lie reward electrocommunication radio; citizen arrest community policing

identity parade, globalisation policing;

football hooliganism, security and protection;

42. **Q:** Explain where and how CCTC use to detect crime?

A: C CTV; In supermarkets, banks, shops and on the street, most of them have install CCTV which monitor the area twenty-four hours. Some are connected to local police station.

The problem is that some of the professional thieves uses face mask and hand. There is CCTV on police cars when surveying suspect on the road

There is CCTV on police cars when surveying suspect on the road suspect on the road

43. **Q:** Explain where and how Alarm is used to detect crime?

A:most households and businesses have alarms which when intruder activate it the control centre calls the police and the owner

44. **Q:** Explain where and how car alarm is used to detect crime?

A: There is car alarm fitted to most modern cars now that goes off when someone attempt to break into, this act as deterrent and also help to arrest the unauthorized intruder

45. **Q:** Explain where and how Police is used to detect crime?

A: The police have vast resources aim to detect and arrest criminals which include sophisticated hidden cameras, tape recorders hidden on their body or the police station or in their cars.

46. **Q:** Explain where and how CCTC used to detect crime?

A: DNA are used to help to conform the criminals, this has been a positive identification, this can be done by taken swab from the mouth, or taken sample of blood or hair or seamen from the man or the woman vagina and are then sent to laboratory to be tested.

47. **Q:** Explain where and how Lie detectors are used to detect crime?

A: LIE DETECTOR: has been used with the consent of the accuser, but latterly this has proof not to be reliable as it has been successfully challenged.

48. **Q:** Explain where and how communication been uses to detect crime?

A: COOMMUNICATION RADIO; on foot or patrol police or those on bicycle or cars use this to communicate with their colleague on suspect or to call for help to arrest.

49. **Q:** Explain where and how citizen arrest been uses to detect crime?

A: In some cases citizen arrest can be done by anybody that can proof that someone has commit crime

50. **Q:** Explain where and how community policing been uses to detect crime?

A: Police rely on the community at large to report any suspected crime by dialling emergency telephone number 999

51. **Q:** Explain where and how reward has been used to detect crime?

A: in serious crime police has offered reward to the public for information leading to the arrest conviction of a specific crime

52. **Q:** Explain where and how identity parade been used to detect crime?

A: IDENTITY PARADE; Where the complainant find difficult to identify a criminal, a selection of about 10 people had been line up with numbers pin to their front, the accuser or complainant stand behind translucent class and pick up whom he or she think committed the crime

53. **Q:** Explain where and how identity parades have been used to detect crime?

A: GLOBARISATION POLICING helps Drug trafficking are being detected due to the cooperation between other countries who have signed treaty to combat crime. They also help to deport suspect to face trial for the sake of the public interest and justice

54. **Q:** Explain where and how football authority been used to detect crime?

A: FOOT BALL Hooliganism's police and the football authority work together by segregating the teams supporters, and in most cases the teams barn the trouble supporters from coming to the studio or traveling abroad to support the team

55. **Q:** Explain where and how security and protection been used to detect crime?

Police and local authority have issued guidelines to the public of how to prevent criminal such as secure their homes, business, etc.

Television programmes have helped the community to identify criminals Computer records have improve police records to identify criminals Police powers of questioning arrest, reporting and search.

56. **Q:** Explain where and how Whistle blowers been used to detect crime?

A; Some get reward by exposing other especially rich people for crime done.

Chapter 5

Theory

57. Q: Do humans need "theory" and why?

A: human beings require theories to live. Example it is theory that stove burners are hot; therefore life would be dangerous indeed if people had to touch glowing stove burners every time to determine that they are hot. We operate using theories all the time without even thinking of them as theories.

58. Q Give examples of generalisation theory?

A: People in our society accept the theory that cold-water faucets are on the right, other drivers will stop at stop signs, that doors are ways to enter buildings. Daily life would slowly stop if we couldn't make these *generalisations.* It is the nature of humanity to generalise.

59. Q: What is the problem of theory of generalisation?

A problem that arises out of the natural tendency of people to generalise is the tendency of overgeneralisation. Which result many social problems in our society. People commonly treat others unfairly because of overgeneralisations.

60. Q: When do people turn to over generalise and why?

A: Generalisation can be perceived as theory the less people know about something, the more they are likely to over generalise. Example comments ,professors are absent minded, men like to watch football. Overgeneralisations like these are easy to spot; most people will have encountered at least a few men who do not watch football and conclude that the generalisation is unfair.

61. Q: In what areas can over generalisation be harmful?

A: The obviously unfair and potentially more harmful are overgeneralisations made about people of other races, religions, and national origins.

62. Q: Define acceptable behaviour and how it could unfairly lead to suspect of crime.

A: acceptable behaviour is what one internal and external environment accept. This means, it may be normal acceptable behaviour in a house or country but not acceptable in next door house or another country.

63. Q: What are the main types of theories?

A: A common distinction between types of theories uses the terms abstract and concrete but can also generate "common sense Theory and Scientific theory

64. What is concrete theory?

A **concrete theory** is one that explains observable, verifiable facts, such as in the hot stove example. Humans can observe the red light, and can use measuring tools, such as a thermometer, to identify precisely the amount of heat present.

65. Q: What is Abstract theories?

A: Abstract theories are not directly verifiable because they involve concepts that researchers cannot directly measure. Humans use abstract concepts all the time. Things like joy, sadness, and love cannot be seen, but most people accept that they are there, example, researchers cannot directly measure ideas such as justice, integrity, and love.

Common Sense Theory **v.** Scientific Theory

66. Q: What is common sense theory

A:Individual daily activities or theories are mostly based on "common sense." The critical element of here is the term *common.* example knowledge is *common* to many people does not mean that it is true because it depend on the acceptable knowledge within society one lives.

67. Q: Give example of some believe which is not true?

A:Some people believed that the earth was flat and was the centre of the universe. That once people get university degree they can get any job. That the colour of your skin make one superior or inferior. these widely held beliefs are not a matter of common sense anymore. Some beliefs are commonly held today that are untrue.

68. Q: What is the problem of common-sense theory?

A: The problem is that we have no way of knowing right or wrong except for systematic inquiry.

69. Q: What is the way we think?

A:The way of thinking is by systematic inquiry which is either philosophical or scientific.

70. Q: What did Fred Kerlinger view about common sense and scientific theory in relation to the current trend in criminal justice research

A: Fred Kerlinger (1992, pp. 4-7) describes five important differences between common sense theory and scientific theory

71. Q: According to Fred Kerlinger, what is common sense theory based on?

A: "Common sense" theory is developed based on "conceptual schemes" that may be "fanciful" and not subject to evaluation. Scientific theory is based on evidence that can be observed and measured.

72. Q: According to Fred Kerlinger, what is scientist theory based on?

A:Scientists verify their theories in ways believed to be objective. People often validate common sense theories by selecting examples that fit the theory.

They maintain their stereotypes by ignoring examples that do not fit their them

73. Q: According to Fred Kerlinger, how is control in science, explain control in this context?

A: Control is important in science. In this context, control refers to the efforts of scientists to rule out other explanations for a phenomenon that their theory does not consider. For example, a non-scientist who believes that children become delinquent because of drugs will not likely consider delinquency in children who do not use drugs.

74. Q: According to Fred Kerlinger, what is the reaction of non- scientist.

A:The non-scientist is likely to seize on a chance occurrence and immediately develop a cause and effect theory to explain a relationship that is not there. A “lucky shirt” is an example of this sort of unscientific logic.

75. **Q**: According to Fred Kerlinger, what do people think of metaphysical explanation?

A: Scientists, unlike most non-scientists (and Philosophers) rule out "metaphysical explanations" for events.

76. **Q:** What does metaphysical explanation mean and give example?

A:Metaphysical explanations is based on something that cannot be tested, which usually means that the proposed cause cannot be observed. Example, If someone proposes that serial killers kill because they are possessed by demons, then they have offered a metaphysical explanation. Or a voice told the person to commit a crime (auditory hallucination).

77. **Q:** While it is true that scientists reject metaphysical arguments as unscientific?

A: The scientists are saying is that they cannot or do not know how to test it because If a scientist cannot test a theory by observation, it is not a scientific theory. Similar, it does not mean that they do not agree with them or think them to be untrue.

78. Q: why scientists do not attempt to answer many important questions, such as "what is justice?" especially in criminal cases?

A: The basic idea of science is to establish a method of knowing with evidence things that is independent of people's opinions about them.

79. Q: If scientist cannot give metaphysical explanation, which areas of study can?

A:The metaphysical question is no doubt important, but is not a question that science can answer. People trying to answer this question can never entirely separate it from their personal opinions and beliefs, so it is more properly answered within philosophy or theology (religion).

80. **Q:** Why do scientists disagree about theory?

A:When scientists disagree about theory, the arguments usually centre on the lack of evidence, the quality of evidence, or the interpretation of evidence.

81. **Q**: What non-scientific method of knowing that cause problems in criminal justice system

A: tenacity, *authority*, *intuition*

82. Q: Explain "method of tenacity"?

A; method of tenacity. is where people hold to their beliefs simply because they believe them to be true and is non scientific

88. Q: What is "method of authority"

A: method of authority is where people believe what they believe because an important authority (e.g., the Bible, Quran the doctor or a professor) said so. This method is not necessarily unsound and is used by scientists all the time. It becomes unsound (from a scientific perspective) when there is no willingness to question the authority.

83. Q: Give an example of why authority sometimes needs to be challenged?

A: Laws are amended or abolished, or policies are changed. Consider where we would be today if Einstein blindly accepted the work of Newton as absolute fact and never questioned it.

84. Q:Explain the method of intuition.

A:The method of intuition is alternative to the scientific method

By this method, people believe what they believe

because it “stands to reason.” This is essentially the method of the philosopher, and explains why there is no general agreement among philosophers on important philosophical questions. Well meaning, honest people can consider a problem in a perfectly rational way and still reach different conclusions

85. Q: Explain different meaning of “theory” between scientist and non-scientist?

A:The term theory means something different to scientists than it does to the average person. Scientific theory is usually based on evidence, unlike the unsupported speculation of non-scientists. while scientific theories are generally based on facts, scientists seldom regard a theory as “proven.”

86. Q: Why is it that scientist reluctant to use the word proven?

A: Scientists are too conservative to use the word *proven* because there might be an exception to the rule that they have yet to find. The strongest commitment that can be found is scientific writing will be something along the lines of a particular theory being "strongly supported by the evidence."

What Makes a Good Theory?

87. Q: From scientific point of view, what is good theory?

A: Since the scientific method has dominated modern criminology, it is generally accepted among criminologists that good theory must be empirically testable, and that evidence gathered from research supports the theory. This requirement is obvious from a scientific standpoint, because empirical validation is the foundation of scientific inquiry.

88. Q: What is the difference between social science and natural science

A: Williams and McShane (2004, p. 4) suggest that there is essentially no difference between what a good theory in the social sciences is and what is a good theory' in the natural sciences (e.g., physics and chemistry). The primary difference comes in how variables of interest are measured. Generally, the more concrete a concept is, the more accurately and precisely it can be measured. Things such as temperature and velocity (important variables in the natural sciences) can be measured with a high degree of precision. Abstract concepts, such as depression or socio-economic status, are far more difficult to measure. For this reason, measurement is a difficult issue for social scientists.

89. Q: Name two method of measuring and test theory of not knowing?

A: The measurement and testing approach suggest types of research known as quantitative and qualitative research.

90. Q Explain Quantitative *research*?

A: Quantitative comes from the same root as the term *quantity* and is talking about numbers.

91. Q: What is qualitative research

A:The term qualitative suggests an interest in the quality of the theory. Qualitative research focuses on the substance of a theory. The first of the qualitative requirements of a good theory is that it be logical. A logical theory is one in which concepts are clearly

92. Q: How do we regard good theory?

A:For a theory to be good, it should explain a wide range of behaviour (Akers, 2000).

93. **Q:** What is parsimonious?

A: Another common requirement of a scientific theory is that it be parsimonious. The law of parsimony is the logical principle that theorists propose no more causes than are necessary to account for the observed facts

Chapter 6

Crime problem solving

94. **Q:** What are the two-problem solving method use in solving in crime?

A: Two examples of successful problem-solving initiatives PROCTOR to enhance SARA

95. **Q:** What does PROCTOR stand for?

A: PRO=Problem, C=Cause, T=Tactic or Treatment, O=Output and R= Result (PROCTOR)

96. Q: What does SARA stand for

A: S=Scanning (problem), A= Analyse (cause), R= Response (tactic/treatment, A= Assessment (output)

97. Q: SARA, if the problem Accidental drug related death involving methadone , what will be the Analyse cause

A: Leakage of prescribed methadone into the illicit drugs market

98. Q: SARA, if the problem Accidental drug related death involving methadone , what will be Response for tactic or treatment

A: Pressure on doctors to agree changed prescribing practices; incentives to pharmacies to provide supervised daily methadone taking. Monitoring of prescription practices and reminders to those prescribing inappropriately

99. Q: SARA, if the problem Accidental drug related death involving methadone, what will be the assessment output

A: Reduced overall prescription of methadone, especially the tablets most associated with deaths, increased daily prescriptions, increased provision for supervised drug taking in pharmacies

100. Q: SARA, if the problem Accidental drug related death involving methadone, what will be the expected result

A: Reduction from 1996 high and then elimination from 1999 of drug-related deaths involving methadone.

101. Q: SARA, if the problem is Disorder late at night at pizza parlours What will be analyse cause?

A: Irritation of waiting whilst pizzas cooked: those waiting under the influence of alcohol

102. Q: SARA, if the problem is Disorder late at night at pizza parlours What will be Response Tactic/Treatment

A: Enable customers to avoid waiting around to collect their orders after closing time when disturbances are apt to take place.

103. Q: SARA, if the problem is Disorder late at night at pizza parlours What will be assessment output?

A: Pizza parlours install direct lines from pubs to pizza parlours for customers to make orders

104. Q: SARA, if the problem is Disorder late at night at pizza parlours What will be expected result.

A: Reduced late night fast food pizza parlour troubles

105. Q: What does PAT stand for

A: PAT stands for Police Arbitral Tribunal

106. Q: What does PAT element use for and what does it focus.?

A; to determine possible results/response and it focus on investigate "Place", "Offenders" and "Victim"

107. Q:Using PAT, if there had been a crime, what will be the response regarding "Place"

A: Tackling the lack of lighting by bringing the problem to the attention of the relevant authority

108. Q: Q:Using PAT, if there had been a crime, what will be the response regarding "Offenders"

A; Considering why the youths hang around the area, to establish whether there is something that brings them there, or whether there is a lack of other places to go

109. Q:Using PAT, if there had been a crime, what will be the response regarding "Victim"

A: Enlisting the help of the local community by encouraging them to keep a special watch on the area and to lobby the local authority to provide better amenities for young people

110. Q; What other measures can be done?

A: Targeting police resources such as foot and car patrols in the area at the particular times identified by analysis when the incidents are most frequent

111. Q How can the community reputation improve?

A:Bringing the problem, and efforts to tackle it, to the attention of the local media to try to improve the reputation of the area

112. Q Using SARA, what do the investigators do?

A: In the final stage of SARA, practitioners review attempts to deal with a problem and evaluate how successful they have been.

113. Q: Give three major reasons why the assessment stage in SARA is very important

1. A: To find out whether a particular problem still

exists and_requires continuing attention. This is important in deciding whether to continue to deploy resources to respond effectively to the problem.

2. To improve problem-solving skills by finding out what seems to work in_ differing circumstances. This avoids reinventing the wheel and contribute to the "what works" knowledgebase and the dissemination of good practice.

3. To enable effective problem-solving to be recognised within the police service and other organisations, acknowledging individuals' efforts.

114. **Q;** What is assessment of how a crime been dealt with

A; Assessment is not an evaluation of the performance of those involved but what happened when a problem was tackled. Assessment can be difficult to do well and as a result is often largely overlooked. It must be a routine feature of any problem-solving structure.

115. Q: Do investigator get rid of successfully assessment?

A; No, an assessment that concludes that a problem has been dealt with successfully does not always mean that it has been eliminated.

116. Q; List about four different types of successful investigations by police.

1. **A:** The problem and its impact remain the same but the volume of police effort to respond to it may be reduced.
2. The harm to the public may be reduced even though the number of incidents remains the same.
3. The number of problem incidents may be reduced.
4. The problem may be entirely eliminated.

117. **Q:** Describe good assessment

A: Needs a clear definition of the problem and a description of how it is being addressed in order to focus measurement where success is most credibly to be predictable.

Needs a good description of what was actually done and when action was taken as there is often a difference between what was planned and what was actually done.

Needs to classify whether a response failed to achieve its hoped-for outcomes because it was not applied as had been intended, or whether it honestly failed to make an impact.

Needs a collection of incident and other data about the problem before and after the response and the identification of the precise action taken to resolve the problem, rather than basic before and after measures at an cumulative level.

118. Q: Why must investigators be careful when using SARA for problem solving.

A: SARA can be used as a controlling process for problem solving, it would be wise not to see it as the answer to everything as it can be limited in its efficiency if it is employed in too automatic a fashion.

119. Q: Give examples of poor use of SARA within problem solving include:

A: By not making full use of past data available when skimming

Needs a group of occurrence and other data about the problem before and after the response and the identification of the precise action taken to resolve the problem, rather than basic before and after measures at an cumulative level.

Needs a good account of what was actually done and when action was taken as there is often a difference between what was planned and what was actually done

Needs to classify whether a response failed to

achieve its hoped-for results because it was not applied as had been intended, or whether it sincerely failed to make an impact

120. Q: What are criminology theories:

A; theories must be grouped in some way before they can be systematically studied.

121. Q: Describe how Akers (2000), how many theories divide

A: Akers (2000), for example, discusses a simple scheme where theories are divided into two groups:

122. Q; What is the first group of theories?

A: The first group consists of theories of making and enforcing criminal law,

123. Q; What is the second group of theories?

A: the second group consists of theories that attempt

to explain why people break the law. As Akers points out, there are many more theories of the second type.

124. **Q:** Describe Classical criminology?

A: . Classical criminology defines theories that focus on legal statutes, the workings of government, and human rights. Classical criminological theory is generally not considered scientific.

125. Q: Describe Positive criminology,

A: . Positive criminology, refers to efforts at making criminology scientific; that is, positivists use the scientific method.

Chapter 7
STATISTIC

126. Q Why are statistics taken and who takes them?

Statistic is normally taken by the police and other agencies to gauge the trend of the crime and to identify which crime are going up or down. This helps the police and the government to plan where to target the resources

127. Q; What was crime in 1995

A: British Crime Survey which includes unreported and unrecorded crimes estimated that there were 19 million offenses in 1995

128. Q: What was police statistics of crime in 1997?

A; In 1997 petty theft increase by 47 % from a year

before, violent crime decrease from about 20% to 6%

129. Q: What was the crime rate in Wakefield, United Kingdom.

A: Drugs; in wakefief U.K 70% of all theft, burglary and violent crime was drug related (drug addict).

130. Q; Why are some crimes not detected especially computers?

A: Computer fraud has increase and most are undetected due to experience professional computer knowledge.

131. Q: Name other crimes that statistic is carried out?

A: Criminal damages, recklessness, theft, robbery, taking without consent obtaining by deception making off without payment, rape indecent assault manslaughter, murder and intent

132. Q: What was statistics of crime in 2013?

17/10/2013 · Statistics on hate crime, racist incidents, crime outcomes, crime against businesses and drugs misuse. National Statistics on crime previously published by the Home Office

133. Q: What was statistics in 2018

A: In the year ending March 2018, an estimated 2.0 million adults aged 16 to 59 years experienced domestic abuse. The latest 2018 figures from the Crime Survey for England and Wales show little change in the occurrence of domestic abuse in recent years.

134. Q: Crime in England and Wales in 2019/20

Total all Crimes in England and Wales: last 2 months

Crime	**Jan 2020**	**Feb 2020**	**Change**
Anti-Social Behaviour	85,176	82,747	-2,429
Robbery	6,818	6,549	-269
Burglary	31,718	28,667	-269
Vehicle Crime	38,797	35,774	-3,023

Crime	Jan 2020	Feb 2020	Change
Violent Crime	152,436	146,480	-5,956
Theft - Shoplifting	27,814	28,685	+871
Drugs	15,242	13,728	-1,514
Criminal Damage and Arson	43,265	37,930	-5,335
Theft - Other	37,277	35,929	-1,348
Bike Theft	5,048	4,683	-365
Theft From the Person	7,627	7,945	+318
Possession of Weapons	3,459	3,143	-316
Public Order	31,934	31,024	-910
Other Crime	8,453	8,019	-434
Total Crimes Plus ASB	**495,064**	**471,303**	**-23,761**

135. Q:global What is the crime statistic in Northern Ireland?

A: Northern Ireland's crime rate has fallen from 84 crimes per 1,000 people in 2002/03 to just 54 in

2017/18. During this time period Norther Ireland's crime rate saw the biggest decline in its crime rate between 2002/03 and 2003/04 when it dropped from 84 to 74

136. **Q: In a table form give List of Top Ten developed nations/ Countries with Highest Crime Rates**

Rank	Country	No. of Crimes
1.	United States	11,877,218
2.	United Kingdom	6,523,706
3.	Germany	6,507,394
4.	France	3,771,850
5.	Russia	2,952,370
6.	Japan	2,853,739
7.	South Africa	2,683,849
8.	Canada	2,516,918
9.	Italy	2,231,550

10.	India	1,764,630

137. Q:How is international crime classified?

A: The crimes can be classified into big lists, but majorly can be the following:

On the basis of offense (Seriousness)

- Felony
- Misdemeanour
- Offense against an individual
- Assault
- Murder (Homicide)
- Kidnapping
- Sexual Assault
- Battery
- Criminal negligence
- Robbery
- False imprisonment
- Mayhem

138. Q: Name top ten countries with highest crime

A:The countries with the ten highest crime rates in the world are: x 1000

1. Venezuela (84.49)
2. Papua New Guinea (81.93)
3. Papua Guinea (81.39
4. South Africa 77.49

5. Afghanistan 76.23
6. Honduras 76.11
7. Trinidad & Tobago 73.19
8. Brazil 68.15
9. El Salvador 67.96
10. Guyana 67.66

139. Q: Name top ten safe countries in the world?

A: These are the 10 best countries in the world in 2019

1. Switzerland.
2. Japan.
3. Canada.
4. Germany.
5. United Kingdom.
6. Sweden.
7. Australia.
8. United States.

9. Norway.
10. France.

Chapter 8

Courts

140. Q: name some courts in united Kingdom?

A. There are various courts dealing with specific offence; Magistrate 2) County court 3)Crown court **4**) court martial for military 5) Coroner's court 6) High court 7) High court Queens Bench division, 8) High court Chancellor division 90 Appeal court, 9) Supreme court(formally house of Lords

141. Q which of these deals with crime

A: Magistrate, Crown court martial for military 5) Coroner's court, appeal court. Supreme court(formally house of Lords.

Magistrate court

142. Q Who are the decision makers in Magistrate court.?

A: This usually consist of three magistrates, who may not legal trained but assisted by a legal train person who advise them the point of law.

143. Q what is another name for magistrate court and why.?

A:It is referred to as police court since all cases including criminal cases has to pass

144. Q: What cases are heard in magistrate court?

A:They hear minor cases which are not serious enough to be tried in crown court, All major crime or offences that are to be trailed in crown court has to start at the magistrate court, who decides the gravity of the crime before transferring to the crown court

145. Q: What restriction on magistrate court?

A; If the accused is found guilty, they passed the sentence, but they have limitation and must not exceed that including the length of sentence and the amount of compensation

146. Q: What happen if accuser is found guilty?

A: The accuser alone can make application to the crown court to appeal against the conviction or the sentence,

147. Q: How do magistrate deals with juvenile cases?.

A; Magistrate court deals with juvenile cases in private chambers and no publicity allowed. In most cases the proceedings are held in private no publicity to protect the young offender.

148. Q: How can magistrate deal with under nine years old?

A; Magistrate can make an order for young person less than 9 years for the local authority care which consist of probation officer, social worker, police, and health and education team.

Crown court

149. Q: name some crimes heard in crown court?

A: This include; control drugs, indecent assault. Sexual assault; reckless driving; handling; fraud, burglary

150. Q: What cases are heard in crown court?

A: All crimes are heard in crown court; the case having been referred from the magistrate court.

151. Q: Give brief description of drugs cases heard in crown court?.

A; DRUGS—class A and class B, Supply or possession with intent to supply, depending on the amount will determine if it is for personal use especially for the drug addict who is registered to have them. Police can cease them and may prosecute, caution or warning.

152. Q: Give brief description of INDECENT ASSAULT.

heard in crown court.

A: These include violence especially towards vulnerable people or threat.

153. Q: Give brief description/example of Sexual Assault heard in crown court.

A: These include rape, attempted rape, and sexual intercourse with underage (under 18)

154. Q: Give brief description of RECKLESS DRIVING heard in crown court.

A: Especially under the influence of alcohol or drugs, speeding and coursing injury or death

155. Q: Give brief description of HANDLING; heard in crown court.

A: Of stolen goods is regarded as theft and carry substantial custodial sentence if the property worth more.

156. Q: Give brief description of FRAUD; heard in crown court.

A: This could be individual or organise gang. It could be towards vulnerable elderly or infirm.

157. Q: Give brief description of Give brief description of BURGLARY;

A: These could be in business or private dwelling house and it could happen day or night.

158. Q: Give brief PUBLIC ORDER;

A: This involve affray and weapons; include attack on public officers such as police ,nurses ,ambulance or any violet disorder

159. Q: Give brief description of Violence

A: involve weapons with intent or if it cause injury including domestic violence or to the public example ticket wardens, police, taxi drivers shop keepers, vulnerable people such as elderly, sick and infirm, shop keepers

160. Q: Give brief description of Give brief description of Children

A: include neglect, violence or cause injury or even slight smack, sadistic violence.

161. Q: Name other crimes?

A: Highway robbery, 2) Riot, 3) Smuggling, 4) Poaching 5) Witchcraft 6) car theft 7) Setting fire to properties. 8) Criminal damage to properties.

162. **Q:** who act for the state or the prosecutor in crown court?

A; The crown prosecution services (UK) or the severing state prosecute the individual

163. **Q;** What is the first stage in hearing?

A; There are different stages that the case goes through before the final hearing. First the accuser is taken to court to plea. If he or she pleads not guilty then the Judge gives direction.

164. **Q:** Who are involved in crown court prosecution?

A: It consists of one judge and the case for both the CPS and the defendant has to be presented by barrister or Queen Council (QC).

Chapter 9
Jury service

165. Q: Which court uses Jury services?

A: Jury service is used in criminal cases crown court, but very occasionally it has been used in civil cases, coroner's jury inquest, anonymous jury.

166. Q How are Jury selected?

A; All jurors are randomly chosen
prior to the commencement of the trial, about 20 selected men and women from the registered of electors or voters registrar between the ages of 18 and 70 and who have been in U.K for over five years come to the court, 12 men names and 12 female names are in separate boxes and the usher pick them at random, hence one ends up with 6 men and 6 women to serve.

167. Q; who are excluded to serve Jury service?

A ; Those who are excluded are barristers, solicitors clergy, mental ill, one who is on bail in criminal proceedings, those serve prison sentence in the past 10 years

168. Q; What obligation do the Jury undertake?

A; The jurors are then asked if there is any reason that they are unable to serve example if they know any of the accusers or the accused, or if they may not last the duration of the case then the person may be replaced In some cases the accuser may be asked if she\he knows any of the jurors. When all this has been done and both sides are happy, each juror is sworn in the court room.

It is against the law to disclose or solicit a jury deliberately.

169. Q: How do jury come to decision?

A: Jury people are (usually 12) are selected according to the law and they are sworn to give a verdict on another according to the evidence. Jury decide the facts as they hear it in court.

After they have heard all the evidence, the judge gives the summing up include argument inference to be drawn in an understandable language. And then instruct and directions relating to the burdens of proof them on question of law.

During their deliberation the jury are entitled to seek the judge help, but the judge must say openly in open court any note received from the jury unless natter of unconnected with the trial

170. **Q:** Who can stop a crown court proceeding?

A: When criminal cases states, it can only be stopped by the attorney General (who have the authority to issue)" Do not prosecute" " Noelle prosequi" order

171. Q: What sentence can crown court deliver and give example?

A: In criminal, the accuse receive custodial sentence and or an order to restore or confiscation and compensation, Example Theft act 1968. In 1973 power is given to the crown to deal with compensation, This is used mainly in crown court but concessionary it can be used in other court

172. Q: What rule is used in crown court?

A; The main criminal rules in this Act include; RULE 2.1,2.4, 2.5, 4.1., 5.1.5.4e, *5.6.57*

Chapter 10
Appeal in court system in the United Kingdom.

173. Q: where does the convicted person start appeal?

A: From Magistrate court the guilty person who has previously pleaded not guilty can appeal to the crown court.

174. Q: Who is involved in crown court appeal?

A: The crown court appeal consists of a judge and two magistrates.

175. Q: What is meaning of "A TRIAL DE NOVO"

A: The grounds of appeal must be on point of law against conviction or sentence.

This is a rehearing or new full trial and is known as (A TRIAL DE NOVO).

176. Q: What happen if the appeal failed.?

A: If the magistrate accuser appeal failed in the crown court, he or she can appeal to the High court Queens division.

177. Q Who can appeal to the High court?

A; Both the prosecutor and the accuser can appeal, and it must be on point of law or the magistrates exceed their jurisdiction. The appeal is called "BY WAY OF CASE STATE"

178. Q: What happen if the appeal is unsuccessful in High court?

A: If unsuccessful in the high court, the per can appeal to the Supreme Court (formally House of Lords)

179. Q: what condition can one appeal to supreme court?

A: One can only appeal on point of law and it must be public interest or application to the Supreme Court for permission to appeal.

180. Q: What next if appeal failed in supreme court?.

A: If still not happy to apply to the European court

181. Q: If one is found guilty in Crown court, what is option?

A; The procedure is to make appeal application within 28 days of the guilty verdict for conviction or 28 days from the sentence if one wish to appeal against the sentence.

182. Q: In High court who hears the case.

A: The appeal will be heard first by a single judge and if he\she approve goes to the full court, which consist of two judges and one Lord.

183. Q: What happened if the single judge refuse the appeal?

A: If the single Judge refused the appeal, the person can still appeal to the full court within fourteen days

.

184. Q: What happened if the full court refuse the appeal?

A: If the full court refused one can make application to the CCRC (criminal case review council) who have the power to refer the case back to the appeal court for reconsideration to quash the conviction or to reduce the sentence.

185. Q: What happened if the full court and CCRC refused the appeal?

A: If this failed the person can go to the Supreme Court and then finally to the European court of human right.

Chapter 11
ECHR EUROPEAN COURT OF HUMAN RIGHT 1998

186. **Q;** What is rule 2.4?

A; There must be evidential requirement in any pre-charge procedure

187. Q: What is rule 4.1

A: Prosecution will only start when the case has passed the two stages of full code of criminal justice procedure.

188. Q:What is rule 5.1

A:This is also called First code test or first consideration evidence "If the case does not pass the evidential stage it must not go ahead no matter how important or serious it may be"

189. Q; What is rule 5.7

A; for public interest there must be enough credible evidence for prospect of conviction.

190. Q: What is rule 5.6

A: Lord Show cross (Britain attorney general) said; it has never been the rule in this country. I hope it will never be—that suspected criminal offences must automatically be the subject of prosecution (29\01\1951) House of Commons debate volume 483 column 681.

191. Q: What is rule 5.4e?

A; Police must consider the motive of the witness that might affect the case.

192. Q; What is ECHR ARTICLE 6.2

A; ARTICLE 6.2Every one charge with criminal offence must be presumed innocent until proven guilty

193. Q; When was Brexit referendum?

A: 23/06/2016

194. Q; When was the schedule for Brexit to happen

A; 29/3/2019

195. Q; when was Brexit extended to?

A; 31/10/2019

196. Q: When did Britain actually left the European union

31/January/2020

197. Q: What is the likely consequence of Brexit

A: Variation in Supermarket Prices

Additional Regulations while traveling to Europe

The increase in Medication Cost

Advice for UK residents staying abroad

Advice for EU Citizens

The custom border between Northern Ireland and Great Britain

The increased cost of imported goods

Impact on House Value

The upsurge in Mobile Roaming Cost

Chapter 12

CRIMINAL AGENCIES

198. Q:Name few criminal agencies

A; Police, U.K prosecution authority
DPP, probation service
local authority, trading standard, serious fraud office, inland revenue, custom and excise commissioners.

199. Q: How many police forces in England and Wales?

A: There are 43 forces in England and Wales which are task to maintain public order.

200. Q: When did the number increased?

A: In 1996 Police acts.1 requires place force to be maintained in each area (the forces have increased from 41 to 43).

201. Q: Who heard each force and when did the law passed?

A: Chief constable head each force, they are appointed by the police authority and had to be approved by the government. S.2 of the Act stipulates that each area is to have police authority. Section s.4 (1) state that, there must be 17 members in each authority.

202. Q Briefly describe Police duty?

A: The police do carry out criminal investigation for both the crown and the defendant as such they are deemed to be independent, and in theory they are neither agent nor servant to the crown

203. Q: Can police use force on suspect?

A; They are allowed to use reasonable force to carry out their duties.

204. Q: Name some powers that Act 1996 gave to police.

A: The Criminal justice Act 996 Act gave the police wide range of powers including power to carry gun, right to question suspect (suspect has the right to be silence) right to detain suspect for specific time after which they have to obtained further extension from magistrate court.

205. Q: Can one obstruct police arrest?

A: NO, It is an offence to obstruct police office or to assault them 1996 act s 89 (2)

206. Q: Why should police keep community consent?

A: Police must keep the consent and support of the community. Failure to keep this could lead to civil disobedience such as the Brixton riot in 1981.

207. Q: What did Lord Scareman said in 1981 about police force?

A: Lord Scareman who was the chairman of the enquiry said at the time that police had become out of touch with the community and had lost consent.

208. Q; When did the United Kingdom introduce measures to help police?

A: In 1990 the government introduced many measures to help police build good relationship with the community they serve.

209. Q: What is the function of the DPP?

A: The director of public prosecution heads the CPS (Crown prosecution service) in criminal cases. Which have a barrister and solicitor in each proceeding?

210. Q: Who advice the police?

A: DPP also advice police on matters related to criminal offences (s.3 (1) of the 1985 prosecution of offences.

probation

211. Q: When was probation service form?

A: This was formed in 2001 called Unified national probation service (UNPS).

212. Q: What was the initial duties of probation services?

A: It was initially established to cater for young offenders and adult

Probation officers will document their findings and hold meetings with other individuals responsible for the case to discuss different options that may be available. Ultimately, the job of a probation officer is to serve as a **mentor and supervisor** for offenders who are trying to re-join society.

213. Q: What is the probation service now?

A: Its function is to rehabilitate offenders to remain in the community under supervision of probation officer and to assist the protection of the public from harm from the offender.

214. Q: Elaborate brief details of probation service?

A:Now probation officers in the community are also given responsibility of adult prisoner. They work with the offender's managers who supervise prisoner in prison. The probation officer prepares yearly report on the progress of the prisoner and prepare plan for the prisoner when released. The probationer officer continues to supervise the prisoner in the community. This is in line with the probation service Act 1993 and crime (sentence) and the Act 1997

.

215. Q: Which act deals with prison service?

A: Prisons are run by prison officer headed by the director or the governor under the prison Act 1952 s.7 in England and Wales.

216. Q: Give summary of prison officers job?

A:

Enforcing rules;

Maintaining order in prisons and jails;

Supervising inmates;

Supervising various activities;

Offering counselling to offenders;

Helping convicts with rehabilitation;

Inspecting the facilities;

Making sure that the facilities meet the standards;

Searching inmates;

Checking for contraband items;

Reporting on the conduct of inmates;

Keeping account of all those in charge;

Searching visitors for contraband items;

Supervising visitation hours;

Going on patrol duties;

Escorting prisoners for both internal and internal visits and transfers;

Helping conduct prisoner reviews;

Making sure inmates get access to professional help;
Functioning as part of a team to resolve crisis situations;
Responding to first-on-the-scene incidents;
Making use of authorized physical control and restraint procedures to control situations;
Protecting the prisoners' property;
Respecting the prisoners' dignity and rights;
Building relationships with other staff members;
Offering educational opportunities to inmates;
Inspecting the prisoners' mail and personal items;
Collaborating with enforcement authorities to prevent crimes.

Chapter 13
INTERNATIONAL CRIMES (summary)

217. Q: Name some international crime and countries involved?

A: International crimes include torture, genocide, illegal logging and counterfeiting. Organized crimes are also becoming prevalent. There are, however, organized gangs like Yakuza in Japan. Mexico, Italy, Mozambique and El Salvador also records higher rates of organized crimes.

218. Q: Define Aggression?

A: An aggression is the act of interfering with the sovereignty of another nation. Such also entail the act of political interference as determined by the United Nations

219. Q: Is there international proviso on aggression?

A: No, there is so far no international convention for stipulation of what aggression means (Stancu 90).

220. Q: Give an example of aggression?

A: An example of aggression is the first trial under the statute of Conradian the king of Sicily. The act was endorsed as an international crime by a 1998 statute of the International Criminal Court (ICC).

221. Q: Is there limit in ICC?

A: The statute however limits the prosecution to a mutual interpretation of the underlying acts to constitute a crime

Genocide

222. Q: What is the definition of Genocide?

A: An international convention has been ratified to define genocide as mass killing undertaken either in times of peace or war.

223. Q: Is there any conditions on states

A: The stipulations are hereby enshrined in Article I of the convention. It further stipulates that the individual states ought to put in place local mechanism of dealing with such crimes including adoption and implementation of penalties (Lemkin 5)

224. Q: Give an example of Genocide?.
An example is the Rwandan genocide affiliated to Fellicien Kabuga where numerous Hutus and Tutsis were killed.

225. Q: How can genocide be control
A: The control of such crimes is however centralized for implementation under the national criminal law of states.

226. Q: Briefly explain genocide convention?
A: The fourth chapter of genocide convention further stipulates that there is a probability that some of the crime charges might be tried in an international tribunal. It was through such stipulations that the ICC curves a modulation.

War crimes

227. Q; Why do countries have defense department?

A: The aim of establishing a military department in a country is to ensure the safety of its jurisdiction.

228. Q what has contributed more hostility among states?

A: Advancement in technology has, however, led to the intensive development of hostility among the nation. As a result, some military extensions result in the application of military force than what might be necessary (Andreopoulos 322).

229. Q: What do you consider foreign superpower destroy other less powerful state?

A: Such an expedition is considered to be not only illegal but also immoral and contrary to the objective of having a military within a jurisdiction.

230. Q: Give an example of war crime?

A: An example is the first trial of Peter Von Hagen Bach by the Roman Empire in a claim that he was just following orders.

231. Q: Why was the Roman empire criticized on trial of Peter Von Hagen Bach.?

A: Though the international legislations acknowledge the military units, they dispute excessive use of military power by a nation against another sovereign nation.

232. Q: How did the definition of international crime derived?.

A; Such leads to a definition of war as an intentional application of military power aimed at with a negative intent hurt a sovereign jurisdiction; hence it is an international crime.

233. Q: who normally act as mediator in international wars?

A: The United Nation mediates in international wars, for protection of the disabled state. The prosecution is subject to the ICC (international criminal court).

Crimes against humanity

234. Q; Initially who is responsible to define and implement humanity that is how citizens are treated?

A: The matter of humanity was previously left at the hands of the state government. It has, however, been argued that individuals have, in some instances, been suffering at the hands of such administration in atrocities.

235. Q: Name a case of concern regarding humanity?

A:Some of the cases are, on the other hand, not attended, including enslavement.

236. Q: Who has intervened on humanitarian grounds?

A; The United Nations have gone at length to develop interventions to deal with crimes against humanity (Andrianopoulos 321).

237. Q: Briefly explain Nuremberg charter?

A:The Nuremberg Charter standards were, for instance, endorsed by the General Assembly through a consensus resolution after what can act as an example: the Axis war that resulted in less humane actions.

238. Q: Who drafted codes for international law.

A United Nation General assembly drafted codes: International Law Commission's to counter crimes on security and peace of the humankind.

239. Q: Why was 1998 ICC statute enacted?

A: The inception of ICC statute in 1998 was also majorly based on a narrowed intention of protecting humans against the crimes contrary to humanity.

Torture

240. Q: Who accepted to end torture?

A; The fight against torture has been profoundly adopted by domestic nations, thus curving a way for the declaration as an international crime.

241. Q: When was agreement to end domestic torture?

A: The domestic punishment against torture was mutually agreed upon by the Geneva Convention of 1949. The Torture convention similarly borrows from the stipulations of the Geneva Convention.

242. Q: Give an example of domestic torture?

A: An example is the issue of torture by medics in Japan that led to Declaration of Tokyo in 1975. Torture is thus prosecuted within the local jurisdictions.

243. Q: Why is the convention definition of torture too narrow?

A: The convention's definition of torture is extremely narrow. It excludes acts of torture committed by individuals in a personal capacity, except in cases where there is some government, or official, complicity.

244. Q: what do you think of international crime on torture?

A; The concept of torture as an international crime is correspondingly, constrained.

Drug offenses

245. Q: what has the international community done on drug abused?

A; As a measure to control the use of drugs, the international community has embraced several agreements against trade, manufacture, and, production of drugs.

246. Q: when was action taken on narcotic and chemical drugs?

A: The International Narcotics Control Board was for instance, established in 1961 by a convention on Narcotic drugs. An additional convention was adopted in 1971 intended to extend the legislation against chemical drugs (De Andrade 150). Examples include the drug cartel ling that is prominent in Southern America not excluding Mexico.

247. Q: what action has been taken on psychotropic substance?

A:The convention on Psychotropic substances came closely before an amendment of the 1961 convention in 1972 to regulate its protocol.

248. Q: What action has been taken to combat drug trafficking?

The United Nations eventually adopted an enforcement in 1988 requiring the affiliate nation to domestically charge the culprits of drug trafficking. The convention against illicit traffic in psychotropic and Narcotic substances meant to define the prosecution procedure

.

Terrorism and threats to civil aviation

249. Q: How is terrorism been defined

A:Terrorism has been defined in two diverse ways to amount to an international crime as per the international standards.

250. Q: How did Principal Treaties define terrorism?

One of the crimes is defined by The Principal Treaties on threats to civilian aviation as a hijack of a civilian aviation in addition to other affiliated crimes (Price and Jeffrey 50). The agreement further demanded that the members' states have to handle such crimes within their jurisdiction enshrined in their national law.

251. Q: Give example for international terrorism?

A: The Isis, Al Qaeda and the Al Shabab are a good example of terrorist groups engaging in international ventures.

252. Q: Is hostage a form of terrorism?

A; Yes, taking hostage is also identified as the second form of terrorism by the international convention.

Bribery of foreign public officials

253. Q: How is bribery defined as a crime?

A; The initial version of acknowledgment of bribery to public officials took place in the United States as defined by the 1997 Foreign Corrupt Practices Act.

254. Q: How many countries agreed to combat bribery

A: As a result of the 1997 Act , an additional 34 countries signed an agreement in a 1997 convention on Combating Bribery of Foreign Public Officials. The jurisdiction of the legislation was, however, limited to transactions in international business.

255. Q; Give example of the bribery?

An example is the case of William Jefferson a congressman whose freezer was reported to have a lot of bribery money in 2005.

256. Q: What measures taken to avoid bribery?

A: The treaty further laid platforms to ensure that the parties participating in the agreement implemented standards that would do away with bribery. There was, however, no stipulation for the imposition of transactions on corporations.

257. Q: why did the bribery agreement failed?

A: The legislation yet faces the problem of ratification by a reduced number of nations. Additionally, it lays no set of penalties for the crime.

Human trafficking

258. Q: Define and give example of human trafficking?

A: Human trafficking has been defined and addressed in some international forums as an international crime. The council of Europe convention, for instance, enlists slavery, forced labor, and sexual exploitation as forms of human trafficking (Do Carmo 1430).

259. Q: Give example of human trafficking

The cases have been in a lot of states, as is the case of the abduction of Yazidi women. Also, human trafficking for sale of human parts or use as slave or prostitution.

260. Q; What convention deals with human trafficking

A: The Palermo Convention on organized transnational crime that came into effect in 2003 set out a protocol to punish, suppress, and prevent such crimes. Nations are required to prosecute culprits in human trafficking as per the legislation within their jurisdiction.

Cybercrime

261. Q: Briefly explain cybercrime?

A:Cyber-crime is referred to as the utilization of modern-telecommunication technology in committing an offense intended to indent the reputation of either a group or an individual.

262. Q:Give example of cybercrime?

A: The most prevalent offenses are sextortion, infringement, copyrighting, and hacking (Neto 180). An example of executed cyber-crimes was embezzlement of above 1.5 million dollars by Park Avenue branch of New York chief teller from numerous accounts.

263. Q: How do United Nation fight Cybercrime?

A: The United Nations uses the FBI in the fight against the crime while the European Union incepted a directive in 2013 to run till 2040 in the curb against the crime.

Organ trade

264. Q: Define red market (organ trade)

A: The red market is defined as the commercialization of the body organs in the health market. The aspect is based on the extensive need for organs transplant that the supply.

265. Q:Which country legalize organ trade

A: Iran is identified as the only country that legalizes the sale of organs. . An example is the Iranian mass sales in 2009.

266. Q: Which agenda dealt with prevention of organ trafficking?

A: The African agenda of 2063 coincides with the General assembly's text documented A/71/ 1007 for the prevention of organ trafficking There is, however, variability in the prosecution crimes since countries like the USA and Spain have partial legalization of the crime.

Wildlife trade

267. Q: Is trade of wildlife a crime?

A: The sale of partial or full products of non-domesticated animals is internationally recognized as illegal.

268. Q: How is wildlife trade protected?

A; Protection against the crime is regulated by the United Nations Convention on International Trade in Endangered Species of Wild Fauna and Fauna (CITES).

The legislation has attracted an embrace by 183 countries. The prosecutions on the crime are, however, implemented by individual states.

269. Q: Give one country as wildlife crime?

A: There are reported cases of wildlife crimes in Mozambique

Blood diamond

270. Q: What is blood diamond?

A:Blood Diamond is a selective form of crime where the culprits illegally sell diamonds in a war invaded territory to the invaders.

271. Q: Give example of blood diamond countries?

A: The affected areas include Guinea Bissau, Liberia, and Angola. Such cases are evident in Angola.

272. Q; How was blood diamond outlaw?

The United Security council took up the campaign against the crime in 'A rough trade' label in 1998 and considered such sales of diamonds as funding for the war. World Diamond Congress adopted similar legislation in 2000. Prosecutions are, however, not defined.

Counterfeiting

273. Q: Define and give example of counterfeiting crime?

A: Counterfeiting is the act of duplication of the original product to steal or destroy the original item. Such includes software, electronics, and pharmaceuticals.

274. Q: What measures in place to fight counterfeiting?

A:The United States Secret Service is an example of a strong arm fighting the counterfeit of the American currency.

275. Q: How do forgery classified?

A:The United Nations classifies forgery under counterfeiting intended for deception.

276. Q: Give example of counterfeit crime?

A; An example is the Interpol discovery of 85 tons of counterfeit olive with Copper Sulphate. The prosecution is conducted in the domestic states as per the legislation.

Illegal mining

277. Q why is mining illegal?

A: Mining is considered illegal when it is undertaken without the consent of the states. It happens typically in areas where there are no land rights.

278. Q: Who carried out illegal mining?

A:Illegal mining can be undertaken by large organizations where it is referred to as organized crime or carried out subsistent.

279. Q: Why and Where do illegal mining take place?

A:Due to widespread poverty, there are rampant cases in sub-Saharan Africa. Organized crimes are also rampant in Latin America. Illegal mining crimes are prosecuted in the local jurisdiction.

Money laundering

280. Q: Define money laundering?

Money laundering is the act of illegally obtaining lump sum amounts of money from groups or organizations.

The crime has recorded higher cases of domestic implementation primarily by higher-ranking officials.

281. Q: How is money laundering organized?
A: Such crimes are undertaken through a series of complex transactions aimed at losing track of the money. Nations have thus made an implementation of transactions complex as a measure to counter such crimes.

282. Q: What is affiliated to money laundering and who prosecutes?
A:The crime is also affiliated with assisting other crimes like trafficking financing. Prosecutions are implemented locally.

Illegal gambling

283. Q: Define gambling?
A: Gambling is the act of wavering money with the intent of making a profit. The act, however, involves a risk, consideration, and a price. The term gaming is used to refer to a legal process of wavering.

284. Q: Give an example of illegal gambling
A: An example is the numerous Chinese slotting machines in African countries. The gaming activities are regulated by gaming control boards that are internationally adopted. Prosecutions are implemented on an individual basis.

Arms trafficking

285. Q:Define Gunrunning?

A: Gunrunning is the act of selling illicit arms as well as ammunition mostly undertaken by the criminal organizations. Such ammunition is used by communities to engage in power battles rather than economic propelling.

286. Q: Who keep records of illegal arms?

A; The United Nations adopted a Register for Conventional Arms in 1991 to maintain a record of the arms obtained illegally. Such cases are highly recorded in Islamic countries like Iran. The domestic jurisdictions prosecute the culprits

287. Q: Give an example of illegal arms?

A:Examples include sales of ammunition to terrorist groups like the Al Shabab and the Boko Haram.

Illegal unregulated and unreported fishing

288. Q: When does fishing become illegal?
A: Illegality occurs when fishing activities take place against the law, while failure to report such cases to national authorities leads to unregulated practices.

289. Q:What effect is such crime?
A: The crime is said to have adverse economic and environmental effects on the local communities whose benefits from the fishing activities are deterred.

290. Q:Give an example of illegal fishing
A: An example is the rampant cases in West Africa. Marine Stewardship Council (MSC) is an example of a regulatory body that implements certification of the seafood. Cases of contradiction to the laws lead to domestic prosecution.

Illegal logging

291. Q:Define illegal logging?
A: Illegal logging is defined as transportation after harvesting timber against the law. The process primarily needs to be conducted illegally or in a corrupt manner.

292. Q: Give an example of illegal logging?
A: An example is the 2004 incidence where Greenpeace interception of a cargo ship transporting timber to UK and France.

293. Q: What laws prevent illegal logging?
A: The East Asia Forest Law Enforcement and Government and Governance were undertaken in 2001 in Bali. The European Union also implemented legislation after a lengthy process pioneered by the European Commission. The prosecutions are enforced in individual nations.

Chapter 14

International Gang Crimes (Countries)

Mexico

294. Q; Why is organize gang crime in Mexico?

A: Mexican organized crime is based on its popularity as a tourist's destiny. It is noted that the drugs in the United States originate from Mexico. Besides cases of human and ammunition trafficking to the United States comes through the Mexican boarders.

295. Q: What does Mexico gang trade in?

A; The gangs' majors in sale of drugs, trafficking of human and ammunition as well as targeting the tourists (Diniz 498).

296. Q: Give an example of Mexico gang?

A: An example is the capture of Joaquin' El Chapo.'

297. Q: What action has the Mexico government taken to combat gang crime?

A:The government, however, has been using detectives not to mention with the assistance of international special detectives to unravel such activities.

El Salvador

298. Q: What organize crime is EL Salvador involved?

A: The countries record higher incidences of murder per capita. The rates are affiliated to higher amounts of ammunitions at the hands of organized gangs

299. Q: When was the EL Salvador gang started?.

The gangs took a foundation during the 1979 civil war. They, as such conduct both urban crimes as well as guerilla attacks.

300. Q:Give example of organize gang in El Salvador

A: An example is Barrio 18 and MS-13, whose prominence is based on both higher literacy levels and poverty (Diniz 502). Precautions are issued by international governments to their citizens against travel

.

Italy

301. Q; Name one gang group in Italy and where it originated?

A: Italy records higher rates of organized crimes in poor urban areas like Sicily. The crimes are associated with the Mafia group that emerged in the 19th century.

302. Q: What do Italy gang deals with?

A: The gangs engage in smuggling drugs and people to Europe (O'Deane 221). They additionally loan shark, extort money, and kill to steal.

303. Q; What action has the Italian government taken against gang crime?

A: The government has, however, adopted an anti-extortion charter to safeguard the start-up businesses.

Mozambique

304. Q: What is Mozambique gang associate to?

A: The gangs in Mozambique are affiliated to the civil war, whose effects remain eminent. Though the country has a rich history of diverse heritage and wildlife, the crimes are inhibiting economic growth.

305. Q: What do Mozambique gang trade in?

A: The gangs thus engage in human trafficking, drugs, and wildlife products (O'Deane 400). They, however, carry out non-violent crimes. The government prosecutes the culprits domestically.

Japan

306. Q: Briefly describe Japan gang crime?

A: The population of Japan is vastly based on its vast harbor of arts, festivals, and cultural heritage. Yakuza, however, conducts gang crimes in a manner that makes it like a form of Mafia.

307. Q: Why is the gang activities appears to be accepted by the local people?

A; Their activities are, however, seen to protect the interest of the local citizens as they target international personalities.

308. Q: What do Japan gang trade in?

A; They engage in human, firearms, and drug trafficking. They also offer sacrifices by cutting their fingers as atonement for their sins.

309. Q: why there is no control of the gang in Japan?

A: There is no recorded effort of controlling the gangs' activities locally as they organized the rescue mission in 1995 after the Kobe earthquakes. Such inclusion is seen as a way of entertaining crimes (Schoultz 100389).

310. Q: why are some states crimes are regarded as international?

A: The advance in crimes as well as international integrations has led to recognition of some crimes as international. The United Nations and other regional blocs like the European Union are as such adopting Conventions to define such crimes, penalties and the Jurisdictions of prosecutions.

Chapter 15

Sources of International laws

A critical evaluation of the Sources of International Law;

311. Q: What is international laws

A:International law governs the conduct between nations in their sovereign status.

312. Q: Where is the source of international laws?

A; The definitive statement as to what constitutes International Law can be deciphered from Article 38 of the Statute of International Court of Justice (ICJ).

313. Q:what has been the aim of Article 38 of ICJ

The Article, which is more of an imperative directs the Court to decide disputes by applying; International

Conventions, International Customs, General Principles of law recognized by civilized nations, and, judicial decisions as well as teachings of highly qualified publicists.

314. Q: How is the Article 38 of ICJ described?

Although not initially intended to be the authority on the sources of international law, it has been described as a convenient catalogue (D'ASPREMONT, BESSON, & KNUCHEL, 2017).

315. Q: What does article 38 of ICJ direct international courts?

A: The article is the focal point from whence identification of sources proceeds. Nonetheless, though subject to debate, the listing under Article 38 aforementioned doesn't create a hierarchy of the sources but is rather prescriptive to what the court ought to consider in making decisions

316. Q: Does Article 38 of ICJ helps judgement to be made in courts?

A: Yes, it is posited that Article 38 is neither a depiction of the normative system, nor a listing of the sources but rather gives a basis upon which the ICJ can found its judgments and opinions.

Treaties and Conventions

317. Q: Briefly explain treaties and conventions?

Treaties and Conventions are express ways of creating rules and principles that govern the conduct of states.

318. Q: What is the significance of treaties and conventions?

A: Their significance can be deduced from the principle of Pacta Sunt Servanta and have been touted as a formal source of international law (THIRLWAY, 2014). The concept of treaties is to bind member state into performing obligations even when onerous to perform them.

319. Q: Where was the concept of Article 38 found?

A: This concept is found in the Article 26 of the Vienna Convention on the Law of Treaties which requires good faith in performing obligations under treaties. This reliance on the principle of Pacta Sunt Servanta has been questioned by scholars who argue that the principle is customary. That notwithstanding, the principle can be categorized as jus Cogen in that it is overriding to any contrary law.

320. Q: What other ways can treaties be perceived?

A:Treaties can also be understood as sources of legal obligations with the overriding principle that those obligations must be observed.

321. Q: what is "soft law" treaty

A: Some treaties in themselves contain mere guidelines with no substantive requirements and have come to be referred as 'soft law.'

322. Q: What do some treaties provide?

A: Other treaties provide a new regime with parties committing to specified behaviors that in the absence of a treaty would not be required of them.

323. Q: Who has to abide by treaty?

A: The extent of such treaties, any variations thereof and the performance of the same is limited to member states. In this case, treaties become a source of law rather than mere guidelines.

324. Q: Give example of treaty deal with specific agenda.?

A: An ideal example would be the Geneva Conventions that restrict the behavior of member states engaged in armed conflicts.

325. Q: What treaty can be source of law?

Treaties, particularly the multilateral ones can be described as direct sources of law. Some prescribe the creation of further instruments and thus the subsidiary instruments have their foundation on the main treaty.

326. Q: Can treaties create organisation?

Yes, Some treaties create bodies like the United Nations and the United Nations Security Council. These bodies have their mandate defined in the treaty. Therefore, in performing their mandate, the organs so created by a treaty, act within the provisions of the treaty and their decisions, whether binding or not can only be premised on the treaty.

327. Q: What happens if decision under treaty not binding?

A: In the circumstances where the decisions are not binding, they are influential and may end up in creating customary law

328. Q; What is Bilateral treaties?.

A: Bilateral treaties as an instrument of law making primarily regulate certain aspects of international law such as extradition treaties creating a network of bilateral treating addressing a single object.

329. Q: How is treaty form?

A; The formulation of treaties is a long and protracted process which requires the consent of member states to be binding. The Law of the Sea Convention was initiated in 1973 and took up to 1994 to complete entry into force with only sixty member states.

330. Q: how can treaties be policed?

A: The effectiveness of treaties to police international relations is further influenced by its signatories.

331. Q: What influence effectiveness of treaties?

A: Politic play a major role with the failure of a powerful state to ratify a treaty undermining its effectiveness. Reservations to treaties by signatory states further reduces the effectiveness of treaties as sources of international law by excluding the applicability of the specified provisions of the treaty in matters relating to that state in particular.

International Customs

332. Q: Describe international custom?

A: International custom is depicted by Article 38 (b) as evidence of general practice accepted as law. International customary law is the foundation for modern international law and emerges from patterns of behavior among states which practices must be backed by the concept of *opinio juris*.

Q: Who are involved in international custom?

A: These are Practices amongst nations that have been mutually accepted as a right and an obligation by the states.

333. Q: How can custom be accepted as international law?

A: For a custom to be considered an international law two essential elements have to be met being *opinio juris* and practice.

334. Q: Give an example of international custom?

A: The ICJ in *North Continental shelf case, ICJ Rep. 1969, at p.3, p.44* explains that the act in question should not only be considered as a settled practice but should also be carried out in such a way as to evidence a belief that this practice is an obligation required by the existence of a rule and the states concerned must feel they are conforming to what amounts to a legal obligation.

335. Q: Explain Opinio juris?

Opinio juris is often referred to as the psychological element of international customary law. It differentiates acts taken by states as comity and out of behavioral regularity. It is the conclusion that a practice has the status of International Customary law.

336. Q: What is regarded as international customary law?

International customary law is universal, unitary and exogenous (Goldsmith & Posner, 2005). It is binding on all states and sovereign entities to the exclusion of those that persistently object to the practice in question during its development to law. It is an embodiment of external factors that are meant to influence ad direct state actions (Goldsmith & Posner, 2005).

337. Q: Where can practice of international practice law be found.?

Part of the practices amounting to international customary law can be found in the form of resolutions passed by international organizations evidencing the acceptance by their member states of the legal obligation backing such practices.

338. Q: Give some examples of customary international law.

A: United Nations General Assembly resolutions and other nonbinding statements and resolutions by multilateral bodies are often viewed as evidence of customary international law. Domestication and incorporation of international customs into national and state legislations also evidences the acceptance of these customs as having the force of law. Legislation, policy documents and diplomatic correspondences also serve as evidence of the acceptance of customs as international customary law.

339. Q: How is customary law used

A: Customary law is used as a source of law and to aid in the interpretation of written laws in international criminal law. The International Criminal Tribunal for the former Yugoslavia applies international humanitarian customary laws with its jurisdiction limited to crimes existing under customary law.

340. Q: Give example of customary laws used in criminal case?.

A: International customary law has been invoked in criminal cases with explicit treaties in place as can be seen in the *Nahimana Case UNSC Res 955 (8 November 1994) UN Doc S/RES/955* before the International Criminal Tribunal for Rwanda where an imprisonment for a period beyond what is prescribed by article 77 of the Rome Statute was upheld based on the international customary law in place in 1994.

341. Q; Can customary law be used by ICC(international criminal court?

A: The International Criminal Court has held customary law to be a secondary source of criminal law has been applied in the interpretation of the ICC written rules (Tan, 2018).

342. Q: What is the weakness in customary law?

A: International Customary Law can however be vague and open to conflicting interpretations. It is prone to influence by a shift in the national interests of states and other sovereign entities and as such prone to challenge overtime.

343. Q: Is it easy to prove state practice and customary law if no treaty exit?

A: The process of determination of general practice as an international custom is also devoid of practical implications due to the uncertainty of what amounts to state practice and state consent to such practice as international law. It is difficult to conclusively prove the existence of an international custom in the face of disputes (Bodansky, 1995).

General Principles

344. Q: What is General principal of Law?

General principles of law recognized by nations are those principles that are common to all national legal systems, in so far as they are applicable to relations of States. These are principles that are repeatedly present in developed national legal systems owing to a common origin or addressing a common need in human association that are applied on the international level (Ellis, 2011).

345. Q: How is the General principal applied?

A: their international application is not influenced by their domestic capacities.

346. Q: What are the sources of General principal of law?

A: General principles are an autonomous source of international law meaning that legal interpretations and legal solution to problems can be based on a General Principle exclusively (Ellis, 2011).

347. Q: Why can they be used in any develop country?

A: They are obvious maxims of jurisprudence of a fundamental and general nature that can be expected from any civilized national legal system.

348. Q: How can General principal be regarded as independence?.

A:Scholars while insisting on the autonomy of general principles have held that the same can be applied in the interpretation of treaties and international customs.

349. Q: In what other areas can general principals be applied?

A: They are an independent and a primary source of law in areas where treaties and customs have not regulated or have left a lacunae.

350. Q: How can General principal be used to assist judges?

A:They further appear in jurisprudence as a form of coordination and to assist judges in determining which rules are to be applied and the validity to be attached to these rules where a complexity has resulted from the application of treaties and international customary law (Ellis, 2011).

351. Q: What areas of law has judges applied municipal principles?

A: Judges have overtime applied municipal legal principles and norms on the international level especially in areas of international criminal law.

352. Q: How is criminal law treated on international platform?

A: While criminal law on the international place is quite new and vintage, national legal systems possess extensive experience in this area. This should however not result in the international stage being treated as a *tabula rasa* for creation of international criminal norms.

353. Q: how has the international economic law benefited?

A: International economic law has also benefited from the creation of general principles from domestic/ national norms (Panezi, 2007). With the states being interconnected by Bilateral Investment Treaties, when a provision appears in every BIT, then there is a heightened normativity in this rule, because we can infer a consensus on its existence.

354. Q: Name one of the principles of general principles?

A: One of such principles is the principle of fair and equitable treatment applied to foreign investments (Panezi, 2007).

355. Q: What do member states share in general principle?

A: It is however important to point out that, as states share important values, interest and principles under the concept of solidarism, not every pattern of regularity result in a legal general principle unless the legal system allocates some normative value to the regularity.

356. Q: How can general principle be cumbersome?

A: General principles are rather unwieldy, and positive proof of their existence and application can be complicated. General principles applied international are also derived from a representative of the domestic legal systems for it practically impossible to compare all national legal systems.

Judicial Decisions and Teachings of highly qualified publicists

357. **Q:** What do we mean by Judicial decision?

Article 38(1)(d) refers to judicial decisions as a subsidiary means for the determination of rules of law.

358. Q: Why does judicial decision rely on considered Article 59 of ICJ?

A: With courts of law and legal scholars lacking the authority to make law, and the doctrine of binding precedent being un-established on the international level.

as is expressly provided for in Article 59 of the Statute of the ICJ, judicial decisions are relied upon to shade light on existing laws and as clarification to legal provisions.

359. Q: How is the decision of the permanent court of justice valued?

A: The Court has in practice however quoted its own decisions and the decisions of the Permanent Court of International Justice as its authority for holding certain positions in law (Goldsmith & Posner, 2005).

360. Q: What does Article 38(1) (d) says

A: Article 38(1)(d) makes no distinction in the application of international or domestic judicial decisions. However international decisions have in practice been considered authoritative evidence of law.

361. Q: How does domestic legal system compare with judicial decision?

A: Judicial Decisions from domestic legal systems on the other hand act as evidence of state/ national practices and can therefore and have actually contribute directly to the formation of customary international law.

362. Q: What is used to determine legal rules?

A: Judicial decisions are key in determination of existing legal rules and their content. Unanimous decisions by international courts also progressively develop international law (Goldsmith & Posner, 2005).

363. Q: What has influence scope of international law?

A: "Teachings of the most highly qualified publicists of the various nations" such as Gentili, Grotius, Pufendorf, Bynkershoek and Vattel have overtime influenced and facilitated the determination of the scope, form and content of international law (Schreuer, 2010).

364. Q: What has the teachings been used?

A: In modern times such writings serve as evidence of existence of international laws and principles on their subject matter. Such writings have also influenced decision makers in practice. Interactions in professional circles among treaty maker, scholars, state practitioners and adjudicators facilitate the shaping of international law by the opinions of all these players (Schreuer, 2010).

365. Q: Give summary of Article 38

A: Article 38 of the ICJ statute lists the sources of international law in their order of applicability. In the determination of any matter legal provisions in treaties and conventions are taken into consideration first and where none exists international customary law and then general principles are called to play.

These three sources of law are independent and autonomous. They continue to develop overtime to cover new areas in international relations influenced and informed by the growth of domestic / national systems. Judicial decisions, both domestic and international, and the legal writings of experts have played a key role in this legal advancement at the international plane. The influence by domestic legal systems in the development of international laws achieve consensus/ consent to the laws once developed as they tend to reflect what the states and other sovereign entities have already consented to in their domestic systems.

Chapter 16

Drug

definition

366. Q What is the definition of Drugs

A: Drugs is a substance that contain chemical compound (period table) which can alter the behaviour of the mind, the characteristic symptoms depend on the class (ABC) a being the most effective and most seriously harm the person's mind.

367. Q:What is the WHO(World health organisation) definition of drug addiction

A: WHO define drug addiction as " Repeated use of a psychotic substances, to the extent that the user (refer to as the addict) is periodically or chronically intoxicated, shows a compulsion to take the preferred substances or substance and has the great difficulty in voluntarily ceasing or modifying substance use, and exhibit determination to obtain psycho active substance by almost any means.

368. Q: How does criminal law define an addict?

A: Criminal law deflation of illegal drugs An addict is someone who has become dependent upon those drugs so much that he cannot live normal life without it. S 1 1973\99 amended s 1 1989\99

369. Q: Who is regarded as Drug abuse or misuse?

A: This applies to person a take drug which does not conform to medical direction.

370. Q: who is classified as Utilitarian drug user.

A: Is a person taking drugs for specific reason such as for fatigue or insomnia but not for medical or pleasure?

371. Q:who is classified as Recreational drug user.

A; Taken drugs because of the effect and not for medical reason

372. Q: Who is casual drug user?

A: Person who takes drugs occasionally but not regularly

Route

373. Q: How can drug be taken?

A:. Drugs can be taken by 1) orally 2) Inhaling 3) injection By snorting or sniffed up nostril. Crack is smoke in pipe; Cocaine can be smoke using free basin

Law.(Definition of the drug Act)

374. Q ; Under which section of the 1983 act will judge disregard drugs intake.

A: Regulations\ Legistrations mental health act 1983 s37, In some serious case like murder the jury will be directed to disregard the intake of the drugs or alcohol as mitigation factor to commit a crime

375. Q: What has the accuser to proof?

A: The accuse has to proof abnormality of the mind and not the intoxication of the drugs or alcohol

376. Q: What does the medicine act. 1968 covers?

A: It covers manufacture and supply of drugs

377. Q: what does Custom and excise management act 1979 deals with?

A: Deals with punishment for import and export, including payment of fine in lieu of prosecution

378. Q; what does Drug trafficking act 1986?

A: Laid down the penalties for administration and preparation of illegal drugs

379. Q: what does Control drugs act 1985 covers?.

A: Increase the penalties of class a drug;

380. Q: what does Intoxicating substances act 1985covers?

A: Penalties for sale and supply of solvent to fewer than 18 people

381. Q: what does Road traffic act 1972

A: Illegal to drive motor vehicle whilst under the influence of drugs

382. Q: what does Health and Safety at work act 1974

A: Section required employers to make sure there employee are not in possession of drugs

383. Q:what does Section 7 of Health and Safety

A: Section 7 require employee to take reasonable care not to bring or take drugs during, before work.

384. Q: When was drug offence Act?

A; 1971

385. Q: Give summary of the control drugs Act 1985?

A:

This act specifies when drugs crime has been committed;

Is an offence to have Possession of control drugs?

Possession with intent to supply (the quantity is considered).

Is an offence to Supply or offering intended to supply a control drug.

Is an offence to allow premises you occupied or manage to be used for the purpose of drugs takers; the registered tenant or the Landlord will be liable for prosecution

Is an offence to manufacture control drugs?

Is an offence for produce control drugs?

Drug trafficking is an offence

386. Q: What does section 4 of 1971 Act?

A; Offence to transport, store, import, export drugs

(misuse of drugs Act 1971 s 4 (1) to supply

387. Q: What and why did Act introduce during the first world war on drugs?

A: In **1916** an act was introduce during the war under control substance called DORA) Defence of Realm Act 1916 was introduce to control Cocaine and Opium

388. Q: What was the prohibition Act?

A; In **1969,** an Act to prohibit the use of the drug LSD In **1971** The Misuse of drugs Act.

389. Q: When was poison Act?

A; In **1858** the poison Act was introduce to control substances (DRUGS).

390. Q: Can accuser use intoxication as defence?

A: No, In criminal cases the accuser can't use intoxication of alcohol or defence, Drunkenness is no defence. O'Grady (1987) QB995 (CA)

391. Q: What does symptoms of drugs depends on?

A: The symptoms depend on the class of the drugs and categories; example stimulant (uppers) Depressant ((downers), Flallucinogen (psychedelic)

392. Q: Can drugs cause mental disorder

A; Drugs could result person acting mental abnormality and his action could be diminished responsibility beyond reasonable doubt. The accuser will need to produce medical evidence that cast doubt on his mental state. In such cases the court may make a hospital order

393. Q: Give an example of Class "A" drugs?

A: opiates, opium, morphine, cocaine,
heroin, methadone, LSD (acid)
hypnotic, sedative, volume,
Glue, shoe polish, paint Thinning

394. Q: What is the reaction of class A?

A: Slow down the brain and make

the person less aware of surrounding

395. Q: what is court sentence for possession of class A?

A: Up to 7 years and\or unlimited fine

Q: What is the sentence for supply punishment?

A; Up to life in prison and or unlimited fine

Class B

396. Q; What is the street name of Hallucinogens?

A: Street name is PSYCHEDELIC CLASS" B"

397. **Q**: Give some example of class B drugs

A; ,(acid), pop (angel),dust, crystal, peace pill, magic, mushroom, mescaline (buttons
ketamine cannabis

398. Q: What are some signs and symptoms of class B?

A: Distort the senses and awareness or perception, hallucination of the Sight, hearing and feel

399. Q: what is punishment for possession class B drugs.?

A: Up to 5 years or and unlimited fine

400. Q; What is punishment for supplying class B drugs?

A; Up to 14 years in prison and or unlimited fine.

Class C

401. Q: Give the name of class c and street name?

A; Class C drugs is called STIMULANT and the street name is UPPERS)

402. Q: Give some example of Class C?.

A: Cocaine, Crack, Amphetamine (Speed), Nicotine, Tobacco, Caffeine

403. Q: What are some of the signs and symptoms?.

A: Euphoria, speed up excite nervously centre system stay awake, have no appetite

404. Q: What is punishment for possession?

A; Up to 2 years in prison or and unlimited fines.

405. Q: What is the punishment to supply class C drugs?.

A; up to 14 years in prison and or unlimited fine

406. Q; How is investigation carried out?

A: Investigation by taken and testing urine, sample, blood, swab from the mouth, stool

407. Q: What are some signs and symptoms of class A illegal drugs?

A; Paranoid, hall nation, agitated, anxiety, tactile, users, injection result HIV, hepatitis, tetanus trebly

Cocaine class A

408. Q:What is the street name for cocaine?

A: people called it different names include; Coke, Charlie, white Percy, Snow, Toot.

409. Q:What is the appearance of cocaine?.

A: White Powder, Often wrapped in Small, packets of paper or, cling film

410. Q; How is Cocaine administered?

A; Snorted up the nose or by injection

Crack

411. Q: How is Crack classified?

A; Is class A drug

412. Q: What is the street name for Crack?

A: Rocks, wash stone, pebbles, base freebase

413. Q: What is the appearance of Crack?

A: Small lumps or rocks about the size of raisins

414. Q: How is Crack administered?.

A: smoked in pipe, grass tube, plastic bottle or foil or can be injected

Ecstasy

415. Q What class of drug is Ecstasy

A: Class A

416. Q: What is the street name?

A: E Pills, brown, Mitsubishi's, Rolex's Dolphins, XTC

What is the appearance of Ecstasy

417. Q: What does Ecstasy look like?

A: Usually in tablet form in all sorts of colours, some of which have picture or logos stamped into them or as powder

418. Q: How is Ecstasy administered?

A; Usually swallowed or smoke or snort them.

419. Q What is the side effect of Ecstasy

A: **Side effect** include 1) dry mouth2),sweating 3),blurred vision 4),Inco -ordination 5),fatigue, acute liver failure

Heroin

420. Q: What class is heroin drug?

A: Class A

421. Q: What is the street name for heroin?

A: Brown, skag, ,horse, gear, snack

422. Q: How does heroin look like?

A: White powder when pure, brownish after a while

423. Q: How is it administered?

A; Smoked, dissolve in water, inject or snorted

LSD

424. Q:What class is LSD?

A: class A

425. Q what is the street name?

A: Acid, blotter, cheer, dots, Drop, flash, hawk, Lightening flash, liquid, acid, Lucy, micro dot, paper mushroom;

Rainbows, smiles, stars, Tab, trips

426. Q: What is the appearance of LSD?

A; Sold as tiny squares of paper with pictures on them but it can be found as liquid or as tiny pellets

427. Q How is LSD administered?

A: Sucked or swallow.

428. Q: What is the side effect of LSD?.

A: Include paranoia, panic, unaware of their surroundings, blurred vision, psychosis- manic depressive.

429. Q Is LSD addictive?.

A; Not addictive and not withdrawal

Mushroom

430. Q: What is mushroom classification?.

A: Class B

431. Q: what is the street name of mushroom?

A; Liberties, Magics, mushies, liberty cap, shrooms, Amani, agaric

432. Q: what does mushroom look like?

A: Brown, dried-up, mushrooms

433. Q: How is mushroom taken?

A; Eaten raw, Dried-up and stored.

Amphetamines

434. Q; What classification is Amphetamines?

A: Class B

435. Q:What drug and colour is Amphetamines?

A; This is synthetic drugs and it comes as powder in white, yellow or pink

436. Q What is the street name of Amphetamines?

A: Speed, pelt, billy, whizz, sulpha, Base, paste, dixies.

437. Q: What is the appearance of Amphetamine?

A: off white, or pinkish powder or white pills

438. Q: How is Amphetamines administered?.

A; Snorted, Swallow, mixed in drugs or by injection

439. Q; What is the side effect of Mushroom?

A: chest pain, palpitation 3)blurred vision, confusion, depression ,irritable ,fear, aggression, delirium, paranoia, ,aggression, 12) headache 13)insomnia

Cannabis

440. Q: What class is cannabis?

A; Class B

441. Q: What are the street names for cannabis?

A: Black blow, Bob hope, dope, draw, ganja, grass, hash, hemp, herb ,hashish, marijuana, pot, puff, resin sinsemilla, skunk, soap, spliff, wacky backy, weed, Dried Chopped plant.

442. Q: What does cannabis look like?

A; Blacky brown lump made from the raisin of plant grass or weed is made from grass leaves and look like lightly packed dried herbs

443. Q how is cannabis taken?

A: Some people mix it with tobacco and smoke it as a spliff or a joint. Or put in a pipe or Bong, makatea with it or put it in food

444. Q: What is the side effect of cannabis?

A: There is not much side effect Side effect, but overdose is life threatening. 2)it is harmful to pre-existing heart problems

445. Q: Give example of Stimulant drugs

A: Stimulant drugs include cocaine, crack and crack cocaine

446. Q: What is general side effect of stimulant drugs?

A:) Agitation, 2) anxiety,3) paranoia, 4)hallucination of sight hearing and tactile(feeling of crawling under the skin,

If snorting or sniff, it could 5) damage the lining of the nose and nasal septum. If injection, it could cause 6) ulcers, 6)abscesses, 7)inflation of the veins,8) tetanus, 9) hepatitis 10) HIV.11)High blood pressure,12) increase pulse rate 13) high temperature, 14)damage lungs, 15)death.

Mothers who took cocaine during pregnancy will usually have small baby who is irritable, suffer trembling and poorly.

447. Q: name some Depressant drugs?.

A; Opiates and Heroin class A

448. Q List some side effect of Depressant

drugs?

A; Overdose result toxic reaction which could be life threaten, 2) Cyanosed due to decrease respiration, 3) running nose, 4) constipation 5) brain or cerebral oedema, heart or pulmonary oedema.6) withdrawal (opiate) this start after 5 days to 10 days. Watery eyes, 8) sweating and yawning within 12 hours, restless sleep Dilated pupils, loss of appetite, goose bumps, back pain, tremor. Insomnia, 11) weakness, 12) stomach upset, 13) chills and flushing. Spasm of the muscle, 15) stomach pain 16) Quick tolerance.

449. Q; What is the consequence to possess solvent class c drugs?

A: If caught in possession and supply to less than 18 years person could result either 18 months in prison or £2,000 fine.

450. Q; What are the side effect of Solvent Class C drugs?

A: includes!) dizziness,2) unreality world of their own,3) slurred speech, 4)double vision,5)disorientation to time and person., 6)Risk of cardiac arrest, brain, stomach and liver damage

Chapter 17

Trafficking

Drug

451. Q: Give some specific international fraud?

A: Some international fraud include; Trafficking of drugs, weapons, body parts, human, nuclear material, money laundering, human smuggling, boiler room frauds, investment fraud, private section fraud, 419 fraud

452. Q: What is the effect of drug trafficking?

A ; The symptoms depend on the class of the drugs and categories; example stimulant (uppers) Depressant ((downers), Hallucinogen (psychedelic)

453. Q: What effect on mental health?

A: The individual might develop symptoms of schizophrenia, bi-polar (manic depressive) or endogenous. The person losing money would lead to deep depression and anxiety and possible suicide.

Agitation, anxiety, paranoia, hallucination of sight hearing and tactile (feeling of crawling under the skin,

454. Q: What happen if individual travel to meet criminals?

The individual be kin nape or physical hurt if he\she travel to meet the gang master

455. Q; Give example of drug trafficking countries?

A: These could have originated from different part of the world for example from Trinidad, Tobago, Jamaica.

456. Q: Who handle drug trafficking?

A: These are handling by professional fraudster who have link in different part of the world.

457. Q: Give example of how drug trafficking take place.

A; The carrier may be a woman who may swallow the drug in a plastic or hidden in their private part, shoe, luggage or suitcase or food.

458. Q: Give example of the carrier route

A: Their carrier leaves Trinidad airport, and may have connection (fraudster) at the airport who will give save passage to the plane. The carrier will have all the details telephone and address which may be fictitious.

459. Q: What happen to the drug carrier on arriving at the destination example U.K airport?

A: On arriving at Ukase will go through the check out and when she collect her luggage will go through the exist that is marked nothing to declare. If she is lucky and come out, she will meet someone to pick her up and takes to the dealers address.

460. Q: What happens to the drugs?

A The drug is then supply to well-known agent for the money.

Weapon

461. Q: How can WEAPONS undergo trafficking?

A: WEAPONS; may be diverted to a country example Iran from UK (who has no trade agreement with Iran by cartel agreement. The weapons can then be used against UK citizen in the Middle East.

462. Q: How can the stock market be frauded?

A: COMMERCIALLY; companies trading on the stock market in London, New York or Paris could be subject to frauds that may create bogus company.

463. Q: How can investment be affected?

A: U.K citizen or any country may be tempted, to invest in a bogus company and latter find out that they have lost their money

Boiler

464. Q: Explain what BOILER is?

A; **BOILER:** to invest in foreign bogus company but mislead people to think that it is base in Britain, by the time they become aware, they would have lost their money.

465. Q How is the effect on United Kingdom economic?

A: These cost UK a lot of money to investigate and to bring these foreign fraudsters to face justice.

466. Q; Where do the trial of drug trafficking start?

A: In most cases the juridical process start in the country of origin of crime

467. Q: What measure has the United Kingdom government put in place to prevent illicit drugs?

A: The government had put in place how they propose to reduce the number of people taken drugs.

Which include given police extra powers to deal with drugs takers and suppliers? Persuade the drug takers to ask for treatment.

468. Q: What is another way for community to help each other

A:Create neighbourhood policing to report drugs dealers

Extend the arrangement between foreign countries to combat drugs and to bring the suppliers to face punishment.

Focus on families to offer help and to encourage the parents to discipline the young people. Increase community sentence and treatment. Increase the support for treatment within the community or rehabilitation.

469. Q How can drug trafficking be solved?

A: Drug trafficking is serious problems and can only be solve through close co-operation of international countries and implementing legal assistance, extradition, law enforcement.

470. Q: What measure needs to be put in place to prevent drug trafficking?

A: Drug trafficking is globalise and therefore needs international collaboration, exchange with effective protocol and policies.

It need well organise Interpol to coordinate intelligence between national law enforcement agencies. There must be effective "Interpol" which is international police force working with national laws.

471. Q: How did Russia defence comment on criminals?

A: RUSIA DEFENCE SAID; "Transnational criminal rings are becoming more and more powerful and their mobility is growing.

These means that all resources of any country state are not enough to seriously harm them

472. Q: How do fraud affect individual?.

A: All form of fraud will have degree of psychological, emotion economical and physical effect on the individual.

473. Q: What has United Nation warn countries?

A: Trans-national organise crime effect individual person and nation that is why it is one of the "ten threats which United Nation warn by high level threat panel

474. Q: What favours the criminals?

A; This fraud take advantage of increase travel trade, rapid money movements, redenomination, advance technology in computer link and mobile phone. The main objective of this crime is money

475. Q: Does crime be transferred across countries boarders

A; The crime affecting UK will also affect other nations who share boarders known as transnational organise crime

476. Q: Why is Belgium considered the main smuggling country in Europe for hand rolled tobacco?

A: Belgium has legalised all class of “ABC" drug, hand roll tobacco including cocaine, cannabis) and prostitute

Flight to and from Belgium and other European countries are very cheap especially weekends hence people take advantage of the flight and lack of strict control at the Hence drug addict or casual drug takers goes to Belgium to satisfy their drug and prostitution habit

It is easy to divert smuggling goods with forged or substituted documents use to cover the tracks of diversion.

Belgium provides smugglers high profits associated with low risk and penalties

Belgium economic rely heavily on drugs, hand rolled tobacco, alcohol and prostitution which can be obtained from the cafe or on the Belgium street without being challenge

Eastern European cigarette counterfeiting operation had been uncovered in Belgium.

Belgium bad was the primary source of hand-rolled

tobacco for long time, hence counterfeiting illicit cigarette have historically originated from china, Malaysia, Singapore, Vietnam to Belgium

Chapter 18

STATISTIC on crime

477. Q; Give the statistic on drugs by British crime survey in 2006/7?

A

The following is from the British crime survey 2006\7

Over 11 and quarter people in England and Wales between the age of 16 and 59 have taken drugs in their lifetime.

35% of between the age of 16 and 59 had used illicit drugs in their lifetime

Drug related offences increase by 23% 9 from 14546 to 178,502 between 2004\5 and 2005\06

2005\06 45.1% of between 16 and 24 years old have used illicit drugs in their lifetime

In 2005\06, 41.1% of cannabis users use drugs regularly

In 2005\06, the most illicit drug was cannabis

United Kingdom spent £16.4 billion a year on illegal drugs.

In 2006, UK provided £560million to class A but the direct cost of processing all drugs users through the criminal system comes to £2.6 billion

Statistic by NCDAS(national centre for drug Abuse statistic

478. Q: In 2017 how many people died in United states of America from drug overdose

A: 70,000

479. Q; In 2017 how many people died in United states of America with substance abuse disorder

A;18,000

480. Q: In 2017 how many people died in United states of America who had illicit drugs

A: 30,000

481. Q: What is the most used illicit drug I America in 2017

A; Marijuana is the most popular illicit drug in the nation. In fact, a 2017 Yahoo News/Marist survey indicated that approximately 35 million Americans use marijuana on a monthly basis. A 2015 study by Jama

Psychiatry concluded that marijuana's popularity has risen considerably over the past decade.

55 million Americans admitted to having used marijuana within the past year, and at least 78 million people surveyed reported having tried the substance at some point in their lives.

482. Q: According to CDC (Centre for Disease control) in America, give statistic of death from drugs misuse?

A; Every year, the number of drug overdose deaths in America increases. According to the Centre for Disease Control (CDC) in 2016, 64,070 people died from drug overdoses. That is a 21% increase from last year alone. Bloomberg reported that for every 100,000 residents, nearly 20 died from drug overdoses. While some states have higher rates than others, it is undeniable that substance abuse is a critical concern for citizens' lives.

From National Statistic

Statistic on misuse of drugs in England 7/February/ 2018 (PAS)

Drug misuse related hospital admissions (England)

483. Q: How many people had mental health problem as result of drugs

A: There were 7,545 hospital admissions with a primary diagnosis of drug-related mental health and behavioural disorders. This is 12 per cent lower than 2015/16 but 12 per cent higher than 2006/07

484. Q: How many in 2018 hospitalised with drug poison?

A: There were 14,053 hospital admissions with a primary diagnosis of poisoning by illicit drugs. This is 7 per cent lower than 2015/16 but 40 per cent more than 2006/07.

485. **Q:** How many deaths related to drug misuse (England and Wales) in 2016

A: In 2016 there were 2,593 registered deaths in England and Wales related to drug misuse. This is an increase of 5 per cent on 2015 and 58 per cent higher than 2006

Deaths related to drug misuse are at their highest level since comparable records began in 1993

486. **Q;** What percentage of adult took illicit drugs in2016/17 in (England and Wales)

A:In 2016/17, around 1 in 12 (8.5 per cent) adults aged 16 to 59 in England and Wales had taken an illicit drug in the last year.

This level of drug use was similar to the 2015/16 survey (8.4 per cent), but is knowingly lower than a decade ago (10.1 per cent in the 2006/07 survey).

487. **Q:** In 2016, what percentage of children use illicit drugs drug use among children (England)

A:In 2016, 24 per cent of pupils reported they had ever taken drugs. This compares to 15 per cent in 2014.

The probability of having ever taken drugs amplified with age, from 11 per cent of 11-year olds to 37 per cent of 15-year olds.

According to Statistic by Michael House Drug Addiction

488. Q: Name the top five counties with worst or severe drug problem?

A: Iran, Afghanistan, Russia ,unites State of America and Great Britain

489. Q: Which country is first free illegal drug use

A: Timor Lester or East Timor. in Southeast Asian nation claimed its independence from Indonesia in 2002. So far there hasn't been evidence of drug production or some great trafficking in this 'most drug free country'.

490. Q: Which country is second free illegal drug use

A: Qatar; because drugs laws are quite similar to Oman's, thus helping them qualify as a drug free region.

491. Q; Which country is third free illegal drug use

A: Oman ; because the drug laws are severe, too. What is a prohibited drug? Just don't ask that question in Oman. There is no difference between "soft" and "hard" drugs, so drug dealers can face the capital punishment

492. Q: Which country is fourth free illegal drug use

A; Maldives

493. Q: Which country is fifth free illegal drug use

A: Brunei; which is a tiny state on the island of Borneo in Southeast Asia. Two people were sentenced to death earlier 2020 for trafficking a little over 800 grams of the forbidden substance

494. Q: Which country is sixth free illegal drug use.

A: Saudi Arabia: Their drug laws are not to be interfered with. Bearing in mind that alcohol is illegal here, what do you think possessing drugs could lead to? Possession of either of these substances can be punished by public flogging, fines, long imprisonment, or even death.

495. Q: Which country is seventh free illegal drug use

A; Gambia. it's a very small country in Western Africa, right in the middle of Senegal

496. Q: Which country is eighth free illegal drug use

A: Gabon; This country along the Atlantic coast of Central Africa is more concerned with human trafficking than opiates.

497. Q: Which country is ninth free illegal drug use

A: Niger

498. Q: Which country is tenth free illegal drug use

A:Singapore that is one of the most common questions, and the answer is positive. As for drugs, this island city-state off southern Malaysia is very strict. You can be sent to prison for possessing a small amount and even be sentenced to death.

Chapter19

Court orders

499. Q: Summarise ways to solve crime?

A; Policing, the court, heavy sentences, reform laws, imprisonment heavy fines, law enforcement. Death penalty or bloody code was abolished in earlyl800 in United Kingdom.

500. Q: What can the court do?

A; The court have the power under F.L.A Family liability Act 1996-part IV grant order to prevent this such as the violent person stay in one part of the house or to leave the dwelling house or part of it.

501. Q: What is injunction?

A; Where a child (molesting a child),the court may deal with this family domestic violent in chambers and may issue non-molestation order or prohibition order preventing the perpetrator (man) from molesting the

child.

502. Q: Name few types of injunction?

A; The court has the power to issue various injunctions 50such as prohibition mandatory interlocutory

503. Q: What is Prohibition?

A: PROHIBITION orders to forbid the person from

carry out wrongful act.

504. Q: What is mandatory?

A; MANDATORY injunctions which include continue restraining by direct performance of a positive act.

505. Q: What is interlocutory?

A: INTERLOCUTORY—emergency temporary injunction aim you maintain the status quo until the trial

506. Q: What is Perpetual?

A; PERPETUAL injunction is usually granted after court hearing.

507. Q; What is interim?

A: INTERIM injunction where restraining ordering on the defendant until specific date; Ex.Parte, Quia timet.

Chapter 20

VIOLENCE

508. Q: Define violence?

A; Most of the crime major or minor involves violence. It could be verbal or nonverbal or actually physical violence (violence brings fear). An offence which is likely or could leads to cause injury (physical or psychological) Or death to a person. (. KHAN (1995) 16 Crapo R (s) 180.

509. Q: What are violent conduct?

A; There are violent conducts towards person or the property which could cause or intended to cause injury or damage, these include domestic violence; use to enter property or violent disorder

510. Q: Name types of violence?

A: threat murder, Assault, Robbery Taken without consent, Deception, Blackmail, Manslaughter, intoxication, wounding bodily harm etc

511. Q: Define domestic violence?

A: In per Thorp J in home secretary v.Robb (1995) 1FLR 42 “Every person's body is violated and proof against any form of physical molestation "These include physical, sexual and emotional abuse occurring within the home.

512. Q: define Battered women?

A: In R.v.Hobson (1977) the times 25 June describe battered women syndrome.

A repeated serious physical injury from a man (or woman) with whom he\she lives"

The law reform committee on marriage violence was in (1974)

513. Q: How does violence end up?

A: Violence always ends up with physical and or mental injury or causing impairment one physical or mental condition.

514. Q: Name other types of violence?

A; terrorist violence, religious violence theft, violence assault violence, bullying violence, psychological violence. Capital punishment has ceased but there had been continue demand it back

515. Q: Is battering women acceptable in some culture?

A: Yes especially in most Africa countries and Muslim

516. Q: When did control of women started?

A; Being in control of women started before Jesus Christ. One can trace it back in historic, culture social experience, realities.

517. Q: What did the Bible say about women?

A; In fact the says "Women must submit to their husband; The Quran and the Bible did not say barter your wife

518. Q; Who is violence towards?

A; A stronger person intimidates, violence which connects to societies or oppression of ;

Women, children, pet, people of colour disabilities, lesbian, gay, bisexual, Trans sexual, elders, Jewish people

Not all are visible example Older women who are vulnerable, isolated or in care homes

Women in rural areas are isolated and may lack of resource

Same sex (lesbians or gay) in which one use physical, sexual or emotional violence or threat.

The fear of homophobic and hostile law enforcement

Chapter 21

Property

519. Q: Define property?

A: According to the law dictionary, property must be definable, identifiable by others, capable in its nature or assumption with degree of performance or stability, To have right to possess example money, including real and personnel plus intangible (things in action.

520. Q; What does property come under?

A: Property falls under tangible or non-tangible or things in action (not physical) and something one owns?

521. . Q: What is tings in action?

A: THINGS IN ACTION is property without physical existence (cannot be torch) example copy right, patent, right to overdraw a bank, right to sue to recover department, cheques direct debit, Good will.

522. Q: Describe property from criminology point?

A: In criminology a property must "BELONG TO ANOTHER" in simple form, but it can be treated under civil law.

523. Q: How does the law define property?

A: The property Act section 4(1) define property as

"money and all other property, real or personnel including THINGDS IN ACTION and other intangible property"

Both civil and criminal laws use some definition.

524. Q; How does the theft Act define property?

A; The theft Act 1968 $5(1) " Property shall be regarded as belonging to any person having possession or control of it or having in it any proprietary right or interest—(The civil law version state that "Not being equitable interest arising only from an agreement to transfer or grange an intent.

525. Q: Is Anatomic specimen property?

A: ANATOMIC SPECIMEN; is properties because it can be stolen. See Kelly (1998) 3 ALLER 761 (CA)

526. Q; Name other property?

A: Other property: The container that held urine,

blood specimen, and human organs can be stolen so they are property

527. Q: What is export Quotas?

A; Export quotas are intangible property

528. Q; Give example of General property?

A; General property include goods and not merely a special property sGA.1979, s 62 (1), (2). -that arise under a bailment.

529. Q:What is criminal damage as per case law?

A: In A (A is juvenile) .v.R (1978) Crime LR 689 (crown court) “A property is damage if it is rendered imperfect or inoperative, or if the harm impairs its usefulness or value

530. Q: What is criminal damage as per case Division court

A: Divisional court went on further "damage includes not only permanent or temporary impairment of value or usefulness" Morphite v. Salmon (1990) crime LR48

531. Q: What is criminal damage as per case Concise dictionary?

A: Concise Oxford Dictionary defines damage as "Injury impairing value or usefulness

532. Q: What is criminal damage as per case Lord Lane?

A: Lord Lane CJ in appeal court said "Any alteration to the physical nature of the property concern (computer) may amount to damage, whether it does so or not will depend upon the effect that alteration (computer programme) has had upon the legitimate operator,(Whitely (1991) 93 Cr App R. 25 computer hacker (joint Accident network.

533. Q: How do one regard dishonest in relation to Actus Reus?

A; The following comes under ACTUS REUS; that person dishonesty is irrelevant in criminal law.

534. Q: Based on the definitions of damage, give example of property not damage?

A: Base on this definition, the following are not property damage. Example 1) trade secret cannot be damaged 2) water flowing under or above land cannot be damage

535. Q: Give example of intangible property that qualified as property damage?

A: Intangible property is excluded, also excluded are flowers fruit, mushroom, wild animals are all not do not have test of commercial purpose as define in the Theft Act.

536. Q: Define Destruction?

A: A destruction can only be dealt with criminally if "The Act of destruction must be one having at least the element of FINALITY AND TOTALITY about it" Barnet LBC .V Eastern electricity board (1973) 2 ALL ER 319 (divisional court)

537. Q: What does the law say about Property mis-description

A: Property misdescription Act 1991 s 1 state that it is an offence to make false or misleading statement about any matter relating to land which is specified by an order made by secretary of stat.

538. Q: Under actus Reus, is death or water flowing regard as stolen?

A: Under actus Reus is causing (death), actus Reus of theft is property.

Not property: Service (because it cannot be stolen, water flowing under or above ground, human body or corps (cannot be stolen)

539. Q:Is cheque or cash property?

A: Theft of cheque and cash is a debt a thing in action and is stolen so is property.

540. Q: What do the court say about one partner cash a cheque with only his or her signature?

A: If one partner cash a cheque with only his\ her signature and the bank pays. The court of appeal stated that, the lack of other partner not signing was irrelevant, appropriated because the account was within credit limit and therefore THINGS IN ACTION means his property.

541. Q: what happen if the cashing of the cheque with one signature result the account being overdrawn?

A: If however when the cheque was cash, it result the

account in red or over the agree limit, then there is no property to steal

542. Q: explain the implication of transferring money from one country to another?

A; If one transfer money from one country to say England, but the bank staff DIVERTED it to another country (say to his bank in another country), the court in England has no jurisdiction to because the money in was not bank in England account as NO THINGS IN ACTION .This loophole was amended in 1993 in the criminal Justice Act

543. Q; What happen if someone steal a cheque?

A; If someone steals a cheque, he is guilty of theft of piece of paper

544. Q: When can land be regarded as stolen?

A: Land (including soil, manure) cannot be stolen unless a trustee or liquidator sells the land for his own use.

545. Q; What offence if a tenant pick fruit from tree?

A; A tenant who picks fruit from the garden has not committed theft because fruit is not property,

546. Q: What happen if the tenant visitor or partner picks fruit from the tree of the tenant?

A; if his visitors or his partner does then it is theft because they are not legally renting the property.

547. Q: What happen if someone pick flowers etc from somebody land?

A; If any one pick flowers, mushroom fungus, fruit or foliage, plant shrub or tree from a land, it does not constitute stealing s. 4 (3),what he pick unless he go and sell them for his use

548. Q; What happens if someone picks fruit to use and then decides to sell it later?

A: If someone pick fruit ECT. For his own use but later decide to sell them (commercial) is no appropriating property as it could be one off.

549. Q: What happens if someone purchase and unpaid goods, but no invoice issued.

A; If the person has such goods and decides to keep and not to pay, the goods now become his possession or ownership therefore he is not guilty of theft despite his dishonesty.

550. Q: When do property burglaries occurs?

A: In England and USA the lowest is February when is very cold and the highest in August when is worm and people on holidays or out on picnic or seaside or taken the children to fanfare or children activities during the school holidays

551. Q: What happen in warm seasons?

A: During the warm seasons some people tend to leave their windows and door open for fresh air which opportunity thieves take advantage. In United Kingdom the season changes plays major part in burglaries.

552. Q: What time do property burglary occurs?

A; The times depend on various factors, such as when mum had gone to work or gone to pick the children from school, or when doors and windows open give rise to opportunity burglaries

553. Q: Do victims able to give time to police?

A: The police information is that victim of the crime are unable to give specific time.

554. Q: In United Kingdom what time do property burglary usually occur?

A: Frequent time range include Morning (7 am to 11 am), Afternoon (12 pm to 5 pm), These are evidence of time when the house occupancy is nil., Evening (5 pm to 10 pm), or just before people return from work, or when parents have taken the children to sports activities or to private tutorial. Night-time (10 pm to 7am) these normally happen when the occupant are sleeping, the burglary usually occur downstairs why the people sleep upstairs, or the occupier might gone to night duty or are on holidays

555. Q; What preparation thieves make before stealing?

A: The burglar normally survey the crime site and the pattern of activities that goes on when they go to bed, or gone on holidays

556. Q: What element burglar consider?

A: There are few elements that the burglar selects which include potential reward, securities and vulnerability, accessibility, visibility or unreliability occupancy, convenience of the property location.

557. Q: what do some criminal do with information?

A; The criminal may pass on information to other criminal

558. Q; Where do burglars occurs?

A: The area where a lot of youth drug addict, hoping centres, sport arena, bus station and train station are easy to surveillance without any suspicion of any suspect

559. Q: Why are some houses burgle few times?

A: There are some houses which are burgle few

times and possible the burglar knows the weak point to enter,(easy assesses) or the occupant is wealthy and replaced whatever is taken so the thief revisit, or to take other property which were not take during the first visit.

560. Q: What about unoccupied property?

A; The empty properties attract which may have a sign FOR SALE or no body live there, the fixture and the fitting and any furniture may be stolen and sold. It is also possible that some thieves might pretend to be a buyer and once the estate agent had shown him the house, he comes back to burgle it.

561. Q: What about property near heavy traffic?

A; Houses near heavy traffic or pedestrian are can be survey by burglar easily without being suspected and then it is burgle later on. Houses in close road

(EU de sac) are less likely to be bugle since the neighbourhoods know each other and act as community policing.

562. Q: What other houses prone to bugle?

A; ; those vacant for long period. (Live abroad and comes concessionary, or being sold), Houses which are always empty during the day (gone to work) or night-time (person being on night duty), Short term tenanted houses tend to be burgle possible before the new tenant move in.

563. Q: What property are concessionary burgle?

A: Also houses which are only occupied by old person can become a target day or night.

Some nursing or old people homes tend to be burgled by drug addict by violence means.

564. Q: What property could be bugle?

A; Those vacant for long period of time (Live abroad and comes concessionary, or being sold)

Houses which are **always empty** during the day (gone to work) or night-time (person being on night duty)

.

565. Q: What can deter thieves?

A: Dogs are deterrent, and it is proof that houses with

dogs are less likely to be burgling

566. Q; How can light affect thieves?

A: POOR LIGHTING reduces visibility to others.

Steady lightening prevent burglar as he might thing some on in occupancy

Motion activated lighting may serve as alerting secluded areas.

567. Q: What about the situation of property?

A: Corner houses whose windows and front door face neighbors are less likely to be burgled

Houses with fewer neighbors are more likely to be burgle day or night

Houses with only one or two people may have violent thieves whereby they may enter if the doors are open, tied them up and get away with valuables (day or night)

568. Q: How does accessibility affect bugler?

A: These depend on the houses

The come entry point are the front, but houses in allays have limited visibility and provide access and escape route for the burglars.

They may use the back doors or the windows especially if there is no neighbors visibility

Burglars always look for weak entry points especially older houses, worn out or rusting doors and windows provides easy access to the property.

569. Q: How do security affect beglaring?

A; There are some houses which have alarm system connected to either the police or the alarm, centre which deterred buglers,

Security locks or devise including locks, dead bolt, burglar bars reduce the vulnerability to burglars

570. Q: Explain presentation of cheque and situation of the account in which the cheque is presented?

A: If the account is overdrawn within the normal limit then the bank have obligation to meet the cheque cash, if however a cheque is presented to a bank which the account is over the limit then it is not property because the bank has no obligation to meet the transaction, in this case cash the cheque will be attempted to obtain cash by deception

571. Q: when does a cheque becomes recipients property?

A: When someone receives a cheque make payable and signed in his favour, then the cheque is his property so if the cheque not honoured, the he can sue whomever gave him the cheque

Chapter 22

COMPUTER CRIME

572. Q: What is Hi-Tech crime?

A: HI-TECH crime is using a technique and tools to the network computers and the internet for criminal activities.

573. Q: What is Botnets?

A: BOTNETS;-this name given when home computers are hijacked by criminals and form into network on computers and mobile phone

574. Q: What Act deals with computer fraud?

A: Computer misuse Act 1990 and 1971, state that hacking is fraud or offence involve with computers which include unauthorized access or modification of computers software and hardware.

575. Q: What is Website spoofing?

A; In the criminal duplicate the website with same IP (Address), and genuine users are directed to the duplicate website. The fraudsters obtain all the financial details (card). It is also possible to duplicate the bank website.

576. Q: Name some method the are used to attack computer?

A: Fraudster use other means such as 1) Virus 2) Worms 3)Trojan$ 4)Extortion 5) DoS (denial of service) 6)DDoS(distributed or directed denial of service which use Zombies, 7)Intellectual property crime,8)Criminal communication 9)Encryption 10) adware 11) Spyware 12) Gray ware 13) Phishing, 14) Ping of death 15) e-mail bomb, 16)spam 7)popup windows, 18)Social engineering, 19(TCT\IP attack (protocol site) 20)SYN Flood, 21) Man in the middle, 22) replay 23) DNS poisoning.

577. Q: Give example of hackers?

A: In 2003 the film "THE MATRIX RELOADED" was made available by hackers on the internet very cheaply within hours of release

578. Q; What means do criminals use to communicate?.

A: The organize criminals use the e-mail, internet chat room, instant messaging, web base, client server mail account, website and message boards are used to communicate including share their knowledge.

579. Q: How do the fraudsters use the media?

A: They also use these media to locate other criminals to share ideas, locate vulnerability victims. The fraudsters use the media for all sort of crime; to negotiate, to discuss and to supply stolen goods such as drugs and drug trafficking.

580. Q: How do the fraudster protect themselves?

A: Fraudster use communication and encryption and sophisticated tools to protect themselves from being caught.

581. Q: In computer fraud, what is VIRUS?

A; Is a programme written specifically with malicious motive and then sent by attackers using e-mail in the network.

582. Q: how does the VIRUS operate?

A: The Virus attach to the computer code software or files or document. It then excited and infect computers. Once a computer is affected, it can be transferred to any computer by e-mail file transfer or instant messaging.

583. Q: How can the VIRUS affect the data on the computer?

A: It can corrupt, delete files or erase the entire hard drive, and destroy information.

584. Q; Are there more than one type of virus and which one is more dangerous?

A: There is various type of Virus but the most The most damaging is us to record Keystroke, harvest sensitivities data such as Password, and credit card numbers

585. Q:Explain EXTORTION in computer fraud?

A: Fraudster use electronic intruder into a computer system to locate valuable and sensitive data which contain financial information for customers. The hacker then put fear in the organization about possible adverse publicity to reduce confidence and reputation (Especially banks, large business and financial institutions.)Who rely on reputation become the victim to such threat

586. Q: What does DOS means?

A: DoS means Denial of service

587. Q: Explain how DOS is used to defraud on computer?

A: **DoS** (denial of service) the hacker use virus and worms to attack via e-mail to enslave a lot network of computers. It act by sending large amount of request to the computer which overload the computer resources which prevent the user from accessing normal services including the server and the e-mail

588. Q: What does DDOS Mean?

A: DDos mean “distributed denial of service”

589. Q: Describe how DDOS is used to commit fraud?

A: DDoS (distributed denial of service) use Zombies to attack and hence make the tracing of the origin very difficult. This can affect thousands of computers to obstruct and overwhelm access to the server it can affect different geographical location.

590. Q: What is PING OF DEATH?

A: Ping of Death is using Repeated and large Amount of ping that crash the computer.

591. Q: What is E-MAIL BOMB use in computers?

A; A large quantity and repeated bulk e-mail that overload the e-mail server and prevent it usable

592. Q: Describe INTELLECTUAL PROPERTY crime?

A: This is when the hacker uses digital technology to crack the security features of the company sale product and produce Pirated copies such as software, games films, music .these are smuggle and distributed on CD -ROM and DVD which are sold cheaply hence deprive the company of income.

593. Q Describe STEALTH VIRUS?

A: STEALTH VIRUS has the ability to lay dormant in the computer until summons by the hacker to carry his instruction.

594. Q; Describe WORM for computer fraud:

A: Is self-replicating, using the network to duplicate its code and cause harmful to the host network because it consumes the bandwith.it does not need to attach itself to the host to excite the infect.

595. Q: Describe the activities of TROJANS.?

A: It is like worm but act like virus by reproduce itself soared and cause damage to the computers. It hides in the software, appear to do something useful but does mischief,

596. **Q:** What is ADWARE?

A: Is a software programme that displays advertisement call "POP UP WINDOWS"

597. **Q:** How does POP-UP ACT?

A: The many windows which cover the screen are call Pop -up and it covers the screen to prevent the monitor being used.

598. Q: What is ADWARE activity on computer?

A: Adware are capable of open more windows faster than the computer operator can close then hence it prevent the use of the computer as the monitor screen is cornered with unsolicited adverts.

599. Q: Describe SPYWARE?

A; Is a type of Grey ware and similar function like

Adware?

600. Q: How can SPYWARE affect the computer?

A: ? It monitors all the activity of the computer and the send information to the hacker.

601. Q: What is MALWARE?

A: is software programme use by hackers for phishing attack

602. Q: What is MALWARE activity?

A; Malware is used to persuade the reader to unknowingly provide the attackers access to personal data example to fill online of which the information is then sent to the hacker.

603. Q; How can SPYWARE be installed?

A; Spyware, grey ware, adware can be installed on the computer without the owner knowledge.

604. Q: What other use is MALWARE?

A:.Malware could be used for spyware, phishing, gather information and send to the hacker

605. Q: What is PHISHING?

A: This attach themselves to the e-mail and act like a social engineer why by it pretend to represent legitimate organisation such as the bank and request information of the password or the username,

606. Q: How does PHISHING act?

A: It act by intimidate you with message of something terrible will happen if you fail to give the information.

607. Q: What is SPAM?

A: This is junk mail (unsolicited e-mail)?

608. Q; What is spam use for?

A: Spam is used as advertisement or harm link and or an attack.

609. Q: Who is SOCIAL ENGINEERING in computer fraud?

A; Social engineering is the person who may trick the owner or user for him to gain access to another computer or equipment and will convince one to divulge username and password detail or company directory with e-mail address.

610. Q: What is TCT/IP Attack?

A; This is a protocol suit use to control communication on the internet. But hacker can use it for attack

611. Q: What is SYN FLOOD?.

A: Is an attack whereby TCPNJP is randomly open flood the internet equipment with false request and cause the computer operation to be denied.

612. Q: What is "MAN IN THE MIDDLE" computer fraud?

A: Attack whereby false information is inserted between the two hosts.

613. Q: What is SPOOFING?

A: The attacker gains access by pretending to be trusted computer.

614. Q: What is REPLAY

A: The hacker use network sniffers to obtain username

and password

615. Q: What is WIRELESS

A: Since data traffic flows through radio waves, it makes the data vulnerable to hijackers.

616. Q: what is the motive of website attack?

A; The attack the website to obtain bank details or just for fun or to damage files.

617. Q: What is the main motives of the fraudsters?

A: The main motive is to make money, but they could use the hacking as catalyst or to support them to make the information to help them make money from other sauces

618. Q: Why do some criminals hack computers?

A: Criminals use hacking into computers to commit fraud. They use Hi. Tec tools (e-mail bad internet to communicate with other criminals.

619. Q: What does inexperience criminals do?

A: If the criminals are not expecting in computer, they may employ specialist or expect to help them

620. Q: What is the effect on global business by the computer fraud??

A: Business globally when attacked suffers the biggest losses (in millions or even billions) of pounds in the term of cost and time.

Chapter 23

Statistic on computer fraud

621. Q: Give brief information of Home net providers survey?

A: Home net providers survey shows that 6% of Britain homes computers have been hijack in bonnets. More than one million household in UK have criminal inside domestic PC.Globally, 5 to 10% of all domestic computers are link to criminals network or Botnets. In 2011,6% of the UK 19 million net -using households are under botnets

622. Q: Give brief information of BBC survey?

A: Survey for BBC reveals that 19 out of 20 nations with the biggest botnets, they attack through the internet and ISP

The biggest network has the biggest problem, example the BTs network.

623. Q: What damage did DoS and DDoS cause in 2002

A: in 2002 DDoS attack disable 9 out of 13 main servers in the internet worldwide for several hours

624. Can spam be sent to mobile phone?

A: Some of the network has evidence of sending spam on mobile phones which helps criminals to steal. (By Dutch team)

625. Q: What is VARIANT OF ZEUS and what they can do?

A: Variant of Zeus is one of most threaten botnets which can take over mobile phone and large bank that use mobile phone and on-line in their transaction.

626. Q: What is police survey on computer attack?

A; A survey by police reveals that about 3,000 UK large and small businesses that over 44% had suffered security breach due to malicious attack

Chapter 24

Prevention computer fraud

627. Q; Does the law enforcement have the technical skills?

A: Law enforcement agencies do not have the technical skill and companies PC and ISPs have realized that they cannot get things done with regard to the law being enforced.

628. Q: Why is it difficult to deal with some crime?

A: Serious and organize criminals, 2) Individual or mere thrill seekers.

Extortion; It is difficult to trace the origin (or the country) of attack.

The hacker finds ways to obscure audit trails and frustrate investigators

629. Q: Why is it difficult with Intellectual property crime?

A: Intellectual property crime; provide difficult TO detect the source and penalties but when caught the penalties is low compare to the huge amount, hence it is very attractive to the criminals.

630. Q:How must business or organisations protect themselves from computer fraud;?

A; They must protect themselves by having strict guidelines or security policy tailored to the organisation.

631. Q: What recommendation should be in the organisation security policy?

1) A: Acceptable computer use statement.
2) Identify who is permitted to use the computers
3) Software and device permitted to be install on computers,
4) Use of hardware example modern, wireless access points.
5) Strict instruction for confidentiality.
6) Employee to sign agreement to implement rules and the consequence of misuse the computers.
7) Information of what to do in case of emergency
8) What steps to take after emergency?
9) Strict guidelines of information not to share with customers, vendors and the media.
10) To back up as detailed by the policy and the back up

to be kept by the director

632. Q: What must be aims of hard and soft ware protection?

A: **The aim of implementing security for hard and soft ware is to prevent** theft, vandalism, data loss.

The physical security is to prevent access to the premises (to protect the data and infra-structure.

633. Q: With regard to hardware and software, what do the criminals target?

A; To achieve their aim, they target banks, businesses and individual who rely on IT online transaction where valuable data is stored.

The criminal's hackers know the vulnerability of most of the software and hardware.

634. Q: What do they use to target banks?

A; DDoS and DoS target Banks large company's financial institution.

635. Q: How do some companies protect their website?

A: Large companies purchase internet names similar to what they have, this prevent the large company website from being misuse.

636. Q; what do you regard as the

efficient prevention policy/

A: The best prevention measures are the police and the media to raise the public awareness to protect their hardware and software of other computers.

The protection \ prevention for the programmes that the hacker use

637. Q: What can be used to prevent computer virus?

A; Antivirus; this run automatically and when it detected virus, deleted or quarantine and then warn the user.

638. Q: What can be used to prevent Spyware?

A: Anti spyware remove Keyloggers and other malware.

639. Q: What can be used to prevent Adware?

A: Anti adware delete the programmed that display the

UN wanted advertising

640. Q:What can be used to prevent Phishing?

A: Anti- fishing blocks the IP addresses of known phishing web site

641. Q:What can be used to prevent Firewall?

A: There are fire wall for software and for hardware

The software firewall inspects and filter data packet and denies outside users from establishing connection to a computer or the network. It works by opening and closing. It open to allow permissible programmed and it close to block unwanted ones

642. Q: What can be used to prevent fire ware?

A: Proxy Fire ware inspects all traffic to and from the computer.

643. Q: what can be used to protect hardware.

A: Hardware firewall is physical component which is free standing install on the routers

644. Q: How do one provide protection\prevention of wireless

security?

A: It is very important to use tools to configure the settings

645. Q: What does WEP (wireless encryptment privacy do?

A: This encrypts the broadcast data making it hard for hackers.

646. Q: What does Wi-Fi protected access (WPA) do?

A: Provide better encryption and authentication

647. Q: What does Mac Address filtering function?

A: This restricts unwanted traffic.

648. Q: What is function of SSID (SERVICE SET IDENTIFIER)

A: This identifies the network

649. Q:What is function of WIRELESS ANTENA;

A: It is advisable to use antenna that serves the area to minimize risk from wider source

650. Q:how do you protect DATA SECURITY

A: There are various methods to protect the data

It is always better to use more than one security to protect the data and the physical equipment

651. Q: What is function of SMART CARD?

A; Is a device to store data safely?

652. Q:What is function of SECURITY KEY FOB?.

A: It has small radio system the communicate with the computer over short distance, the computer must sense signal from the key before the accepting password and username.

653. Q:What is function of BIOMETRIC DEVICE;

A: These work by using the characteristic of the user such as eye or the fingertips. It must accept the characteristic of the user before allowing the password and username

654. Q: What do we mean by ENCRRYPTED PASSWORD?

A: This means that the attacker had to decode the encryption to lean the password

655. Q; What is EVENT LOGGING AND AUDITING;

A: This is built in within the operating system which must be enabled to monitor activity on the network.

656. Q: What does Encryption use for?

A: This is used to encode data being transmitted on the net, user should configure to encryption data.

657. Q: What is the function of HASH ENCODING?

A: This makes sure that messages are not corrupted or tampered with during transmission.

658. Q: What is the function of SYNMETRIC ENCRYTION.

A: This requires both the sender and the receiver to use encryption key to be able to decode the data

659. Q: What is the function of asymmetric encryption?.

A: This require two keys, private and public keys, the private key is to be kept secret, but the public key can be use by the public.

660. Q: What is (VPN) VIRTUAL PRIVATE NETWORK?.

A: This is private network that uses encryption to secure data as it was travelling in a private corporate Lengthen data travel in a secure tunnel which prevent hackers to interfere with the data

661. Q: What is the best way to physically protect/secure Hardware?.

A: To protect the hardware. use at least two devices.

662. Q: Name few devices to secure hardware?

A: Lock, conduit, card key, video equipment, security guard to control access. Others are; Laptop docking station locks,

Lockable cases, lockable HD carries, secure storage and transport of back up

Media, US security dongles, Biometric sensors, berg connecters

663. Q: What can BIOS use for?

A: The setting of the BIOS can be used to protect the data

664. Q: Which of those attackers is most dangerous

A: It has been very difficult to choose most dangerous between Intellectual property, Extortion and Dos DDoS but I choose DDoS\DoS.

665. Q Give reason of your choice

A: DOS AND DDOS ARE MY CHOICE because They can do more than intellectual and Extortion

666. Q: Why didn't you choose Intellectual?

A; Need hacker with more technical knowledge and can be used to pirate goods, which will cost companies example films, music such as what happened to the film "Matrix Reloaded".

667. Q: Why didn't choose Extortion?

A: I think a lot of companies by now know or are aware of such threat of blackmail intimidation and fear that the hackers use, and they may take extra precaution to protect their reputation.

668. Q: Why in my opinion Dos and DDos are more dangerous?

A: Damage DoS and DDoS can do include:) Gain unauthorized access, 2)render the network inoperable, 3)damage the computer system 4) cause the company to loose reputation, 5) financial loss for the company

669. Q: How does Dos and DDos affect network?

A: They use network computers or even a computer to infiltrate another computer network.

670. Q: How does Dos and DDos affect access?

A: It has the capability to enabling unauthorised access, one do not need to be expected to use such operation.

They can damage computers with other hi-tech crime such as using virus and Worms.

671. Q: How does Dos and DDos affect servers?.

A: They are able to attack servers and destroy the data. DDoS uses Trojan code (which act like a friendly and doing something useful but in fact aim for mischief.

672. Q: How does Dos and DDos ability to use Trojan cause havoc?.

A: Trojans is like a worm but can behave like virus in that it attach itself to a software and reproduce itself many times and cause damage to computers.

The fact that it produces rapidly via e-mail to terminate or enslave thousands of computers and computer system includes servers using Zombies

673. Q: What is the effect of Dos and DDos using Trojans?.

A: The result of these actions can cause significant financial losses to business of which some become bankrupt and close, other loose reputation. Their attack is more severe than hackers planting virus and worms. DDoS and DoS main motive is to cause more damage although they could behave like intellectual to threat companies to get money. It can also act like Extortion by interfering with the stock exchange market In 2002, DDoS attack and disable 9 of the 13 main servers that power the internet worldwide for several hours (so this proof their capability)

Chapter 25

Computer Hacker

674. Q: How do you define Computer hacker?

A; Computer hacker is someone who obtains unauthorized access to computer which is offence under the computer misuse Act 1990 ss 1-3.

675. Q: What is the Aim of the Hackers?

A: To achieve their aim, they target banks, businesses and individual who rely on IT online transaction where valuable data is stored. The criminal's hackers know the vulnerability of most of the software and hardware

676. Q: Name two date of United Kingdom Act on computer misuse?

A: Computer miss use Act 1971 and 1990.

677. Q: Give case law in which the Act was used?

A: Case; COX.V RILEY.

Damaging a plastic circuit there by erasing a computer program.

It was heard that the programmed was intangible and therefore not covered by the Act,

The judge said, "what is contemplated — is some physical harm, impairment or deterioration which can usually perceived by the sense" (ref, Smith and Hogan criminal law 8th edition, Butterworth, 1996,694.

Wasik suggested in (1988) 17a -alr37,40,THAT THE PRESENT LAW SHOULD be extended to data, but the computer misuse Act 1990 ended that possible road to reform.

678. Q: give another case law?

A: A computer hacker gain access to a system, manage to find out where sensitive files were stored on a large metal magnetic disk. He was able to change the password, deleted and added files wipe the tile which would have detected his use of the programme including the programme to trace him.

He appeals against his conviction for damaging the disks by altering the magnetic particles.

679. Q: What was the appeal grounds?

A; The disk function was not damage by him, no physical damage to the computer, that destructing, or the damage was to the information on the disk which did not impair the usefulness of the disk.

680. Q:What did Lord Lane said on the appeal?

A: The law as it stands that tangible property has been damage not necessarily that the damage itself should be damage — that the magnetic particles upon the metal disc were part of the disc and if the appellant was proved to have intentionally and without lawfully excuse altered the particles in such a way as to cause impairment of the usefulness or value of the disc to the owner, there would be damage" Any alteration to the physical nature of the property concern may amount to damage. Whether it does so or not will depend on the effect that the operation has had upon the legitimate operator— if the hacker actions do not go be young for example the mere tinkering with an inference with the disc amount to an impairment of the value or usefulness of the disc to the owner, then the necessary damage is established Whitely (1991) 93 Cr App R 25 (computer misuse Act 1990 s (6)

681. Q: What does the criminal damage Act 1971 say about computers?

A; a modification of the content of a computer shall not be regarded as damaging any computer or computer storage medium unless it effect on that computer or storage medium impairs its physical condition.(The above information from criminal Law 4 the edition by *Michael Jefferson)*

Chapter 26
YOURTH CRIME

682. Q: Define Youth crime

A: "Crime and disorder Act 1998 state that anti-social behaviour is acting in a manner that cause or is likely to cause harassment, alarm, or distress to one or more persons not of the same household"

683. Q: Legally what does the term youth refer?

A; Youth is referring to as juvenile or young offender. According to the CJA 1991 part 111 this juvenile term apply to children under 14 years. Young person is 14 to 17).

684. Q; Which court deals with youth and who preside?

A; Juvenile court is now youth court CJA 1991 s70 and

normally base in Magistrate court which have to have at least three magistrate and at least one of them must be a woman,

685. Q: How is proceeding in Juvenile court?

A; The proceeding are normally private in chambers **(not** open to the public and the details not allow to be published unless the Home secretary overturn it

686. Q: what sort of sentences are there for juvenile offenders?

A: Court; A young offender may receive warning if he or she has not offend before. If he has offended more than two years he\she will receive another caution unless the crime is very serious and is of public interest.

687. Q: What other sentence available in juvenile court?

A: In most cases the offender will be referred to the young offenders team.

688. Q: What consist young offenders team and under what Act.?

A: The young offenders team which local authority is requires to provide and consist of; probation officer, health officer, police social worker, health officer, education officer. This is requirement under 1997 cl.30

689. Q: What age group are immune from prosecution?

A: The CJA sometimes refer infancy and the immunity from prosecution. Example children below the age 9or up to 9 cannot be convicted of any offence but may be referred to juvenile team of the local authority.

690. Q: what Act provide such immunity?

A: Young person Act 1933 s 50 as amended from 1963 s 16.

691. Q What happen if adult persuade youth under 9 to commit crime?

A: To avoid adult criminals using under 9 ,if an adult persuade a child under 9 to commit a crime, the child is innocent, but the adult is deem as the offender under Actus Reus.

692. Q: What debate had been for children 10 and 13?.

A: Children between 10 and 13, there had been a lot of debate that child of 10 to 13 cannot form Reus which protect them from presumption conviction basically the law base that these age group cannot understand right or wrong.

693. Q: what did Lord Jauncy said about a 12-13 age group?

A; Lord Jauncy said " It almost an affront to common sense to presume that a boy of 12 to 13 who steals a high-power motor car, damage other cars while driving it, knock down uniform police and then runs away when stopped is unaware that he is doing wrong”

694. Q: What did Lord Lowry said about a child?

A; Lord Lowry in CV DPP (1990) IACO “Better formal education and earlier sophistication, do not guarantee that the child will more readily distinguished right from wrong”

695. Q; What is are some of the factors that contribute to youth crime?

A: youth unemployment;, identity;, media;, communication, parental discipline; domestic violence; education, lack of support; lack of resource; lack of activities; material world, opportunity crime, technology.

696. Q: how does youth unemployment contribute to youth crime?

A: This is link to theft, riot and social disorder to satisfy their material, drugs and alcohol needs. They have low self-esteem, loss sense of security.

697. **Q**: how does identity contribute to youth crime?

A: Some commit crime to have identity or feeling of belonging for example "FOLK DEVIL (link to young white criminal or MUGGERS or YOB; which is link to youth black street rubbers. Youth feel an honour or feel **"cool"** to be link to this group.

698. Q: how does media contribute to youth crime?

A: Youth learn from what they see and read such as television, violent films and the news paper

699. Q: how does communication contribute to youth crime?

A: Youth criminals communicate sometimes using coded e-mail; messages to pass on information of crime and how to get access to commit crime.

700. Q: how does parental discipline contribute to youth crime?

A: Lack of family warmth, love and care. Lack of discipline or communication from parent and teachers, result the youth behave without direction or control.

701. Q: how does education contribute to youth crime?

A: No effective peer tutoring or parent help to obtain job or good education.

702. Q: how does domestic violence contribute to youth crime?

A: If the child witness violence in the family such as the

father abuses the mother or the family pet. Or even if the youth, he or she will feel that it is acceptable behaviour.

703. Q: how does lack of resources contribute to youth crime?

A; There may be no resources in their community such as teen centres, arenas, skyboard parks, pool, music, clubs theatre for them to form feeling of belonging.

704. Q: how does lack of support contribute to youth crime?

A: The family unable to give adequate support for their youth due to poverty, drug and alcohol addiction, domestic violence, physical isolation, lack of social service facilities, could not afford recreational activities.

705. Q: how does lack of activities contribute to youth crime?

A: For them to channel their frustration and boredom may lead to crime if there are no positive activities. Lack of activities for them to feel productive hence they commit crime to satisfy their needs

706. Q: how does material world contribute to youth crime?

A: material world; they may want to be like a famous person, the cloths, design clothes haircut, Jewell, posture, speech leads the youth to crime

707. Q: how does opportunity crime contribute to youth crime?

A: Some careless of property owners such as leave their windows or door open, or rotten doors with unsecure lock cars without alarm with valuable left in the car seat.

708. Q: how does technology contribute to youth crime?

A: Some youth are very knowledgeable about hacking computers hacking using various technique to get information of how to get people credit cards or debit cards or financial detail to use to get money

709. Q: How does not being warn contribute to youth crime?

A: The public not being warn of hackers and procedure to protect their computer

Peer group could be dealing with drugs or alcohol or football hooligans, or involve with drugs and alcohol.

710. Q: How does low punishment contribute to youth crime?

A: LOW PUNISHMENT; Some youth aware that the benefit of committing crime is higher than the punishment or sentence or if they are fine the parent have the means to pay.

711. Q: How does low school attendance or drop out from school contribute to youth crime?

A: Could be jealousy or revenge on the ex-girlfriend.

Some adult use the youth to commit crime knowing that due to their age, they will not be charged with any crime.

712. Q: How does abuse contribute to youth crime?

A: Youth who might have been abuse physically or

emotionally or sexually by parents or peer or teachers?

713. Q: How does lack of support contribute to youth crime?

A; Lack of positive support for their needs which include basic human needs, education, recreational and health To deal with their anger, confusion depression and guidance to learn socially acceptable manner.

714. Q: How does Pressure contribute to youth crime?

A; In search of high esteem, self-warmth and sense of belongings, or he\she may find him being pressured from parent, teachers and peers to do things which may lead him to crime.

715. Q: How does low self-esteem contribute to youth crime?

A: self-esteem and feeling and feeling insecure.

716. Q; How does lack of guidance contribute to youth crime?

A; Lack of knowledge of where to go to access information and service when needed for support.

717. Q: How does the lack of CCTC in the area contribute to youth crime

A: In the arrear to monitor any undesirable person Lack of citizen arrest in the area Lack of police patrol on foot Stiffer immigration control At airport and country car and foot boundaries 1) Lack of neighbourhood watch in the area

718. Q:Name as many as possible anti-social problems that can cause youth crime?

A: People could be mindless violence who is likely to cause riot

2) Driving a car without a driving license
3) Anarchist squatters.
4) Litter on the street instead of putting in the bin provided
5) Destruction of property,
6) Clashes with police,
7) Gang fight
8) Disturbance of the peace
9) Rampage,

10) Quarrel,
11) Fight,
12) Revolt,
13) lawlessness,
14) Violent protest and disturbance
15) Muggers (Use for black young street rubbers
16) Folk devil use for white you anti-social behaviour
17)) Troublesome in school.
18) Dishonesty and aggressive
19) Hyperactive,
20) A deficit disorder,
21) Risk taking and poor concentration.
22) His routine activities such as drinking, alcohol, drugs
23) Standing at the side road and shouting abuse and making racial remark to passer-by.
24) Desire for material gain
25) Status among peers excitement
26) Sexual satisfaction
27) Disturbing the public peace
28) Acting in an unruly manner
29) Challenging socially acceptable manner
30) Disorderly behaviour
31) Breaching the rules or expectation
32) Perception of disorder can be just as significant as the disorder that might actually occur
33) Underage consuming alcohol
34. Underage smoking or taken illegal drugs
35. Underage prostitution

34)Uncontrolled animals

35)Harassment including racist and homophobic

36)Riding\ cycling on foot paths

37)Aggressive begging.

38)Rubbish damping and misuse of communal areas

39);Nuisance from vehicle

Vehicle being park or abandonment.

42Criminal behaviour

43 Unkempt garden which attract dumping of goods creating eyesore)

44;Racial motivating aggravated harassment ,wounding, common assaults criminal damage

719. Q: How could anti - social behaviour could be transferred to the public?

A: There are many types and meaning of exhibit example; Gang graffiti

720. Q: Give example of how group of

people express their emotion of violence threat, messages to the owner or to the public and is common

A: Tagger graffiti

This could be few to complex street are common and widespread, conventional graffiti

this sometimes called" youthful exudence"

ideological graffiti, ideological express hate for religion racial, ethnic, vehicle crime, there are two main types namely theft from a car or theft of the car. Vehicle targeted

Chapter 27

Anti-social/delinquency

721. Q: What did Socrates, the Athenian philosopher describe young people BC?

A:) The young people of to-day—"-have bad manners, they scoff at authority and lack respect for their elders. Children nowadays are real tyrants—they contradict their parents—-they tyrannise their teachers '.

This saying is attributed to Socrates, the Athenian philosopher writing around 400 BC

722. Q: How did Daily post paper describe some children?

A; Yobs destroy children scarecrows in “mindless wrecking rampage”

By Daily Post on 29 May 2013 (William, 2003)

723. Q: How did Daily Graphic describe some young people?

A: A gang of roughs, who were parading along the roadway, shouting obscene language —and pushing respectable people down. By The Daily Graphic 25 August 1898 (quoted in the Pearson 1983, pp 4—5)

724. Q:How did Cohen describe anti-social people?

A; "Folk devils" these anti-social people are dangerous, creating a moral panic, threat to society order" "More moral panic will be generated—more talk devils will be created— society will continue to generate problems for some people" (COHEN 1972 p.233

725. Q: How did the media describe youth disorder?

A: The media describe youth disorder as YOB (young white working-class male)

which has characteristic of " lager louts, football hooligans joy riders, foul mouthed, irresponsible, unemployed, violent hangs around council estate, terrorizes local or colour people, some alcoholic,. Drugs and more likely to be criminal domestic violence. They give the look of being mad, bad and dangerous. (COWARD 1994 p.32)

726. Q: Who acknowledges anti-social behaviour?

A: For the first time since—Robert Peel set up the Metropolitan police, areas of our cities are becoming unsafe for peaceful citizens by night and some even by day.

By Sir Keith Joseph Member of Parliament in 1977 (quoted in the Pearson 1983

727. Q: Who developed Farrington et al 2006 on delinquency

A; Criminologist Donald West and David Farrington (a forensic psychologist. Was developed of Farrington study 1995, 2003 and 2005 and join by other colleagues who helped in 2006.delinquent development.

728. Q: List the six categories of

delinquency by Farrington et al 2006?

A; (FARRINGTON et al 2006) SIX CATEGORIES OF DELINQUENCY

The six categories of delinquency include

1.Antisocial behaviour, including being troublesome in school dishonesty and aggressive

2.Hyperactive, attention deficit disorder, risk taking and poor concentration.

3.Low intelligence and poor school attendance.

4.Family criminality, convicted parent, order sibling and sibling with behaviour problems

5.Family poverty, large family size and poor housing.

6.Poor parental, child-rearing behaviour, including harsh and inconsistent discipline, poor supervision, neglect and parental conflict.

729. Q: How was Farrington et al carried out?

A: Farrington et al (1986) and 2006 study on delinquency on 8—10-year-old boys reveal six categories of delinquency. Who carried out observation and feeling (emotion responds) in an environment especially peers or parent form major part of future personality including process of being strong or could cause delinquency

730. Q; How did study by Cambridge university carried out

A; A study by Cambridge university study in delinquent development (Delinquent and criminal behaviour) using longitudinal method (over long period) which started in 1961 studying 411 males from the age 8 to 48 in deprive working class areas.

Parent not happy with them for any apparent reason

Being beaten up just for the father to get satisfaction Always tell the child that he is a failure and that his future is brick

731. Q: Give about thirteen anti-social behaviour and the effect of anti-social on some people

1) A: Ant social behaviour such harassment, violence that frighten me because I am very meek and introvert.

2) These anti-social behaviour lacks consideration for others and may cause harm to society or label attached to the behaviour of some groups of young people.

3) Have had my car damage by pouring paint striper on it and the tires had been punctured

4) Theft from my house and the car.

5) Freighting at night especially coming home after lodge meetings 6} It is a threat to social stability and social order)

1) The racist remark and insulting calling me Negro go home

2) My children being call names such as coconut, half cast mix race

3) The use of four-letter words hurt me, and my children as are brought up strict God fearing.

4) Nasty remarks about my association with freemason society such as Dodgy handshake, all your secret will be revealed

11) Fear of violent crime

12) Fear of intimidation

13) Fear of victimization, cost to put the effect right

732. Q: Name three ways to create a safer and sustainable environment?

A: The three recommended toolkits to create safer and sustainable areas include.

Prevention by crime and disorder partnership aim to combat physical and social environment to prevent anti-social occurring

The housing Act 1996, the crime and disorder Act 1998 give power to the police to eradicate anti-social behaviour, and these must be enforced.

The local authority to reintegration\ resettlement; to avoid repeated anti-social behaviour and provides shelter for homeless

733. Q; What will you suggest for social control?

A; I support and join the agencies of social control include;

The police, communities, probation, citizen's arrest and the criminal justice system

Campaign for tougher policing and tougher sentence

Bystanders could help to prevent crime, but they are at risk of being accused of assault or being assaulted this is the reason why many people will just walk away.

I support the "SUS" law (Right of police to stop any one of suspected muggers (Gave rise to rise to black people became systematic harassment by police.

734. Q; What must be the strategy for

saver environment?

A: The strategic include; Identify and assess the local problem, determine and implement local action

The community partnership with police tackles action to solve the problems by priorities the most serious service

the police and campaign for the police to enforce the crime and disorder laws

735. Q: What is expected outcome?

A: Outcome focused; setting of targets, monitoring and evaluate review the weak point and implemented.

736. Q: Name some ways to avoid anti-social behaviour through education?

A: The government or the local authority need to help people with the following.

Study family, work responsibility have long term goal, and could change ways of decision making.

What is likely to stop reoffending is by realising the risk of higher sentence or punishment, partner disagree threat of incarceration or threat of broken relationship.

Altitude of how to see the future which includes work and family as more important.

737. Q: What can intervention

program include?

A: Also to prevent re-offending is to have intervention programme which include cognitive? behaviour skill training to reduce impulsiveness

promote good child rearing through parental education and supervision.

738. Q: What are some factors to prevent reoffending

A: Factors to prevent reoffending include getting older change of social environment, steady job marriage moving to new area away from the environment, change of their altitude.

People routine activities such as drinking, alcohol, drugs, stánding at the side road and shouting abuse and making racial remark to passer-by.

Study family, work responsibility have long term goal, and could change ways of decision making.

Wharf is likely to stop reoffending is by realising the risk of higher sentence or punishment, partner disagree threat of incarceration or threat of broken relationship.

Altitude of how to see the future which includes work and family more important.

Also to prevent re-offending is to have intervention programme which include cognitive9 behaviour skill training to reduce impulsiveness, promote good child rearing through parental education and supervision.

Also to prevent re-offending is to have intervention programme which include cognitive? behaviour skill training to reduce impulsiveness, promote good child rearing through parental education and supervision.

739. Q: What is Status offending?

A: Juvenile delinquency can also be called status offending

This occurred when one failed to follow the law, often referred to in relation to a young person, for example juvenile delinquency or behaviour by some group of young people that has been labelled as deviant and delinquent.

740. Q: what characteristic result from short term anti-social?

A: For short term anti-social, he may turn to drugs, alcohol, boredom and frustrate

741. Q: How does low income affect crime?

A: Those more likely to engage in anti-social behaviour are people from low income, unemployment, not successful at school. They are more likely to commit crime to achieve their desire such as designer clothes, latest mobile phones.

Chapter 28

STATISTIC on youth crime

742. Q: What is the 2005 British crime survey?

A: In 2005\2006 British crime survey estimate that 45.1% of 16 to 24-year-old used at least one illicit drug in their lifetime.

Cannabis used most which was 21.4%

The survey also reveals that Ketamine is increasing among young people word wide

In 2007, 17% of pupil said they had taken drugs in a month.

A survey conducted by Life education among 9 to 11 years old (1500 pupil revealed 71% know about most illicit drugs; cocaine, then second is cannabis. The worrying was that 38% cited the pressure to look cool as a main reason for using drugs.

Scotsman survey revealed that young girls (9 to 11) are likely to abuse drugs than boys.

About 250,000 neighbour disputes (England and Wales)

The fear of quality of life being affected, minimum impact seems to be increasing but moderate and substantial impact are decreasing

According to British crime survey 2001 victims of burglary, vehicle theft and violence in low and high disorder areas had been decreasing since 1998.

British crime survey 2001 revealed more fear of attack in council estate at night and less in the ruler areas, physical disorder twice as high

743. Q: Which areas in UK are safer?

A: With regard to personal safety in U.K North West and London shows high percentage.

Low areas are Wales, east midlands south west In 1998 the criminal court heard 59,290 for criminal damage offenders.66,747 for public order 1931 for intimidation of harm of witness jurors 80% of all criminal damages were adults.

744. Q: Which areas in United Kingdom suffers more antisocial behaviour?

A: Metropolitan authorities have 8 times more likely to describe anti-social as “BIG PROBLEM OR VERY BIG PROBLEM"

Local authorities estimate the cost of a case against anti-social behaviour to be around £10,000

745. **Q:** What is the cost of vandalism of anti-social.

A:

1998 TO 1999 in Bradford was £895,593 and £114,000 repair but all incidents in U.K was £1.3 billion

NACRO estimate cost of £100,000 a year for dealing with anti-social behaviour

Salford housing spent £2 million and Hull spent £177 million on anti-social per year.

For short term anti-social, he may turn to drugs, alcohol, boredom and frustrate.

746. Q: What is the Characteristic of antisocial?

Give statistic

Characteristic of trend of anti- social behaviour			
TE	who	v	centag
95-1998	ice	reased by	%
96-1997\8	al hority	reased by	7%
93—1997	h	rease by	%
5 years	ial dlords	reased by	%
95—1997	ish crime vey	reased by	%
990-2000	ish crime vey	reased by	

747. Q: In a graph, explain graph

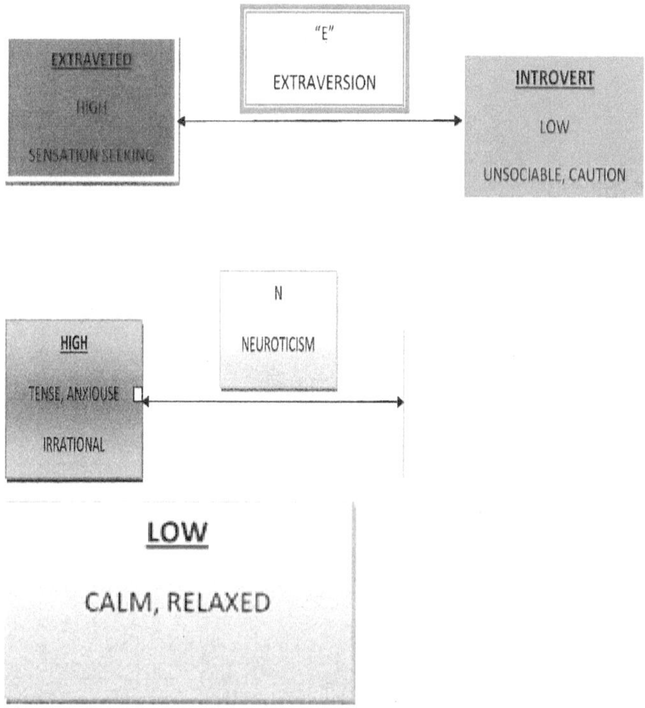

748. Q: In a graph explain antisocial potential?

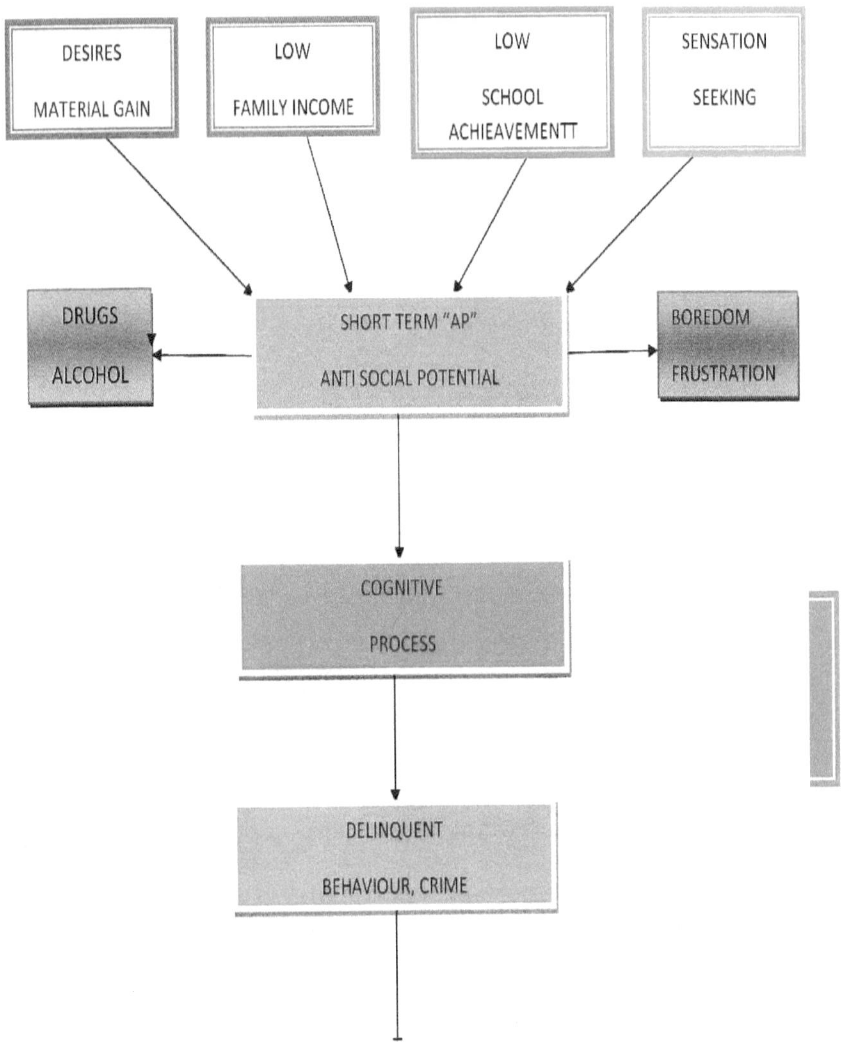

Q: Integrated cognitive antisocial potential theory (igap1 by Cambridge study. Farringdon alone (1995, 2003. 2005) and in **collaboration with colleagues 2006.**

REINFORCEMENT

REWARDS

749. **Q**: How will parent behaviour affect youth?

A: Mother Smash the house when upset.

Parent gave nasty remark even if the child does something good.

Parent violence affects their emotion

Frequent observing violence of a child 17 to 20 will be at risk of becoming criminal is such as theft, robbery, fraud, impulsive, risk taken.

If the family has history of offending or family poverty or child rearing practice will associate to his future behaviour

Chapter 29

Criminal psychology

750. Q: What is psychology?

A: Psychology is the study of the mind, the way the individual plan, think and action. Is a way of searching human thought, feeling, behaviour and interact with our environment since human is unpredictable.

751. Q: What is Forensic?

A: Forensic is the method is use during investigation or the term use in court of law?.

752. Q: What is Forensic psychology?

A; Forensic psychology is the knowledge in human behaviour base on clinical, social and cognitive helps to investigate crime, such as to identify a criminal or intent or insisting a crime. It is also use for research, design policies or correctional facilities and prison. It covers the areas such as academic training and law enforcement and consultation.

753. Q: who also use forensic psychology?

A: Clinical practice psychologist use it for assessing some offender and to determine what type psychological treatment that individual (example SOTP core is use for high risk sex offenders or SOTP rolling use for low risk sex offenders.

754. Q: Name one psychological tool for investigation?

A: One of the psychologies tools for investigation is Stanford-Benet intelligence test.

755. Q: Can psychology be bias?

A: yes it could be It is also important of how psychological bias for understanding individual decision making which could be either mental bias or limits on decision making.

756. Q: Who was the first forensic psychologist?

A; Since 20lh century there had been eminent psychologist notable Hugo Munsterberg who is regarded as the first forensic psychologist.

757. Q: Name some other known psychologist?.

A: Others are William Stern, Alfred Benet and Sigmund Freon, Lewis Term.

758. Q: Describe Psychological economic?

A: Psychological economic is an approach, blend psychology and economic of how individual make decision.

It is also important of how psychological bias for understanding individual decision making which could be either mental bias or limits on decision making.

759. Q: Describe Psychologist Herbert Simon argument about people.?

A: Psychologist Herbert Simon 91950s) argue that people have mental limit in how they were able to process information

When this was put to Simon that standard economic people have almost unlimited capacity to absorbed and to process information when people make decision.

Simon argued that this view of human was unrealistic as people often struggle to compute a lot of information and will suffer from information overload. Simon 1955.

760. Q: Describe Thaler and Sinstein opinion on status Quo?

A: STATUS QUA bias; this point to the tendency that individual has to fall back on existing patterns of behaviour and adopt the status quo.

761. Q:What does Thaler and Sinstein think of over confidence people?

A; OVER CONFIDENCE; Individual tend to overestimate their capacity to filter and understand a mass of information. Also people think that bad things are less likely to happen to them than to others.

762. Q: What is BOUNDED RATIONALITY?

A; Bounded rationality: There are bounds or limits in the capacity of people to make rational calculation. One effect of these is that people rely on rules of thumb when making decision.

763. Q: what can prevent people offending?

A: Factors to prevent individual re-offending include marriage, steady employment, moving to new area away from factors in the environment.

764. Q Why did psychologist Eysenck say about why people commit crime?

A; The factors to be considered why people commit crime and others don't include, link between biology, personality and crime (social process) as per psychologist Eysenck's

765. Q: What is ICAP theory?

A: Factors that could lead someone to commit or reoffending include the size of the family, poverty child rearing practices school attainment and employment (ICAP theory by Farrington's and Cambridge.

766. Q: How could personality be detected?

A: Personality could be detected by Biological approach that is use of anatomical or physiological process to try to explain behaviour example genetic, immune or nervous system.

767. Q: What is criminal behaviour?

A: criminal behaviour is human action that breaks the law and can receive punishment or behaviour that has been labelled as illegal in a particular time.

768. Q; What is white collar crime?

A: white collar crime refers to businesses and office example stealing of office stationery, perk of the job that some people term it.

769. Q: What is Deviance/deviant behaviour?

A: Deviance\deviant behaviour; Behaviour that violates some social norms and thus becomes labelled as deviant. crime and deviance are social disorder.

Chapter 30
Offender PROFILING

770. Q: what is definition profiling?

A; Offender profile is a method of identifying the perpetrator of a crime base on an analysis of the nature and the offense a manner in which it was committed including personality such as his or her choice before, during and after plus relevant evidence\ physical compare with the crime characteristic mental (Wikipedia).

771. Q: What is Crime profile?

A: Criminal profile helps investigator examine the evidence from crime scene and victim and witness reports to develop on the offender description.

772. Q: What sort of description the

police might need?

A: This description may include the analysis of psychological variables such as personality and behaviour Patten as well as demographic variables such as age race or geographic location investigators should use profiling as a means to narrow down the suspect pool or in structuring interrogation of a suspect once apprehended criminal profiling.

773. Q: How does Brent Turvey, M.S.San Diago describe deflation of criminal profiling?

A: Brent Turvey, M.S.San Diego, Academic press 1999.

Criminal profile helps investigator examine the evidence from crime scene and victim and witness reports to develop on the offender description.

This description may include the analysis of psychological variables such as personality and behaviour Patten as well as demographic variables such as age race or geographic location investigators should use profiling as a means to narrow down the suspect pool or in structuring interrogation of a suspect once apprehended criminal profiling.

774. Q: What other waves can be used in criminal profile

A: In criminal profile one can base on three waves which are 1) the study of clues. 2) The study of the crime committed. 3) The study of the psyche of the criminal

775. Q: How is profile of criminal?

A: Profiling of a criminal is very difficult and involve how, when, what manner the crime was committed which might linkage

776. Q: Name few Aims of collecting criminal profile?

A: To assist law enforcement of where to apply investigation.

2) To assist the court to in determining whether or not there is sufficient behavioural evidence to suggest a common scheme or plan in order to address forensic issues.

3) If similar crime may be trailed together

4) Whether any similar crime may be brought as

evidence.

777. Q: How many concepts for assessing behaviour

A: On assessing behaviour evidence or Case Linkage, there are 3 concepts

MO, MODUS operandi

signature

Victimology.

5) To assist law enforcement of where to apply investigation.

6) To assist the court to in determining whether or not there is sufficient behavioural evidence to suggest a common scheme or plan in order to address forensic issues.

7) If similar crime may be trailed together

8) Whether any similar crime may be brought as evidence.

778. Q What main goals that Holms and Holmes (200) considered When investigate a criminal

A:

Provide law enforcement with social and psychological assessment of the offender.

Provide law enforcement with a psychological evolution of belongings found in the possession of the offender

Give suggestion and strategies for the interview

process.

Victimology

779. Q: What are the six steps by Holms and Holms to identify offender?

A

If the crime is crime is break in. Britain there is one criminal law for England and Wales.

In other countries such as USA, one needs to check the characteristics of the jurisdiction and the legal element of the state where the crime was committed.

To assess the physical evidence collected and to interview the victim and any witnesses.

Also find out the motive the who might be the suspect. (This step is known as HYPOTHESIS

Collect data and check the records and also to compare with police record. Depending on the information, obtain, one may need to reinter view the victim and the suspect and compare the information or data to determine similarity or difference

Evaluate the information and to see how truth and reliable they are and also the physical evidence one may have compare to any other physical laws that could suggest possible reinterpret the physical evidence.

Priorities all the evidence and follow up procedure laid out which might prove or disprove a particular suspect to be charged after you feel that you have enough information according to the law of the country or state

Draw a conclusion that is supported by court-admissible evidence leading to the arrest prosecution and conviction of the offender.

780. Q: Explain the Ainsworth (2001) used four approaches to identify the offender?

A: 1) Geographical: analyse patterns regarding timing and location of the crime scene which will help to find where the offender lives works and hobby.

2) PSYCHOLOGICAL; Use psychological theories to find out his or her

characteristic by compare to present offender behaviour and style of offence.

3} TYPOLOGICAL; Special characteristic of the crime scene, these will lead to categories various characteristic.

4) CLINICAL: Psychiatry and clinical psychology technique to determine if he\she suffering from mental illness or psychological abnormalities

5) CASE LINKAGE (Brent E Turvey criminal psychology)

6) This involve compare physical evidence, victim logy crime scene characteristic, modus operandi that is organize or disorganize typologies and signature.

7) This is to determine whether or not there is discrete connection between two or more previous unrelated cases through crime scene.

8) PATTERN Series of similarities that might indicate the same person committing the crime previously known as

9) LEADS can lead to the victim or who must have done it.

10)TIPS the local community might be able to provide any unusual information.

11 (THEORIES The information received may leads to

theories which have been tried and tested

12)CLUES The collection of evidence may be consistent and similar to previous crime committed.

13)One must focus on the deceased Crime scene and crime lab.

781. Q: Why is profiling of a criminal difficult?

A: Profiling of a criminal is very difficult and involve how, when, what manner the crime was committed which might linkage. Some eminent people have used different method to identify suspect.

Chapter 31

Procedure for criminal file

782. Q:Described briefly the five main procedure in gathering information for criminal profile

A:

1) Analyse how the type or nature of the criminal act is made and compare to type of people who have committed similar crime in the past

2)In depth analysis of the actual crime scene

3)The victim background and activities are analysed to look for possible motive and connection.

4)Possible factors for motivation of the crime is analyse.

5) Description of the possible offender is developed, based on the characteristic which has been detected, and compare with previous case

783. Q: Why do police take DNA from suspect.

A: DNA is taken to march the previous burglar the sample can be taken form the saliva the mount, blood or se-men or faeces.

784. Q: What sort of investigation police do on break in or theft.

A;

What time either day or night-time that the crime usually takes place

How he\she entered; through the window or front doors

What did he used to gain access to the properties? As he may use the same method or tools

Type of items he normally take example jewel, money, television

785. Q : How do police get knowledge of suspect?

A: Asked the neighbour or the community if they see any suspect hanging around the arrear and if so to describe his approximately height, build hair colour and style facial shape, colour of the eye, height, accent race voice colour of the teeth male or female complexion (black white and others)

Any characteristic Pattern, trend compare to the previous

description of the crime

Any psychiatry symptoms

786. Q: What about the suspect behaviour?

A: The behaviour as is naturally accruing and cannot be manipulated What he wears might include groves, and was the head covered?

Footsteps, shoes or trainers.

Touching and thing in the house for fingerprint expect

Details of what he has stolen including serial number, receipt.

Watch the CCTV on the street ask the neighbours if any of them have CCTV to watch.

Any tyre mark on the ground might determine the type of vehicle

787. Q:What happens if the victim think he/she saw the accuser

A: If the victim was not sure of the possible

description, Identity parade (about 10 people) could be used whereby the victim stands behind translucent glass (so that the people unable to see her) and he could then select the likely suspect.

789. Q: What happen in difficult and serious cases?

A: In difficult cases the police might offer the public reward for arrest and convicted.

790. Q: Briefly describe the six steps of the Scientific Method Of Crime Reconstruction?

A: Crime reconstruction typically starts with inductive reasoning, then proceeds to deductive reasoning, then involves a breaking down or analysis of facts, and then involves a building up of facts or synthesis. The number and kind of facts, together with any ambiguity' or doubt associated with them, determine the level of evidentiary value. The process is almost exactly the same as the scientific method:

791. Q: What is the first step in the reconstruction of crime using scientific method?

A; Step 1 - State the problem by looking at what type of crime was committed, the legal elements of the crime, and the characteristics of the jurisdiction where the crime was committed

792. Q: What is the second step in the reconstruction of crime using scientific method?

A; Step 2 - Form a hypothesis by looking at the physical evidence and interviewing the victim or witnesses to determine motive and possible suspects

793. Q: What is the third step in the reconstruction of crime using scientific method?

Step 3 - Collect data by doing records checks and police checks, re-interviewing the victim, witnesses, and suspects, while trying to obtain additional witnesses and exemplar or comparison samples from suspects

794. Q: What is the fourth step in the reconstruction of crime using scientific

method?

A: Step 4 - Test hypotheses by evaluating how truthful and reliable the stories are of each party to the crime, and weigh their stories against the physical evidence and any known physical laws that could possibly reinterpret the physical evidence.

795. Q: What is the fifth step in the reconstruction of crime using scientific method?

A: Step 5 - Follow up on the most promising hypotheses (theories) with any and all procedures (e.g., surveillance, stings) that might prove or disprove a particular suspect is the offender.

796. Q: What is the sixth step in the reconstruction of crime using scientific method?

A: Draw conclusions that are supported by court-admissible evidence leading to the arrest, prosecution, and conviction of the offender.

797. Q: What should the conclusion of crime reconstruction highlight

A:The conclusions of a crime reconstruction should take one of four (4) forms about the sequence of events:

(1) it can be shown to have occurred in a given manner; (2) it can be shown to have likely occurred in a given manner; (3) it can be shown to have unlikely occurred in a given manner; or (4) it cannot be shown to have occurred in a given manner.

798. Q; What is status quo bias?

A; Status qua bias is the point to the tendency that individual has to fall back on existing patterns of behaviour and adopt the status quo.

799. Q What are some factors why some people do, and others do not commit crime

A: The factors to be considered why people commit crime and others don't include, the link between biology, personality and crime (social process) as per psychologist Eysenck's.

Environmental include neighbourhood also plays major part

Chapter 32
psychological autopsy

Factors to consider when investigate a victim as in a psychological autopsy

800. Q; Name few reasons why Psychological autopsy carried out?

A; Psychological autopsy is usually 'carried out when there is a sudden unexpected death.

If the victim had been ill but not seen by doctor for about two weeks then the police have to be involve

If the body is found being dump somewhere or recover from river, then psychological investigation have to start immediately.

801. Q; what must be done when one discover the body?

A: The victim body and what is within the immediate

environment must not be torched.

The first thing is to get a doctor usually the General Practitioner to certify the death.

The police must then be called to start their investigation

802. Q; What will the police do in their investigation.?

A: The police will take some fingertips and may take some of the material within the vicinity for further forensic

The police will inform the coroner who may either come to the scene or see the victim later.

803. Q; what happen to the victim body when the police finish their investigation?

A: The victim can then be taken away by the undertakers when the police have completed. And will be kept in a freezer until post-mortem is carried out (using the standardize checklist accepted for coroner investigation

804. Q: When will the body be released to the family?

A: The body will not be buried or cremated, (in fact it will not be released to the family until and the police and coroner finished their investigation. Sometimes it would take weeks or months before the body is released to the family

805. Q: Why is study of the victim important?.

A: The Victimology or the study of the victim is very important as sometimes the insurance may require more detail before they pay out.

Detective has different generic protocols and check list which is used for reconstruction.

806. Q: Describe three areas using Turvey theory?

A: Turvey in 1999 consist of three areas namely:

1) WOUND pattern which must be fully examine before the victim is taken for autopsy.

2) victim state of mine and 3) mental health which can be gathered by interviewing and looking through records.

807. Q: What items do police investigate near the victim?

A: Most of the items within the vicinity of the victim such as alcohol, drugs food syringe clothes bed linen, pillows rope (if it is hanging or strangulation)

808. Q: What is the first thing police might consider?

A: Depend on the age of the victim, the first thing detective might consider is suicide or murder signs.

809. Q: Why do police check the victim records?

A: Psychological autopsy is a process of elimination.

After the body has been taken away, the police will start to study the records. Some victim might leave a not given reason why he or she has suicide,

810. Q: Give an example of an actor who committed suicide?

A: example is the actor Mrs Doubt fire who left a note stating that he was poor and did not wish to rely on anybody.

The victims background which includes employment, school and hospital records.

811. Q; Why is it necessary to interview people after unexpected death?

A : One of the aims of interview people is to determine warning signs such as giving away possession, money, check the date of the Will and the benefactors

812. Q; why do police need to check deceased victims medical records?

A:

For natural death, medical history, family medical history may give the clues.

Compulsive sliming or special diet will need the dietary history

To assess his or her personality and academic intellectual; military history, employment history, educational history,

813. Q: Why do police interview other people after the unexpected death?.

A: To provide link to people; Interpersonal relationships, writings by the decease, books and music owned by the decease, web site visited, phone calls, made, recent conversation with friends, acquaintances, relatives, co-workers, and teachers, interests and hobbies shared with other.

For possible murder then details of old and current enemies will be useful

Reaction by any of the above parties to the victim's death, especially as to the degree of lethality, as well as the usual questions about early warning signs and who might have intended harm

Assessment of intention about the role of the decedent in their own demise, including any sub intentional, covert, or unconscious role, this obtain by analyse.

Time of events leading up to the day of the deceased's death

The pattern of how the victim went about accomplishing their goals or life plans Fantasies, dream, thought, premonitions, fear, or phobias of the victim, socio-emotional mood swings, mental status exam, concentration and judgement abilities, IQ

814. Q: What can be used to trace a murderer?

A: The result or the information of the psychological autopsy could help to trace the murderer

815. Q: What do police consider in case of murder?

A: Police consider how the body was disposed; does the body and disposal take place at one scene or different\multiple.

There may be reconstruction of how and who might

have committed the crime and the reasons behind it. Gregg .o. Mac Cray concluded that behaviour reflect to personality which may be identify questions in four stages

What is Antecedent:

The fantasy or and plan do the criminal have and he\she act in some days and not others

816. Q: What else do the police investigate?

A;

1) Methods and manner

2) Type of victim did the criminal choose, what method and manner of the crime (stabbing, strangulation)

3) Post offence behaviour

Does the murderer try to help with the investigation through the media or contacting the investigators?

Chapter 33

International Terrorism definitions

Research and studies have found that there are more than one hundred definitions of terrorism by different nations.

DEFINITIONS

817. Q: What is United Nation definition of terrorism

A: criminal act intended or calculated to provoke a state of terror in the general public, a group of persons or particular persons for political purpose in any circumstance, unjustifiable, whatever the considerations , ideological, racial, ethnic, philosophical religious or any other nature that may be invoked to justify them.

818. Q: What is United Kingdom definition of terrorism?

A: The 1978 act was suppression of terrorism which gave the police extra powers the act 1990 was aviation and maritime security.

819. Q: What does Act 1989 s. 18 says?

A: According to prevention of act, terrorism act 1989 section 18 "it is an offence for a person to fail, without reasonable excuse, to disclose to a constable as soon as reasonably practicable, any information which he knows or believe might be of material assistance in preventing act of terrorism or in securing the apprehension, prosecution or conviction of a person for an offence involving the commission, preparation or investigation of an act involving terrorism

820. Q: What does the terrorism Act 1996 s. 58 say?

A: The terrorism act 1996 section 58 prevention of terrorism (Northern Iceland emergency provision.)

A person who is or has been concerned in the commission of any act of terrorism or in attempted commission of any act of terrorism or in directing, organising or training person for terrorism.

821. Q: Use a case law to define terrorism?

A: Terrorism is use of violence for political and religious and social, ethnic and violence aim at putting the public in fear.

Case laws

R.AL-Mograbi (1979) 70 Cr App R.24 P and CEA 1984 s 116 (5), CJA 1993 s 43,

CJ.P. OA 1996

822. Q: What is United States of America definition of terrorism?.

A: "A premeditated, political motivated violence perpetrated against non- combatant target sub national groups or clandestine agents, usually intended to influence in audience"

This definition was supported by Paul Pillar (ex-deputy chief of the CIA counter terrorist centre). He cited four key elements in terrorist namely,

Premeditated (that is planned in advance) not impulsive at of rage.

Political. (Designed to change existing political order.

It is aimed at civilian (Not at militancy target or troops.

carried out by sub national groups (not by army).

823. Q: Give as many examples of terrorism attack in the world?

A

Oslo. Norway An illegitimacy or unlawfulness act of violence example!) Immediately after the 2011 terrorist attack in Norway perpetrated by Anders Behring Brevik.

A Bagdad bus station was the scene of triple car

bombing in August 2005 that killed 43 people

FRANCE Mass killing in the Vendee during the Reign of Terror in France 1793.

BOLOGNA attack at the Bologna railway station on 2 August 980 by the neo-fascist group

ITALY Nuclei Amati Revolutionary which killed 85 people. It was the deadliest massacre in the history of Italy as a republic nation.

USA United Airlines flight 175, which had been taken over by hijackers, hit the south Tower of the former World trade centre on 11 September 2001 in New York city USA.

TEHRAN 1979Seizure of American embassy hostage in Tehran.

MUNIC OLYMPIC -In 1972, the Palestine group black September took Israel athlete's hostage in the Olympic village.

OKLAHOMA BOMBING. Oklahoma City bombing killed 168 people.

824. Q: What are some of the reasons for terrorist attack?

A: The reason for terror attack include:

It is aim at an influence wide audience using violence .Brian Jenkins in 1974 state "Terrorism is theatre"

Psychological impact of violence or the threat of violence aimed to change political decision.

Attack are carried out such a way that as to cause a maximize severity and the length of the psychological impact.

In most cases it has a political impart

The suffering of the people and the nation accomplishes the terrorist goals of instilling fear, getting the message out to a wider audience or otherwise satisfying the demands of their often-radical religion and political agendas

Example. Terrorist over the control of ancestral homeland or holy site that is Israel Jerusalem.

Terrorism wants maximum publicity so they tend to target the public who are defenceless and vulnerable so that their message can be passed through to the government and religious people.

The media are the main source of publican hat the terrorist act.

Timothy McVeigh who admitted and convicted of the 1995 Oklahoma City bombing, killing 168 people said that he targeted the federal building because it has "plenty of open space around it to allow the maximum possible news photos and television footage.

Media love dramatic or negative news to attract more readers.

It may be regarded as spiritual failure by death of innocent civilians

Nelson Mandela was once treated as terrorist, yet he became president of South Africa and the most prisoner and person on earth.

Northern Ireland, southern Ireland and England Wales had suffered long time terrorist attack.

PUBLICITY; Terrorist is intensely interested in publicity and they aim for target to bring publicity example as list above.

IEKBQ.R1SM ORIGINATED

Terrorism originated during France's Reign of terror in 1793—1794—using "Traitors "which was then accepted, but since then the terrorist motive have change for worse.

In the first century, it was termed holy warriors where

Romans head were cut off by the Palestine, Jews Zealots.

TYPES OF TERRORISM

825. Q: Give example of nationalist terrorism?

A:These group aim to form separate state by using violence 1) Oppose to French rule in Algeria in the 1950's

1) British rule in Palestine in 1940.

826. Q: Give reason and example of religious terrorism

A: Their purpose is divinely commanded example;

To create Kurdish state in Turkey

Osama Bin Laden's al- Qaeda network.

Yigal Amin who assassinated the Prime Minister Yitzhak Rabin in 1995.

In 1994, Machine gunned Muslim worshippers in Hebron Mosque by Hezbollah radical Jewish group.

827. Q: what is State sponsored terrorism

A: This is deliberately by radical state as foreign policy tools.

Hoffman said accost effective way of wagging war covertly through the use of surrogate warriors or gun of fire.

828. Q: What is Narco terrorism?.

A: This group involve in the cultivating, transporting or distributing illicit drugs.

This is mainly group who use the drug trade to funds or raise funds example Columbia FARC who form close ties with the powerful drug Lords. They may have other agenda including political Narcoterrorism is mainly used to raise funds for the terrorist.

829. Q: What is cyber terrorism?.

A: They use computer and computer network by blocking web server or deface website. It is clear that Cyber terrorism is used more to cause havoc or to destroy a country.

830. Q: Explain computer Hackling?

A: The hackers block communication, cut off essential such as water, electricity, telecommunication use bombing which contain biological, chemical or radiation attack. To make aeroplanes collide, can destroy machinery of the information infrastructure including bank, stoke exchange, telephone switch enchant.

Use for electromagnetic weapon,

831. Q: How does computer use to steal classified files etc?

A: Use Denial of access to steal classified files, sabotaging operations, erasing data, disrupt financial market, breaching dams, colliding airplanes shutting down power grid. X-ray machines, country borders, prevent their true identity or their location

832. Q: What is the funding for terrorist?

A: Terrorist need money to sponsor their aim, so they turn to support others such as the drug (Heron, Cocaine, marijuana) trafficking or support a state to fight for them.

833. Q: What do they use the money for?

A: The terrorist use the money they get from drug trafficking and other source for weapons, equipment, training, computers bribes, safe houses, forged passports, other document pay rolls

United Nation estimated that in 1998, illicit drug business generated about $ 400 billion per year for the terrorist.

834. Q: Give example of money earned or country spend on terrorism?

A: Afghanistan for Taliban rulers earned 40 to 50 million dollars a year.

In 2000, Americans spent almost 63 billion dollars on illicit narcotic

Possible prevention of terrorism

835. Q: What must we do to do to prevent terrorism

A: Demand by terrorise must not be meant as this will show weakness and must not even be negotiated especially if they start violence prior to stating their demand.

836. Q: Must we have discussion with terrorism?.

A: If they request to discuss their demands before

starting the violence then I suggest this must be given a chance as it may result compromise before any aggression.

837. Q: what biblical evidence to support give chance to enemy?

A: In fact Prophet Muhammad stated that we must exhaust all counselling before war.

Even God gave people enough time to change before He destroyed the country i.e. Sodom and Gomorrah

838. Q:How can agencies help to prevent terrorism?

A; For effective and efficient crime prevention, all agencies must cooperate\co-ordinate to work together include community safety partnership (CSPs); Police local authorities, fire brigade, rescue, health, hospital ambulance, probation service, schools workers parent, teacher's youth, education media, and community news booklet.

Chapter 34

International FRAUD

Tobacco fraud

839. Q; what percentage of illicit tobacco smuggle in freight?

A; Most (perhaps 70 to 80 percent) illicit cigarettes are smuggled in freight by serious and organised criminals

840. Q: What successes UK had in the 2000s.

A: Since launching its Tackling Tobacco strategy in March 2000, HM Customs and Excise has disrupted over 100 serious and organised criminal groups involved in tobacco smuggling, and in 2001-2002 seized 2.6 billion cigarettes. Of these, 1.6 billion were seized in the UK. The remainder was seized on-route in joint operations with overseas agencies.

841. Q: Why do people carry out cigarette fraud?

A: HM Customs and Excise assesses that the high profits and relatively low risks and penalties, compared with other forms of serious and organised crime, has encouraged some criminals to move away from drugs trafficking and switch to tobacco smuggling, and others to diversify into tobacco and other forms of excise evasion.

842. Q: How organised is cigarette smugglers?

A: For a significant number, tobacco smuggling is a core activity. Serious and organised criminal groups have also become more sophisticated over the past decade, often operating in large gangs, and some have used violence, including the use of firearms, to protect their interests

843. Q: Where in 2015,United Kingdom (HMRC) found illegal tobacco?

A: The largest tobacco factory ever encountered by HMRC inside a farm unit in Crook. The factory had more than 24 tonnes of tobacco inside, along with 500,000 cigarettes, old imperial tobacco machinery and products used to make the cigarettes. Officers also discovered caravans that were being used by the factory workforce.

844. Q: Which town in UK involve in UK's largest illegal tobacco factory

A in a County Durham town, in 2020, £10million fraud was jailed after they were caught running the UK's largest illegal tobacco factory which produce 140 packs of cigarettes a minute.

Alcohol

845. Q: How much does it cost United Kingdom in alcohol fraud in 2000s

A:Frauds involving alcohol cost a total of £750 million in lost revenue during 2000-2001. Of this, £500 million was lost on spirits, amounting to 15 percent of the legitimate market, while £200 million was lost on beer (four percent of the legitimate market), and £50 million was lost on wine (two percent of the legitimate market).

846. Q:What was the losses consist of?

A: The losses were mainly from cross-channel smuggling of duty-paid products, mostly beer and wine, smuggled in light vehicles, and from the diversion of duty-suspended products, mostly spirits, transported as freight.

847. Q: What is targeted in diversion fraud?

In the case of diversion frauds, less well-known, non-proprietary brands of spirits tend to be favoured, as these, unlike 'premium- brands, can be obtained duty-free for as little as £10,000 per lorry load. The fact that the excise duty payable on a load of spirits can be as much as £100,000 gives some indication of the potential profit to be made.

848. Q: How is illegal alcohol sold?

A; HM Customs and Excise estimates that most illicit alcohol is sold through legitimate retail outlets, such as off-licences, pubs and clubs, at close to normal duty-paid prices. This leads consumers to believe they are buying legitimate products, and in the criminals making greater profits.

849. Q: What measures are there to combat alcohol fraud?

A: ELM Customs and Excise has introduced a number of initiatives to tackle alcohol diversion fraud, including more x-ray machines, new penalties for hauliers who allow their vehicles to be used, and new controls on the 1,100 UK excise warehouses. In addition, agreement has been reached with the National Lottery operator that retailers that knowingly sell illicit spirits will have their Lottery franchise revoked.

850. Q: Apart from alcohol, what other fraud criminal do at the same time?

A: Many serious and organised criminals engaged in large-scale alcohol diversion fraud are also involved in tobacco smuggling. The easy interchange between cigarettes and alcohol not only highlights criminal opportunism, but also the potential flexibility and responsiveness of serious and organised criminals when faced with targeted enforcement measures.

851. Q: which countries are targeted in alcohol fraud?

A: Where successes have been recorded against

diversion frauds from Belgium, France and the Netherlands, for example, the organised criminals have had the flexibility to source supplies from elsewhere.

852. Q: how many people died in United State of America of alcohol misuse in 2012

A: In 2012, 3.3 million deaths, or 5.9 percent of all global deaths.

853. Q: In 2010, what was the cost of alcohol misuse for USA

A: In 2010, alcohol misuse cost the United States $249.0 billion

854. Q How do criminal carry out alcohol fraud in UK and Europe?

A: Alcohol duty fraud in the UK often involves exporting untaxed alcohol to the EU, and then bringing it back into the UK with false paperwork. This method exploits EU rules which state duty does not have to be paid on alcohol when it is being transferred between registered producers or wholesalers

Fuel

855. Q; what does oil include?

A; petrol diesel Kerosene and gas oils

856. Q: Are fraud of fuel the same in every

part of UK. And give loss of revenue by various UK government.?

A: The nature of oils fraud in the UK differs significantly between Great Britain and Northern Ireland. In Northern Ireland, HM Customs and Excise estimate that in 2001 approximately £370 million in revenue was lost from use of non-UK duty paid petrol (£130 million) and diesel (£240 million). A substantial proportion of the losses in Northern Ireland come from legitimate cross-border fuel shopping, but there is also a large element of fraud, resulting from the smuggling of fuel from the Republic of Ireland, and the misuse, 'laundering' and mixing of rebated and duty-free fuels.

857. Q: Explain is Red diesel

A: Kerosene and gas oils (red diesel) are duty-privileged fuels. Red diesel, so-called as it is artificially coloured red to aid the detection of misuse, carries a duty rebate for use in off-road vehicles and machinery, making it substantially cheaper than ultra-low sulphur diesel. Kerosene is fully rebated when used for heating purposes. Duty-privileged fuels can either be put into road vehicles neat or mixed with road fuel as an extender. Red diesel can also be 'laundered', or treated, with strong acids to remove the colouring agent and then sold on in the guise of a non-rebated road fuel. The resulting fuel contains strong acids and severely damages the engines of unsuspecting motorists.

Oils fraud

858. Q: What is oil fraud?

A: Oils fraud, involves the misuse of duty privileged fuels supplied for non-road use, began in Northern Ireland. It rapidly spread to mainland UK where criminal organisations were laundering rebated fuels with other fuels to sell to hauliers, evading both excise duty and VAT. Many of the fraudulent suppliers became in HMRC terminology 'missing traders' and disappearing without paying VAT.

859. Q: Name some oil fraud types?

A: The key fraud types are Laundering Mixing- Misuse Smuggling Decanting, Biofuel/vegetable oils

860. Q; Explain laundering in oil fraud

A: Laundering – treating red diesel and kerosene with chemicals to remove their markers and dyes and make identification

861. Q; Explain Mixing in oil fraud

A:Mixing- combining kerosene or 'tied' oils with lubrication oils to make an illegal road fuel or to dilute road diesel

862. **Q;** Explain Misuse in oil fraud

A: Misuse – illegally using red diesel in road vehicles when it is only intended to be used in off road vehicles.

863. **Q;** Explain Smuggling in oil fraud

A: Smuggling; importing quantities of oil without payment of UK excise duty. Smuggling of oil (both red diesel and laundered fuel) from the Republic of Ireland (RoI), where duty rates on road fuel are lower, across the border to Northern Ireland is a significant problem. There is also some smuggling from the RoI to the UK mainland by ferry.

864. Q; Explain Decanting in oil fraud

A: Decanting– involves bringing fuel into the UK in the running tank of a commercial vehicle (which is legal) but then decanting it for use by other vehicles (which is not legal)

.

865. Q; Explain Biofuel/vegetable oils in oil fraud

A: Biofuel/vegetable oils– used to mask laundered fuel and produced and sold commercially without payment of excise duty.

866. Q; How do criminals in oil operate in Northern Ireland (UK)?

A: Oil fraud is profitable criminal enterprise in Northern Ireland, with the proceeds often used to fund other forms of serious crime. In particular, serious and organised criminals in Northern Ireland are active in smuggling and laundering both UK red diesel and the equivalent 'green diesel' from the Irish Republic. Some criminal groups are capable of generating tens of thousands of pounds in a day from their activities, and possibly millions of pounds over the course of a year. Since April 2000, HM Customs and Excise has increased the number of staff engaged in tackling this form of fraud in Northern Ireland. As a result, seizures of fuel in Northern Ireland have more than doubled, vehicle seizures have more than trebled, and 17 laundering plants have been dismantled. In 2001-2002, 1.85 million litres of illicit fuel were seized, eight laundering plants were broken up, and seven of the major gangs behind oils fraud were dismantled. This success is reflected in the fuel retail market in Northern Ireland with an increase in legitimate fuel deliveries for the first time in five years. The volume of petrol delivered was up by six percent, and diesel by eight percent.

867. Q: In other part of UK, what does oil fraud involves?

A: In England, Wales and Scotland, the vast majority of oils fraud involves the misuse of duty- privileged fuels supplied for non-road use. HM Customs and Excise estimated that the revenue lost from non-UK duty paid petrol was £50 million in 2000. In 2001, this doubled to £100 million. The main area of concern, however, is with diesel where losses resulting exclusively from fraud are estimated to have been around £600 million in 2001, amounting to five percent

.

868. Q: What is tied oils?.

A: Tied oils relates to misuse of duty-free oils, known as tied oils. These oils are used in certain industrial processes, for example as lubricating oils. They are unmarked and can be misused in much the same way as red diesel. Tied oils frauds are large-scale and complex, indicating the involvement of serious and organised criminals.

Oil fraud in UK

869. Q: What and why did the government introduce a strategy on oil?

A: In his 2002 budget, the Chancellor of the Exchequer announced a new oils strategy aimed at reducing fraud in England, Wales and Scotland to no more than two percent of the market within three years. This strategy, launched in September 2002, combines an authorisation and assurance scheme for the distributors of red diesel and kerosene with a significant enforcement regime.

VAT FRAUD

870. Q: Name the three types of VAT fraud?

Value Added Tax fraud can be broadly divided into

three categories: registered evader fraud, unregistered evader fraud, and thief fraud.

871. Q: What method do they use to defraud?

A: They reclaim purchase for re-sale, but reduce the amount of income which in effect the amount claim is larger than the amount to be paid to the VAT custom and excise

872. Q: Explain Registered and unregistered evader fraud?.

Registered evader fraud

A: Registered and unregistered evader fraud

Registered evader fraud occurs when VAT-registered traders fail to declare their true liability by suppressing transactions. Unregistered evader fraud involves genuine traders who have turnovers above the VAT threshold in 2020 is about £85,000 but fail to register for VAT. These two categories of tax evasion are usually concentrated in cash-based businesses, such as those found within the leisure or construction industries, restaurants, pubs, taxis, and repair and maintenance services. Serious and organised criminals are probably attracted to VAT fraud by the large profits and the relatively low penalties compared with other serious crimes. Registered evader fraud does not usually attract serious and organised criminals, except gangmasters who organise illegal labour in the agricultural, construction and contract cleaning sectors.

873. Q: Who are these people and why do they defraud the system?

A; These frauds are gangsters who organize cash in hand labour. Due to the policy of inspecting business every 3 to 5 years, these gang masters can make large profit but if caught the penalties is low.

874. Q: Who are not requested to register for VAT?

A; The Custom and Exercise rule that business whose turnover is £61000 or more must register for VAT with little exception such as nursing or care homes, education, hospital college food).

875. Q: How do unregistered evaders fraud occurs?

A: This fraud occur by manipulating the financial

statement especially the profit and loss account to show less than the thresh hold of £61000 or loss. The Ledger account which is also subjective may be manipulated

Thief fraud

876. Q: Briefly explain VAT theft fraud?

A: Serious and organised criminals feature most prominently in the area of thief fraud. This involve setting up bogus VAT registered number and print them on their invoice and letterhead so that they can charge customers VAT but never pay back to the HM Custom and Exile and cannot be traced unless somebody report them.

877. Q: Name the types of VAT thief fraud

A: There are three main types of thief fraud: missing trader intra-community fraud; repayment fraud and third country export diversion fraud.

878. Q: what type of business do commit vat theft/

A; These types of fraud occurs in agriculture, construction, motor repair sale ECT.

879. Q; Explain and give example of country export fraud?

A; Third country export fraud, are mainly used in luxury goods including, Jewells, cars and basic consumer goods. It is simple by diversion of goods from export to home use without charging VAT

880. Q: What is country export diversion fraud?.

A: The last of these involves the diversion of goods from export to home use without charging VAT. Basic consumer and luxury goods have been used in such frauds.

881. Q: When can Repayment fraud occurs?

A: Repayment fraud can occur with goods or services. It involves the recovery of VAT on wholly fictitious or exaggerated transactions by a bogus business. More sophisticated criminals engage in multi-cell repayment fraud', disguising their activities and increasing their profits by setting up numerous bogus registrations, each of which reclaims small amounts of VAT.

882. Q: Explain and give example of Repayment fraud?

A: Repayment fraud; The advance technology has made it possible for experience criminal to undertake multi-cell repayment fraud by claiming VAT using nonexistence or grossly exaggerated transaction on bogus business detail using counterfeit sales invoice that appear to look genuine.

883. Q: How has advance technology helped VAT criminals?

A: Advanced technology has enabled criminals to create increasingly authentic-looking counterfeit sales invoices to support these frauds.

884. Q: What is Missing trader intra-community (MTIC)

A: Missing trader intra-community (MTIC) fraud is a systematic criminal attack on the VAT system, and has been detected in many EU member states. It involves obtaining a VAT registration to purchase goods from a VAT-free source elsewhere in the EU, selling the goods at a VAT-inclusive purchase price, and going missing without paying over the VAT. This results not only into a loss to the Exchequer of the VAT owed, but on occasion a further loss in VAT refunds made to traders in the chain.

885. Q: What is another name for MTIC and involve what?

A: MTIC fraud is commonly known as acquisition fraud, and often involves items with rapid turnovers that are transported in high volumes, such as soft drinks and confectionery.

886. Q: What does carousel fraud involves?

A; development of this fraud, known as carousel fraud, involves the continuous movement of goods between collaborating traders in different EU member states, resulting in multiple tax losses.

887. Q: Who is involved in MTIC and Carousel?.

A: To facilitate this, a number of companies are inserted in the supply chain, increasing the distance between the UK missing trader and UK dispatcher, making detection difficult. The result is that goods are sourced VAT-free from EU countries and sold on in the UK for a VAT-inclusive price. The criminals disappear before the VAT is paid over, and a further tax loss occurs with purchasers reclaiming the VAT paid to the original trader.

888. Q: What sort of Goods attract MTIC fraudsters?

A: Goods that are easily traded and have a high value and low volume, such as mobile telephones and computer components, are particularly attractive to MTIC fraudsters.

889. Q: Give history of MTIC VAT fraud?

A: MTIC fraud is HM Customs and Excise's highest VAT fraud priority. MTIC frauds grew rapidly throughout the 1990s, at a rate of £450 million to £750 million each year. It is estimated that the fraud cost the Exchequer between £1.7 billion to £2.75 billion in 2001-2002, although there is some evidence that this type of fraud is starting to decline. A strategy to combat the fraud was initiated in September 2000, and aims to minimise VAT loss and maximise recovery by intervening at an early stage. In 2000-2001, over 1,000 suspect registrations were refused and around 500 existing missing traders were identified and cancelled. Further preventative measures were announced in the 2003 Budget.

BENEFIT FRAUD

890. Q: How many types of benefit fraud and which department in United Kingdom is being defrauded?

A: There are many types of benefits fraud and the victim is DWP(Department of works and pension)

891. Q; Give an example of the magnitude of the fraud and which areas of the DWP?.

A: The Department for Work and Pensions (DWP) estimates that up to £2 billion is lost due to benefit fraud each year, the largest proportion relating to Income Support. In 2000-2001, Income Support fraud accounted for a loss of £573 million, or four percent of the total paid. Jobseeker's Allowance is the second largest type of benefit fraud. In 2000-2001, the loss to fraud was £201 million, which represented seven percent of applications.

892. Q; How does the fraud occurs?

A: Much of the loss is due to small-scale and opportunist offences, for example where recipients do not inform the DWP that they are living together as man and wife, or do not declare all sources of income or levels of savings. However, more sophisticated offences are committed by serious and organised criminals.

893. Q: Who and how investigate the fraud for DWP?

A: The Counter Fraud Investigation Division in DWP assesses that the largest organised frauds against the benefits system involve the theft of instruments of payment (IOPs), such as giro cheques and order books, while they are in the postal system.

Stolen IOPs are often altered to show higher values. The date on IOPs may also be changed enabling them to be cashed immediately. Giro cheques, in particular, can be paid into third-party bank accounts and subsequently transferred into foreign and offshore bank accounts before the genuine benefit claimant reports their loss.

894. Q: how much is estimated loss from benefit order books alone?

A: Estimates of the annual value of order book fraud vary from £83 million to £133 million.
Serious and organised criminals have been known to corrupt staff in post offices to accept fraudulent IOPs and even to place people into sorting offices and other parts of the postal system specifically to steal IOPs and other items of value. Criminals also exploit knowledge of procedures for transporting and distributing IOPs (particularly order books) through the Royal Mail in order to plan thefts. They also counterfeit IOPs, and the number of identified counterfeit giro cheques has been around 1.5 million a year for the last two years.

895. Q; How do the criminal get away with their identities criminals steal ?

A: There is continuing organised use of false and stolen identities to defraud the UK benefit system, although the scale of this activity remains unclear. Stolen identities are used for benefit claims in the UK, and in some cases to facilitate concurrent benefit claims across a number of EU states. Identities may be obtained by corrupt individuals, both in the public and private sectors, who have access to personal details.

896 Q: How do some criminals obtain

records of victim?

A: criminals are known to gather information from public records, which may then be used to purchase birth certificates of deceased infants as the basis for creating false identities.

Fraudulent foreign identity documents are presented for benefit purposes by a wide range of people, including those arriving from the Baltic Republics, Balkan States and the Middle East. Counterfeit documents frequently display features which show that the same criminals have created them, indicating some level of organisation. Criminals from both Britain and abroad have also used false identities to enable crimes such as mortgage and property fraud, illegal working and illegal immigration.

897. Q: What measure was implemented to reduce benefit fraud?

A: From April 2003, IOPs gradually phased out and replaced with direct payment into bank accounts, starting with Child Benefit and War Pensions, and gradually covering all other benefits. The DWP expects this to reduce significantly the instances of IOP fraud. A range of other measures have been introduced to tackle fraudulent applications for benefits, including requiring applicants to produce more evidence to support their claim, and cross-checks with Inland Revenue records. In addition, the DWP is working with Royal Mail to implement a 'do not redirect' scheme to prevent the use of false addresses by bogus claimants

INLAND REVENUE FRAUD

898. Q: Who is responsible for investigating Inland Revenue fraud?

A: The Special Compliance Office (SCO) is the arm of the Inland Revenue that conducts criminal prosecutions against fraudsters. SCO tackles the majority of tax fraud using civil measures for the recovery of tax interest and penalties.

899. Q: Who is more likely to defraud the inland revenue and how?

A: Companies and individuals perpetrate most of this type of fraud. Fraud by serious and organised criminals is only a small percentage of the total volume of fraud against the Inland Revenue. However, it is likely that a large proportion of serious and organised criminals commit tax offences by failing to declare their true income.

900. Q:Name other areas of Inland Revenue fraud?

A:

Capital Gains Tax and company capital gains, Charitable donations and tax reliefs, Inheritance Tax, PAYE and Corporate Tax receipts from the banking sector, Regional employer NICs holiday for new businesses, Personal wealth, Employment Allowance take-up, Non-domiciled taxpayers in the UK

901. Q: What is another way that the Inland Revenue recover some of the tax evaded?

A: taxing a suspected criminal's income or financial gain is one of the tactical options for the new' Assets Recovery Agency, which was established in 2003. Inland Revenue offences are also committed by serious and organised criminals who supply illegal labour to various sectors of the economy.

902. Q: How does paying employee cash defraud inland revenue?

A: Despite a change in the Inland Revenue's construction industry scheme, tax-free payment of wages in cash still takes place. The workers avoid paying both income tax and National Insurance. The employer benefits by employing labour relatively cheaply and by avoiding its share of National Insurance. Sometimes organised suppliers of labour will provide workers on a sub-contractual basis, often knowingly using illegal labour. This also occurs in the agricultural sector. The layering of companies also takes place in order to disguise the identity of the true employer.

903. Q: How is benefit administered by Inland revenue could be used to defraud the inland Revenue?

A: A number of tax credits, such as the Children's Tax Credit and Working Families' Tax Credit, were introduced in 2001 and are administered by the Inland Revenue. To date, there have been relatively few prosecutions for fraud against these schemes, since the Inland Revenue has lacked the powers to obtain information from third parties such as banks. In 2003, however, new tax credits legislation was allow such information to be obtained and used.

904. Q: How is the inland revenue dealing with fraud from 2017

04/04/2017 · The HMRC Fraud Hotline: 0800 788 887. The hotline is open between 8am and 8pm, seven days a week, 365 days a year. Customers can use the new hotline to report all kinds of tax fraud and evasion

PRIVATE SECTOR FRAUD

905. Q: Who might be involve in private sector fraud?

A: Various types of fraud occur within the private sector. The amounts in question can be considerable. Many of the perpetrators of these frauds are not typical serious and organised criminals, although some of the latter are also extensively involved.

906. Q: Name some private sector fraud?

A: Frauds include high-level manipulation of share prices and high-yield investment confidence tricks, such as pyramid schemes, faked instruments of payment, timeshare scams and long firm frauds. The latter involves setting up a company, trading legitimately to build up a credit history with a firm, and then placing a large order before disappearing without paying

419 FRAUD

907. Q: Which countries are notorious for 419 fraud?

A: Nigeria in West Africa

908. Q: Briefly explain 419 fraud

A: West African 419 fraudsters target individuals and organisations offering significant money-making opportunities. Millions of unsolicited letters and emails are sent out annually, enticing victims to offer their bank accounts as the destination for large sums of money (often openly stated as being illicitly gained) in return for a percentage of the funds. Those who respond positively are requested to provide advances in order to overcome various bureaucratic hurdles and free up the promised returns on investment. Victims are often requested to travel to other countries to collect the money, where they unknowingly face further risk from fraud, possible intimidation and even kidnap.

909. Q: Why do people become involve in

the 419 fraud**?**

A: People lifestyle is involved with money making and they may think the 419 is one of the easiest ways

910. Q: How were people deceived?

A: Some people are easily deceived because of the content of the media (letter, e-mail fax) which may appear genuine Some believe that because it is in writing, they could go to the police for help if they lose out

911. Q: Give an example of victim losses?.

A: In 2002, more than £8 million of losses were reported to NCIS alone, with further losses reported directly to UK police forces.

912. Q: Why do some people fall victim to 419 fraud?

A: 419 fraud exploits the gullibility and need of its victims, often drawing them into colluding with the fraudsters. Some victims are too_embarrassed or concerned about the consequences to report their losses, and the true figure may therefore be much higher. Public awareness remains the key to countering this type of advance fraud, so that potential victims are forewarned.

913. Q: Explain how are the 419 fraudsters using improved technology?

A: 419 fraudsters are taking advantage of the latest technology. Letters are still used, the trend being towards the use of post-paid impressions from countries other than Nigeria. However, the internet provides a degree of anonymity and the facility to send blanket emails to multiple potential victims. Predictably, the number of reported email approaches has risen considerably. Emails and fax documents are sent from web-based accounts, which are only used for a short period of time before being abandoned.

914. Q: Have the people aware of technologist?

A; Some people are not aware of the latest advance sophisticated technology, Lack of knowledge, awareness or experience lead people to fall victim

915. ; What are some of the qualities other people?

A: A lot of people are inexperience in the financial market or the loophole. There are a lot of people who are risk takers and will take chance on anything that from the media. It can also be argue that greed lead people to risk taken

916. Q: What sometimes affect or influence people to get them into 419 Fraud

A: Some of the media offer a partnership with millionaire which may attract people

An advert offering money making opportunity is difficult to resist.

When people are asking to travel abroad for the money, they must ask themselves few questions or must be suspicious of the motive.

917. Q: Why do the fraudster create false account?

A: fraudsters create false internet banking sites to dupe victims. The idea is to persuade the victim to part with more cash by convincing them that the deal is genuine and that they retain some control over their money. Potential victims are provided with the web address, an account number and a PIN number with which they can access their 'account'. When they do so they find details purporting to show that a large amount of money has been transferred into it. The identities of genuine companies and financial institutions are sometimes ‘hijacked' to help deceive the victims.

918. Q: Briefly explain lottery prize fraud and give an example.

A: There was a substantial increase in lottery prize fraud in 2002-2003. For this form of fraud, in which serious and organised criminals are thought to be involved, letters and emails are sent to people stating that they have won a large lottery prize. The recipients are asked to send a fee to an address, usually abroad, to secure their prize. The letters are relatively sophisticated and often include certificates and other material to give the feeling of credibility and realism. Of course, the prize never materialises, and the criminals keep the money. As with 419 fraud, public awareness remains the key to countering this type of fraud.

919. Q: Briefly explain data protection fraud?

A:Data protection fraud increased substantially in

2002-2003. This form of fraud involves companies, usually small or medium sized, being contacted by letters purporting to be from companies offering to 'register' them with the Information Commissioner so that they comply with the Data Protection Act. The accompanying documentation is professionally presented, and the company names are convincing. A standard fee of £95 is charged, which is pocketed by the fraudsters.

920. Q: Briefly explain commercial and financial fraud?

A: Some of the highest, value frauds are conducted by company owners or senior employees, rather than victims are shareholders, customers and members of the public, these are typical serious and organised criminals.

921. Q: how do the fraudsters within the company account for their fraud?

A: There have been cases where the fraudsters fail to differentiate between company funds and their own, borrowing the former to finance lavish lifestyles or to speculate, and then finding themselves unable to replace the money.

922. Q: How can senior company employee use their accounts to commit fraud?

A: there have been cases where the declared profits, of companies have been inflated order to keep a company afloat. or to maintain or increase share prices, thus staving off shareholder discontent or safeguarding or increasing the value of a director's share options. These types of frauds are more easily perpetrated if senior staff, non-executive directors and auditors are weak, incompetent, or, in the worst cases, complicit.

Chapter 35

Summary of crime prevention

923. Q:How can the United Kingdom crime and disorder help to prevent crime

A: The involvements of cps (Criminal prosecution Service come under crime and dies order Act 1998 section 5

924. Q: What is the aims and objective of CPS (Crown Prosecution Service)?

A: There are about 300 CPS in England and 22 in Wales.

The aim and objective of CSP for each region or local authorities must work together to protect their local communities from crime and to help people safer. Guidelines to deal with local issues including anti-social behaviour, drug, alcohol, youth delinquency, youth and adult re offending.

925. Q: What is the police involvement in crime prevention?

A: The police carry out assessment of the local crime priorities and the partners draw up plans of how to deal with it, the community safety partnership and police and crime commissioners (PCC) work together Annually the CSPs prepare their report and the strategy and send it to the local PCC (police and crime commissioner).The annual meeting of PCC must have at least one CSPs.

926. Q: What is the function of the PCC?

A: PCC encourage but not impose merger hence CSP submit their annual merger request to PCC. PCC may request CSPs for specific issues.

In England and Wales the Home secretary is responsible for law and order.

927. Q: What is the core role of the crime prevention partnership?

A: The aim or the core role of the partnership including the police is to provide effective and efficient safety and securities including preventing, reducing and detecting crime for law abiding citizen and their families for civil society.

928. Q: Give some example of transnational crime?

A: Examples of transnational crimes include

Money laundering

Trafficking in human beings (THB)

Drug offences (incl. drug trafficking)

Apartheid

Piracy

Corruption

Smuggling

Cybercrime

929. Q: How has technology affect government action?

A: Due to the fast global improving of the technology, the government always invests in new technology. Forensics and better gathering management and use of intelligence in policing.

930. Q: What is United Kingdom objective in tackling crime?

A: United Kingdom government objective includes;

Spread neighbourhood policing, Modernization of the police workforce, greater involvement of communities in determines how their communities are policed (information from home office web site).

931. Q: Why do police have to work with other global crime prevention agencies or Interpol to combat terrorism?

A: This is to stop other ways of terrorist raising money

Which is used by terrorist to raise money for their action by using illegal means to raise funds.

Drug trafficking is globalise and therefore needs international collaboration, exchange with effective protocol and policies.

932. Q: What is the best way to solve world crime problem?

A:The world need well organise Interpol to coordinate intelligence between national law enforcement agencies. This is serious problems and can only be solved through close co-operation of international countries and implementing legal assistance, extradition, law enforcement. There must be effective "Interpol" which is international police force working with national laws.

933. Q: Give few ways of police monitoring (police power)? In crime prevention.?

A: Ability to serve notice issue fines, power to prosecute individual for disordering behaviour. The law of the country is legitimate claim to exercise authority over particular aspects.

934. Q: How can the public help the police in crime prevention?

A: Monitoring; the public to help police to monitor each other behaviour is encourage.

Police may be called for "operation clean sweep that is resident to report anti-social behaviour.

CCTV is used to monitor people behaviour without the public realize that it is being "watch over"

The state plays major part in defining and monitoring social order

935. Q: What measures has the government of United ?

A: Kingdom put in place to prevent crime

The government had put in place how they propose to

reduce the number of people taken drugs.
Which include given police extra powers to deal with drugs takers and suppliers?
Persuade the drug takers to ask for treatment.
Create neighbourhood policing to report drugs dealers.
Extend the arrangement between foreign countries to combat drugs and to bring the suppliers to face punishment Focus on families to offer help and to encourage the parents to discipline the young people
Increase community sentence and treatment.
Increase the support for treatment within the community or rehabilitation.
involving the commission, preparation or investigation of an act involving terrorism

936. Q:Who might be considered as terrorist according to the ACT 1996 section 58?
A: A person who is or has commission of any act of terrorism or in attempted commission of any act of terrorism or in directing, organising or training person for terrorism.

937. Q: Name one publication for solving crime problems?
The following checklist has been developed and included in the following publication: Not Rocket Science? Problem-solving and crime reduction, Tim Read and Nick Tilley, Home Office Crime Reduction

Research Series Paper 6, published 2000.

938. *Q:* What is the aim of the check list to reduce crime?

A: The checklist aims to help local problem-solvers take a critical look at their current working practices and identify points for improvement. It can be used by both individual agencies and by partnerships as a way of assessing progress towards problem-solving.

939. Q: Give brief analysis of crime prevention?

A: An ideal analysis tool for anyone looking at a crime prevention problem within a certain area.

It is based on organisations adopting an evidence-based approach to crime reduction which in practice can be described as making use of data to establish the existence and extent of a problem, to analyse its nature and source, to plan intervention methods to reduce it and to monitor and evaluate the effectiveness of the selected response (whether the interventions have worked, whether they have produced their effects in the expected way, and whether there have been any significant (positive and negative) side effects).

Other things to be taken into consideration include

Drawing on findings from existing research to inform data analysis and choice of responses

Applying informed lateral thought in developing innovative solutions

Using feedback in decisions to adjust, expand, abandon and maintain initiatives.

940. Q: Give brief investigating method of the victim as in a psychological autopsy?

A:

1. Alcohol and drug history, decedent's history of dealing with stress, medical history, family medical history, recent stressors in the victim's life, military history, employment history, educational history, sexual history, dietary history

2. Interpersonal relationships, writings by the deceased, books and music owned by the deceased, web sites visited, phone calls made, recent conversations with friends, acquaintances, relatives, co-workers, and teachers, interests and hobbies shared with others, old and current enemies

3. Reactions by any of the above parties to the victim's death, especially as to the degree of lethality,

as well as the usual questions about early warning signs and who might have intended harm

4. Assessment of intention about the role of the decedent in their own demise, including any sub-intentional, covert, or unconscious role, this obtained by analyse

5. The pattern of how the victim went about accomplishing their goals or life plans Fantasies, dreams, thoughts, premonitions, fears, or phobias of the victim, socio-emotional mood swings, mental status exam, concentration and judgment abilities, IQ

6. Timeline of events leading up to the day of the deceased's death

941. Q: with regard to crime reconstruction, summarise measures considered?

A: Concepts Of Crime Reconstruction include

A number of terms require definition to fully understand reconstruction.

942. Q: What is induction in any case of crime?

A: Induction is the process of reasoning where experience, skill, and observation are applied to the particulars of a case and a conclusion or generalization is drawn.

943. Q; What is Deduction in crime investigation?

A: Deduction is the process of reasoning that starts with a generalization or premise and then considers the logical consequences of any particulars that follow.

944. Q: What is Abduction in crime investigation?

A: Abduction is the process of cycling through both inductive and deductive reasoning by adding known facts until one is able to reject or retain a hypothesis.

945. Q: What is Typology in crime investigation?

A: Typology (a.k.a. classification or taxonomy) is the process of arranging known facts into mutually exclusive categories.

946. Q: What is synthesis in crime investigation

A: Synthesis is the process of combining separate

parts or elements.

947. Q:What is analysis in crime investigation

A: Analysis is the process of starting with the whole and breaking it down into its separate parts.

948. Q: What is apotheosis in crime investigation

A: Apotheosis is a tentative assertion subject to verification or falsification.

949. Q: What is theories in crime investigation?

A: Theories - these are beliefs about the case that take you in one direction, at the exclusion of other possible directions. A theory is a somewhat verified hypothesis. Serendipity is the factor of chance or luck.

Some of these terms, and others, are used in different ways by detectives

950. Q: What is Patterns in crime investigation?

A: Patterns - series of similarities that usually indicate the same person, or the same modus operandi is involved in different crimes

951. Q: What is Leads in crime investigation?.

A: Leads - clues or breaks in the case that help move an investigation forward, usually something in a witness statement that was overlooked, or it could be something that comes up after a records search or lab report

Tips - leads provided by citizens or informants. Tips by definition involve specifics, like names, dates, places, addresses, phone numbers, or license plates

952. Q: What are Clues in crime investigation?

A: Clues - these are pieces of evidence that are consistent with the corpus delicta or elements of the crime believed to have been committed or that the suspect will eventually be charged with.

953. Q: Are all investigation the same?

A: No, there are certain steps or priorities that a seasoned investigator will take depending upon the crime he or she is investigating.

954. **Q:** Draw a chart of how a seasoned investigator would probably investigate the Homicide, Rape, robbery, burglary crimes

Homicide:	Rape:	Robbery:	Burglary:
1- focus on deceased 2 — crime scene 3 - crime	1 - focus on victim 2 - medical reports 3 - crime scene	1 - modus operandi 2 - crime scene 3 - police records	1 - focus on scene 2 — records check 3 — property check

955. Q: Explain Mode Operandi (MO)?.

A: Modus Operandi can be defined as those behaviours, taken by the offender, that were necessary to commit the crime. MO is learned behaviour. It is somewhat dynamic and can change over time (Douglas & Munn 1992). Signature behaviours, by contrast, are those behaviours committed by offenders that serve psychological and emotional needs (Geberth 1994). Records checks are similar to background checks, involving sources of information on people, up to and include garbage ology, since it is not illegal to search through abandoned property. Police records refer to its databases and resources that only police departments have access to.

956. Q: In a table form explain crime investigation?

A: See below a copy for the headings use during investigation to arrive at conclusion

PROOF	Intuition	Probable Cause	Preponderance	Clear and Convin	Beyond Reaso	Scientific Certaint
EVIDENCE	hunch, guess, or gut feeling	facts a reasonable person	Corroborated facts, eyewitness testimony, physical evidence, or evidence interpreted by			Precise facts with known

QUANTITY	articulable suspicion about	Prima facie, presumptive but	Over 50% of facts are in support	Slightly less facts than beyond	Sufficient facts to preclude	Overwhelming facts
CERTAINTY	apparent	possible	Basis for hypothesis formulation		Basis for theory	Seldom achieved
LAW	suppressed	basis for binding	Civil law standar	International law	Criminal law standar	Seldom used
INVESTIGATION	useful during early	basis for arrest	basis for confession and informant law		basis for convicti	Seldom used

957. Q: Explain "A Primer On Logical Reasoning"?

A: Inductive logic is frequently used by seasoned investigators and when you only have small titbits of information to start with. It is sometimes called analogical reasoning or *argument from analogy.* Analogies, synonyms, antonyms, metaphor, simile, rhyme, parable, fable, myth, and poetry form the basis for inductive reasoning, and it is a skill that can be sharpened.

House of Lords

958. Q: Explain the Law Lords in the supreme court of United Kingdom?

A: The judicial function of the UK House of Lords is entirely separate from its role in government; the judicial work is done by a number of senior judges colloquially called Law Lords'. They hear appeals from the High Court and the Court of Appeal and until 1999, were in effect, the final resort for appeal in the UK legal system, at which time the Supreme Court of the United Kingdom became the final resort for appeal. House of Lords rulings are binding on all other courts

Chapter 36

International Law on Self Defence

Scenario

You are a legal advisor working for the Ministry of Foreign Affairs of the state of Odesia. The state of Rotundria, your neighbour, has had a protracted civil war for over 5 years. There are four large factions fighting in the civil war: the Government of Rotundria, the anti-government coalition, the Veleno People's Movement (VPM), and the Church of the Temporary Mortal Affliction (Affliction). the Government of Rotundria and the anti-government coalition, were the original instigators of the conflict. The two others grew in the ensuing power vacuum.

The VPM is a long-standing separatist movement trying to unite regions of three different states where the Veleno People live, including Odesia. It primarily uses political means to achieve this unification, but it also has an armed wing which has participated in the Rotundria civil war, mainly fighting the Affliction, but has also staged some actions in other states, including Odesia. These actions have resulted in the deaths of military and police personnel, as well as civilians. The Veleno People's Movement has grown in power and experience during the civil war, especially in its fights against the Affliction, for which it has received funding and training from one of the global superpowers. That assistance has gradually decreased after the Affliction's defeat.

Odesia is concerned by the rising power and experience of the VPM. Consequently, Odesia's military has prepared a plan for expanding its counter-terrorist actions into Rotundria, with the aim of securing its border regions from possible further incursions by the VPM. The plan calls for creating and maintaining a 10 km buffer zone inside the territory of Rotundria. It plans to use regular Odesia military forces augmented by local militia forces loyal to Odesia. The plan also calls for conducting sweep operations for weapons and members of the armed wing of the VPM in towns and villages in the buffer zone and a limited re-location plan for the members of the Veleno people within the buffer zone. Despite the long civil war, the UN has largely been unable to come to a consensus regarding the proper response to the situation in Rotundria, except to call for an immediate cessation of hostilities by all sides.

The Ministry has asked you to provide them with a written opinion on the legal implications of the military's plan in relation to the use of force, the right to self-defence, and give guidance, if necessary, on humanitarian law implications of the plan.

The following questions leads to my Opinion on the Legal Implications of the Use of Force by the Military

959. Q: What act is right of self-defence?.

A: right to self-defence under ***"Article 51"*** of the "UN Charter." However, the right for self-defence within the Charter of the United Nations is a temporary right that allows the ***"Security Council"*** some time to implement measures that allow the preservation of peace and security globally. This is an indisputable fact that is addressed within ***"Article 51"*** of the Charter.

960. Q: what did article 51 condition of use as self-defence?

A: The article also makes it well known that the use of force in self-defence is a viable option however, only in relation to an armed attack.

961. Q: What are the variable to use article 51 of UN?

A: There are a number of variables that go into exercising the "right of self-defence" specifically if a nation is looking to exercise violence.

962. Q: Considering the scenario given how is the conflict be assessed?

A: It will be assessed given the conflict between two neighbouring nations, Odesia and Rotundria. The assessment is aimed at analysing the countermeasures proposed by the Odesian military against the Veleno people (a core faction fighting the civil war within Rotundria). my opinion on the legal implications of the military's plan in relation to the "use of force," the "right to self-defence," if necessary, on humanitarian law implications of the plan as requested by the Ministry of Odesia.

963. Q: Give The Foundations of the Proposal by the Military in the scenario

A:For over 5 years, there has been a civil war raging

within the neighbouring Rotundria. As of now, there are four main factions that are partaking in the civil war. These factions include the existing *Government of Rotundria;* the *"Veleno People's Movement"* (VPM); the *"Anti-Government Alliance,"* and the *"Church of the Temporary Mortal Affliction"* (Affliction).

964. Q: Who instigate the conflict?

A: The Rotundrian government and the anti-government coalition were the ones who instigated the conflict. The other two factions grew due to the resulting power vacuum formed by the war. The VPM is a long-standing separatist movement trying to unite regions of three different states where the Veleno People live, including Odesia.

965. Q: What means was used to unite the factions?

They use political means to achieve this unification, but it also has an armed wing which has participated in the Rotundria civil war, mainly fighting the Affliction, but has also staged some actions in other states, including Odesia. These actions have led to the loss of soldiers, police personnel, as well as civilians.

966. Q: What has the Odesian propose for self-defence?

A: The Odesian borders had been breached and the matter now is of national security. Due to the turn of events, the Odesian military has proposed that the "right to self-defence" be utilised against Rotundria. However, since this is a matter of international law there are going to various legal implications of this decision and they should be addressed prior to acting against Rotundria.

967. Q*:* What is the Legal Implications under the United Nations Charter?

A: To successfully exercise the "use of force," the nation in question has to consider the ***"Article 51"*** of the "UN Charter" that dictates that the right is only awarded to a state if it is planning to use it against an armed assailant. Thus, it becomes necessary to constitute what is recognised as an armed attacker by the "International Court of Justice." In *"Nicaragua v. United States (1986),"*

968. Q: What did ICJ (international court of justice ruled in this case?

A: The "International Court of Justice" ruled that the attackers must be of a set caliber or "scale and effect." Meaning that not all potential threats can be seen as "armed attackers." According to the "International Court of Justice," an armed attack constitutes the harshest use of force.

969. Q: How did the ICJ view the Iran v USA in 2003?

A: Furthermore, in the case of the "Islamic Republic of Iran v. United States of America (2003)," it was dictated by the "International Court of Justice" that the state is looking for an appeal to use force in self-defence must bear the burden of proof. The use of force as a response to an armed attack (as defined by the International Court of Justice) is a legal action, however, it is specified that it is only deemed lawful against attacks that have taken place.

970. Q: Why was the stipulation in the UN articles?

A; This stipulation is a part of the law to prevent unnecessary armed conflict between nations.

971. Q: What does article 2($) of the UN state?

A: Additionally, under "Article 2(4)" of the "UN Charter" it is stated that all affiliate states are prohibited from the use of forces and even the threat of use of force against other member nations in regard to the political independence, territorial integrity or any other manner inconsistent with the ideals of the UN (Gunaratne, 2011).

Considering the given situation of the conflict, it becomes necessary to learn how a nation might respond to a threat that has yet to happen.

972. Q: When can "Use of force" as a Preventive Action under the "UN Charter" be used

A; When it comes to intellectuals there is a device among them in regard to the given issue. Some scholars believe that the use of force under the right of self-defence as a response to an impending attack is lawful. However, there are others who have a different perspective on the issue stating that preventive actions are not permissible. Scholars who are against the notion of the use of force as a preventative measure call for legislation like "Article 2(4)."

973. Q: What is UN view on threat?

A: On the other hand, the *"UN Secretary-General's High-Level Panel on Threat, Challenges and Changes"* proposes that states that are threatened have the right to take military action against the assailant, the only prerequisite being that the threat should be imminent (Gunaratne, 2011; von Einsiedel, and Fong, 2017). In addition,

974. Q: Explain the Caroline formula on self-defence?

A: "The criterion of imminence correlates with the Caroline formula (1842), according to which the self-defence can only be exercised in the situations where they need to respond is instant, leaving no moment for deliberation.

975. Q: What is the legal definition of imminence?

A: There is no legal definition of imminence. As examples of events that may indicate the presence of the imminent threat of an attack mostly are mentioned: the enlargement of armed forces, procurement of weapons and belligerent declarations of intention to start a war, the other threatening activities and the other evidence that prove that an attack will take place in the nearest future" (Upeniece, 2018).

976. Q: What does imminence refer to in UN terminology?

A; there is a disagreement between what is meant by 'imminence' in the given context. There is the argument that the idea refers to there being an existing threat of an attack at the hands of an enemy. There are other claims that state imminence to be the predictability of an attack, as the variables concerning a given situation are under a constant state of change.

977. Q: Who can stop an attack on another state?

A: As seen by Dinstein, only the victim state can legally intercept the attack even if it is within its initial stages (von Einsiedel, and Fong, 2017).

Therefore, as proposed by this idea the armed attack has to be apparent to the nation damaged.

978. Q: What did the UN Security council view on the Iraq v. Israel war as self-defence?

A: The 1981 attack targeting the “Osiraq nuclear reactor” in Iraq at the hands of Israel was an event that forced the “Security Council” to reassess the criterion of imminence. The conflict came from Iraq’s refusal to sign an armistice agreement with Israel, which was used as a legal justification to exercise force under self-defence (Conte, 2017).

979. Q: How did UK and Sierra Leon used Caroline formula?

A: During that time the UK and Sierra Leone made use of the “Caroline formula” in order to assess the legality of these actions. As noted in the formula, it is stated that for the countermeasure to be lawful it has to be overpowering, immediate, and leaving no moment for negotiation. Considering that the plans were highly planned, Israel took some time in preparation for the many states that saw the actions of Israel as unlawful (Conte, 2017). Furthermore, it was also noted that while there was a potential threat present it was not imminent.

980. Q: Explain Principle of Immediacy, Necessity, and Proportionality in relation to ICL international customary law?.

A: Another opinion on the matter dictates the idea of the use of force to be lawful if the conditions of immediacy, necessity, and proportionality are met. As noted in Upeniece, (2018);

"The principle of necessity and immediacy, as expressed in the ***Carolina doctrine***, is considered to be a part of the customary international law. According to the international customary law, the self-defence is lawful if the response is necessary, proportional, and immediate.

981. Q: Name some of the wars in which ICJ refer to using international customary law?.

The International Court of Justice made references to the principles of the international customary law in such cases as *Nicaragua v. United States*, *Islamic Republic of Iran v. United States of America*, *Democratic Republic of the Congo v. Uganda* and in the other cases.

982. Q: What did the court say about the Nicaragua case?

A: In the Nicaragua case, the Court recognised, that the Charter of the United Nations does not contain any specific rule whereby self-defence would warrant only measures which are proportional to the armed attack and necessary to respond to it, a rule well established in customary international law." Furthermore, it was also evaluated that the actions taken by the US in the context of self-defence was did take place during the Nicaragua attack, but continued long after the incident.

983. Q: Comment on the Oil platform case on self-defence?

A: At the "Oil Platform case" the Court looked upon

the factors of proportionality and necessity (Upeniece, 2018). In doing so it was heled that America was under the obligation to showcase that the actions it partook were both proportional and necessary in comparison to the armed attack it suffered.

984. Q: Comment on the arm activated in Congo?

A: the case of ***"armed activates in Congo"*** the issue of necessity and proportionality did not come up. The reasoning behind that was that as for the given case there was no enquiring the entitlement to self-defence as there were no preconditions for the use of self-defence in the case (Upeniece, 2018). The Court did not evaluate the idea of the use of force as self-defence in the given circumstances where there is a lingering threat from the other side, i.e. an adversary, of armed force.

985. Q: How do the court define necessity?.

A; Under international law, the idea of necessity is defined as the verification that the given conflict is such that it cannot be resolved in a peaceful manner.

986. Q:What other opinion can necessity be understood?

A: Another opinion on the matter states that necessity can also be interpreted as if the impending attack is such that the targeted nation is unable to prevent it, thereby justifying the need for aggressive measures. For instance, if there is a conflict that is posing a direct threat to the survival, or sovereignty of the state and there are no possible solutions to the issue aside from the use of force than an argument can be made for said right (Bethlehem, 2013).

987. Q: What evidence must nation provide for using force as self-defence?

A: The nation in question has to have credible evidence of the impending armed attack. The burden of evidence is placed on the reacting nation so as to ensure that the use of force as self-defence can only be used as a response to a tangible threat to the state in question, and there were no alternative means to resolve the situation in a more peaceful manner.

988. Q: Explain proportionate in relation to international law?

A: The idea of proportionality as proposed within international law looks to describe the limitations placed on the use of force (Bethlehem, 2013).

989. Q: what legislation that govern the use of force as self-defence?

A: While there are conditions where nations are allowed the use of force, however, they cannot choose the severity of the actions wilfully. Rather, there is legislation in place that states that the use force should be enough to only neutralise the attack which the state was under the threat of. As stated by Cassese, the principle of proportionality has particular requirements in regard to insuring balance between the injury caused and the countermeasures being imposed.

990. Q: What measure is in place for nations responding to attack?

A: The nation taking countermeasures has to ensure that it do not seriously exceed the damage caused by the armed attack endured while making sure that the core aim of the use of force is to force the offender to withdraw its wrongful behaviour (Bethlehem, 2013). However, the principle does not dictate that the responding nations has to use the same weapons as were used, or were planned to be, in the armed attack against them.

991. Q: Explain the principle of immediacy?

A: The final criterion for the execution of force as self-defence is the *"principle of immediacy."* There are varying views on this topic making it rather controversial, nevertheless, the principle has to be addressed as it is a core element that to the given issue (Bethlehem, 2013). One view on the subject is that the window for enacting self-defence is right at the moment the attack is taking place. In that way, the principle of immediacy is described as the timeframe between the initial armed attack and the self-preservation measures. Furthermore, as seen by some the delay in the reaction to the armed attack can be lawful if the interval was question is objectivity reasonable (Bethlehem, 2013). The opposing view on the subject finds there to be an interconnection between the idea of immediacy and necessity.

Therefore the idea the self-defence action does not have to be close to an armed attack.

992. Q: After considering all the aforementioned when can a nation implement self-defence by military means

A: The main disputable and controversial question is when or in which point of time the actions for self-defence become lawful. As it was mentioned above there is an opinion that the anticipatory self-defence is admissible if it complies with the requirements, which are set by Webster in the Caroline Case, namely, if the necessity of self-defence is instant, overwhelming and leaving no choice of means, and no moment for deliberation" (Upeniece, 2018).

993. Q: What other option can the nation/Odesian military have?

A: another option that the Odesian military can go for is "*sui generis,*" where the idea is that while the action take was not legal, it was legitimate in the sense that it was the lesser of the two evils (Ker-Lindsay, 2011; Vidmar, 2014).

994. Q: Who make the final decision of using force in self-defence?

A; The final decision still lays in the hands of the *"International Court of Justice"* and the *"Security Council,"* therefore the nation in question is still subject to legal accountability under the *"R2P principle"* (ec.europa.eu, 2011).

995. Q: Why do nations have to take into consideration United Nations guideline before using military as self-defence?

A: The existing international responsibilities upon member States help in making sure that they refrain from such actions and undergo various procedures to prevent/punish war crimes, genocide, ethnic cleansing and crimes against humanity (www.un.org, 2020).

996. ***Q:*** Considering the scenario given what is your opinion?.

A; In my opinion, under the Threat, Challenges, and Changes," the Odesian military does have the right to implement self-defence tactics against Rotundria. However, in order to avoid any legal liabilities, the three principles discussed in the above sections have to be taken with immense care. If not the EU Commission might take legal actions against Odesia like an infringement procedure.

997. Q: Can the military action be preventive measures?

A: Even so, the opinion on the issue remains such that the Odesian military can take preventative actions against Rotundria if they have ample evidence that the armed attack that took place did not occur in the distant past. Furthermore, it has to be addressed whether or not the action was severe enough to be classified as an armed attack or not. Thus, the military will have to prove that the attack was of such a severity that it was a security issue for the nation.

998. Q; What do the military have to do to implement " right of self-defence?.

A; If the military is looking to implement the "right of self-defence" as a preventative measure for future attacks by the Veleno people, they have to first present ample evidence in the "International Court of Justice" in order to lawfully exercise force under the "right to self-defence."

999. Q: In this case, what needs to be addressed?

A; However, a unique issue that has to be addressed is that the main cause of the conflict is a non-state actor (Brunei, and Tope, 2019; Etzioni, 2010). Considering that activities they have undergone in the past, the group can be categorised as a transnational terrorist group (Etzioni, 2010). Therefore, one has to consider whether or not the "right to self-defence" is available against a "non-state actor."

1000. Q: What will be proposer to resolve the conflict supported by resolution?.

A: In order to resolve this **conflict,** I proposed that "resolution 1368" and "1373" of the "Security Council" be considered (Brunei, and Toope, 2019). Both resolutions were adopted by the Council after the events of "September 11th, 2001." The resolutions reaffirmed the "right to self-defence" as "...the inherent right of individual and collective self-defence as recognised by the

Charter of the United Nations" (Wood, 2013).

1001. Q; Can Leiden policy recommendation be used to justify the use of military in self-defence?

A; the *"Leiden Policy Recommendations"* concerning international law and counterterrorism showcase a similar conclusion to the principles by "Daniel Bethlehem" discussed within the previous section (Etzioni, 2010). Therefore, the Odesian military has to follow the aforementioned procedures and principles in order to move away from the consequences that will be imposed due to the illegal use of force under humanitarian grounds (ec.europa.eu, 2011).

1002. Q: If the military have the right for self-defence, what do they have to consider before taken any action.

A; The Odesian military can exercise the "right to self-defence" under International law. However, to lawfully use force Odesia has to showcase that the action is one that necessary, proportional, and the only means available.

1003. Q: What else do the military have to proof before taken any action?

A: The use of force as a preventative measure calls for Odesian to showcase that there is an imminent threat to its national security, one that is unavoidable. If so, "the use of force" as a preemptive measure is seen as legitimate. In addition, the force used has to be in proportion to the damage received, and must only be used to neutralise the threat that being the Veleno people.

1004. Q; What is my final conclusion on the military action?

A: in my opinion, the proposal by the Odesian army may lead to the lawful use of the "right to self-defence" if they representatives are able to provide concrete evidence to the "International Court of Justice" and the "Security Council."

Chapter 37

Immunity for head of state for crimes.

Scenario;

Question from primary source

Do heads of state have immunity before the International Criminal Court (ICC)? The ICC has issued several judgments on the immunities of heads of state in the Al-Bashir case, changing its reasoning several times. The latest judgment of the Appeals Chamber was issued on 6 May 2019 (Judgment in the Jordan Referral re Al-Bashir Appeal, Case No. ICC-02/05-01/09 OA2). Using primary and secondary sources, give a legal analysis and a critique of the judgment.

1005. Q; What is the function of ICC?

A: The institutional obligation of the International Criminal Court (ICC) is to investigate and prosecute crimes listed in the Rome Statute (Schneider, Iglesias, Hallberg and Kuperman, 2014).

1006. Q ; What is article 27 of ICC?

A; While the ICC is governed by several principles, article 27 deals with the fact that position of the accused, such as being the head of state will not prevent the ICC from exercising its institutional mandate. Normative practice based on international treaties coupled with existing customary international law has recognized the fact that senior government officials such as heads of state enjoy immunity relating to both civil and criminal prosecution (Besson, 2016).

1007. Q; What is the degree immunity might apply?

A; However, the extent to which this immunity applies with regard to international criminal law is highly contested (Zappala, 2001). The tension arising from diplomatic immunity of sitting presidents has not been alleviated by the recent jurisprudence from the ICC Appeal Chamber concerning the cooperation of Jordan in effecting the arrest warrant issued against Omar al-Bashir, who was at the time the sitting Head of State of Sudan.

1008. Q; What was reaction of Al-Bashir case?

A: The decision by the Appeal Chamber (hereinafter

the '*Jordan Appeal Decision* [2019]) has received a lot of attention where scholars and the international community such as the African Union (AU) have either condemned or supported the decision.

1009. Q; How did Mudukuti view the decision by ICC in AL-Bashir case?

A: According to Mudukuti (2020), the decision was akin to the ICC tapping into uncharted waters since the arrest warrant was the first to issue by the International Criminal Court against a sitting president. Sadushaj et al. (2017) argue that the approach taken by the ICC Appeal Chamber was legally correct.

1010. Q; How did Nouwen view the decision by ICC in AL-Bashir case?

A: Nouwen (2019) argues that the Appeal chamber should be given an opportunity, such as through an advisory opinion to conclusively address its argument concerning the extent to which immunity of Heads of States applies when contending with international crimes.

The determination by the international Criminal Court was correct. Be that as it may, the approach taken by the court had several instances where the applicable law was misinterpreted.

1011. Q: Give background of the AL-Bashir

case?.

A: The case concerns the warrant for arrest that was issued against the then president of Sudan on March 2009 by Pre-Trial Chamber II (*Jordan Appeal Decision*, [2019]). It issued the warrant for Bashir's arrest following the results from the investigation by the ICC into the situation in Darfur (*Jordan Appeal Decision*, [2019]). It is noteworthy that the investigation concerning the situation in Darfur was initiated following a 2005 resolution by the Security Council (resolution 1593) (*Jordan Appeal Decision*, [2019]) in line with the provisions of article 13 (b) of Statute of the International Criminal Court.

1012. Q; When was the second warrant issued?

A: In 2010, a subsequent warrant of arrest was issued against Mr. Omar al-Bashir (*Jordan Appeal Decision*, [2019]).

1013. Q: How did the Arab League reacted to the two Warrants.?.

A: Communication of the two warrants of arrest were subsequently sent to the member states for purposes of assisting the court to implement the arrest warrant (*Jordan Appeal Decision*, [2019]).

In 2017, the 28th Summit of the Arab League was hosted in Amman, Jordan, where Omar al-Bashir was in attendance (*Jordan Appeal Decision*, [2019]). However, despite having received communication concerning the request for cooperation in arresting and subsequently surrendering Mr. Bashir to the ICC, Jordan failed to either arrest or surrender him to the ICC (*Jordan Appeal Decision*, [2019] despite the fact that it is party to the Rome Statute.

1014. Q: What action was taken against Jordan for failing to arrest AL- Bashir?

A: In 2017, the Pre-Trial chamber found Jordan guilty of failing to comply with its request concerning arresting and surrendering Mr. al-Bashir (*Jordan Appeal Decision*, [2019]). It is the 2017 decision that forms the basis of the appeal.

1015. Q: Name some of other cases where the member states ignored ICC?.

A: it is important to note that the court has issued 8 other judgements against member states that have failed to cooperate with the court. These include *the*

Djibouti Decision [2016], *the U*ganda Decision [2016], *the South Africa Decision* [2015], *the DRC Decision* [2014], *the Nigeria Decision* [2013], *the Chad Decision* [2013], and *the Malawi Decision* [2011]. In all the above cases, as is the case with the *Jordan Appeal Decision* [2019], the ICC ruled that the states parties ought to have arrested and surrendered him.

1016. Q: what was the Appeals chamber decision on the Jordan case?

A; In the foregoing case, the decision of the pre-Trial Chamber was reaffirmed by the Appels Chamber, although while taking different approaches to the pertinent legal issues for determination (*Jordan Appeal Decision*, [2019]).

1017. Q: What does the customary international law views on immunity for head of state?.

A: For purposes of this discussion, the focus will be

on the finding that no provision under customary international law grants sitting Heads of State immunity from being prosecuted for crimes within the Rome Statute, and the determination that article 98 is a procedural safeguard rather than a substantive provision (*Jordan Appeal Decision*, [2019]).

The Legal Framework for Presidential Immunity.

1018. Q: Do head of state have immunity against prosecution?

A: Yes, generally, Heads of States enjoy specific immunities that they may claim as a defense against prosecution from foreign courts.

1019. Q: Briefly explain Article 27 of ICC?

A: Article 27 of the ICC Statute states that, among its principles, the official position of the accused person is irrelevant when prosecuting the individual for the alleged crimes. Among these positions is that of a Head of State or Government. In effect, this means that as per the Rome Statute, in spite of Mr. Bashir being a sitting president, the court was not prevented from issuing the arrest warrant. Similarly, this means that, *prima facie,* once Mr. Bashir was surrendered to the Court, the court had every right to prosecute Mr. Bashir without prejudice to his position.

1020. Q: What is the concept of immunity from

international customary Law perspective?

A; The notion of immunity is derived from the international customary law as well as international treaty law such as the 1961 Vienna Convention on Diplomatic Relations. The conceptualization of the extent to which the court took the correct interpretation of article 27 of the Statute of the ICC is dependent on the proper understanding of the types of immunity that exist under international law. There are two types of immunities that are afforded to the Heads of States; one is based on their position such that by virtue of occupying that position, he/she enjoys immunity whereas the second type focuses on the functions of the Head of State.

1021. Q: Explain personal immunity?

A; Personal immunity (*ratione personae)* refers to the type of immunity that is linked to the office of the individual (Akande, 2004; Akande and Shah, 2010). It has been argued that the existence of personal immunity ensures that the protected individuals are able to conduct their functions devoid of any encumbrances (Fox and Webb, 2013; Murphy, 2014).

1022. Q: give an example of arrest warrant in personal immunity case?

A: The *Arrest Warrant of 11 April 2000* (Democratic Republic of the Congo v. Belgium) [2002] hereinafter "*the arrest warrant case*", presents the position of the ICJ when it ruled that personal immunity applies to the official's personal as well as official capacity.

1023. Q:Explain functional immunity?

A; Functional immunity, conversely, refers to the immunity that the Heads of State enjoys concerning their actions (Akande, 2004) in their official capacity (Shi, 2019). The protection extends to the individual even after he or she ceases to occupy the position, as can be seen at article 39(2) of the Vienna Convention on Diplomatic Relations ("VCDR") as well as article 24 co-read 43(1) of the Vienna Convention on Consular relations ("VCCR"). Notably, the two types of immunity are often applied in the horizontal relationship between the different states (Akande, 2004; Reinisch, 2006).

1024. Q: How does the appeal chamber view immunity?

A: The Appeals chamber argued that the immunity is

a matter of customary international law and its application was limited to the relations among the states (*Jordan Appeal Decision*, [2019]). In effect, the court argued that the immunity did not apply when the states or Heads of State interacted with the ICC (*Jordan Appeal Decision*, [2019]).

1025. Q: Name some statue that the court relied on?

A: In constructing this assertion, the court relied on the establishing statutes of various international *ad hoc* tribunals including the article 7 of the Statute of the International Military Tribunal at Nuremberg, article IV of the Convention against genocide, the Statute of Special Court for Sierra Leone (SCSL) at 6(2), the Statute of the International Criminal Tribunal for the former Yugoslavia (ICTY) at 7(2) as well as International Criminal Tribunal for Rwanda (ICTR) at 6(2) (*Jordan Appeal Decision*, [2019]). The court further relied on the jurisprudence of the above-mentioned *ad hoc* tribunals to substantiate its assertion. For example, the court brought into perspective the case concerning Slobodan Milosevic where the ICTY issued an arrest warrant against him yet he was still in power as the president of Serbia (*Jordan Appeal Decision*, [2019]). It also relied on the fact that the SCSL issued an arrest warrant against Charles Taylor while he was the sitting president of Liberia and subsequently rejected his appeal that was anchored his immunity as a sitting president (*Jordan Appeal Decision*, [2019]).

1026. Q: What is the notion of immunity for head of state?

A: That the notion of the immunity that Heads of State enjoy is not only a statutory provision established by the Statute of the ICC, but a rule of customary international law. One might agree with the reasoning of the court as relates to the extent of the application of the immunity of the Heads of States. Akande (2004) states that the application of both immunity *ratione materiae* and immunity *ratione personae* only apply in the horizontal that occurs when the states interact among each other, rather than in the relationship between the states and the international courts and/or tribunals.

1027. Q: How can immunity be removed from head of state?

A: Akande (2004) contends that the removal of the immunity that is given to the Heads of States by either statute or conventions (whether personal or functional) is dependent on whether such waiver is provided by statute, or if such implications can be inferred from the provisions of a statute. In the instant case, the Statute of the International Criminal Court expressly provides that the immunity enjoyed by the accused is irrelevant in criminal proceedings under international law.

1028. Q; How does customary international law form jurisprudence from ad hoc tribunal.

A: A:According to Baker (2010) customary international law is currently shaped by emerging jurisprudence from the *ad hoc* tribunals. On this premise, since the *ad hoc* tribunals have previously dismissed the allegation that sitting presidents enjoy immunity from the International Criminal Courts, it can therefore be construed that the Appeal chamber was accurate in its assertions.

The Legal Consequence of Article 98 of the Statute of the International Criminal Court

1029. Q: Briefly explain Article 98?

A: Article 98 requires that the Court should not go ahead and make a request for state parties to assist the court (cooperate with the court) if such cooperation by the party will mandate the state to act in a manner that is materially inconsistent with its obligations under international law. This is especially true when the inconsistency related to a third state, or diplomatic immunity, of an individual who is a third state. However, article 98 proceeds to state that the court has to obtain a waiver from the third state first.

1030. Q: Explain what one mean by "third state" as per Law of treaties Article 2

A: According to the Vienna Convention on the Law of Treaties at article 2, the term 'third state' refers to countries that are not states parties to the treaty or convention under consideration. In applying the above provisions to the instant case, Sudan becomes the third state since it is not the contracting party of the Rome Statute (Chigara and Nwankwo, 2015). The foregoing assumption from the above provision is that the effect of the provisions of 98 is to the extent that it recognizes that there is some level of immunity that members of the third state enjoy when interacting with the International Criminal Court.

1031. Q; Does the immunity relevant with reference to Rome Statute?.

A: To that extent, as argued by the court in the preceding section that the notion of immunity is irrelevant regardless of whether a state is party to the Rome Statute, this implies that the contents of article 98 are rendered redundant.

1032. Q: what does the court regard Article 98?

A; In its reasoning, the court argued that the provisions of article 98 are a procedural matter, rather than a substantive matter (*Jordan Appeal Decision*, [2019]). The court further reasoned that the provisions of article 98 do not afford any form of immunity, but simply guide the court on how to proceed when, due to article 21 of the ICC Statute, the court is convinced that there is no form of immunity (*Jordan Appeal Decision*, [2019]). However, the relevant part of the ruling concerning the interplay between article 27 and article 98 is seen at paragraph 131 of the ruling. Specifically, the court stated that the importance of article 98 is to provide a safeguard against a member state violating its international obligations in when meeting its obligations under the ICC Statute (*Jordan Appeal Decision*, [2019]).

1033. Q; Does the court greatly contradict itself by the above interpretation of article 98 section 131, article 21 and 27 of the ICC statute. statement.

A: The argument made by Jordan, the African Union and the Arab League was the fact that article 98 prevented it from exercising its obligation under the international law as related to the immunity of al-Bashir as the then Head of State (*Jordan Appeal Decision*, [2019]). Jordan argued that the execution of the request for cooperation in arresting Omar al-Bashir created a horizontal relationship between the state of Jordan and Sudan (*Jordan Appeal Decision*, [2019]). The paper agrees with this standpoint.

1034. Q:Explain with example of idea of functional and personal immunity?

A: The concept of functional immunity and personal immunity apply when states are interacting among themselves. By virtue of the point that Sudan is not a state party to statute of the International Criminal Court, the notion of the lateral relationship cannot, *strictu sensu*, apply in this case. Regardless, for purposes of identifying the erroneous nature of the interpretation made by the Appeal Chamber, it is imperative to de-link this section from the fact that the court, through relying on the provisions of the Security Council resolution 1593, found that the cooperation expected of Sudan was similar to that of states parties (*Jordan Appeal Decision*, [2019]). Failure to separate the two obscures the identification of the problem. In any case, in interpreting article 98, particularly at paragraph 131, the court addressed Sudan as a third state.

1035. Q; How does immunity applies?

A: It is noteworthy that in its ruling concerning the scope of article 27, the court recognized the fact that the concept of 'immunity' is a matter of customary international law such that immunity only applies in their horizontal interaction (Jordan Appeal Decision, [2019]. the contention is not whether the Head of State has immunity at the ICC; rather that there exists diplomatic immunity when the states interact among themselves (Scheffer, 2005).

1036. Q: How can arrest Warrant be executed?

A: The execution of the arrest warrant, as per the provisions of article 98 depends on the waiver of this immunity.

1037. Q: Why was the arrest of al- Bashir

A: The Appeal Chamber of the ICC took a skewed approach to the conflict brought about by article 98 in terms of the cooperation of the state parties. It did not address the extent which the execution of the arrest warrant would have resulted in the violation of customary international law by Jordan. In any case, the arrest of al-Bashir was bastorred by article 98.

Implications

1038. Q: How does the ICC implement its mandate?

A: The extent to which the International Criminal Court (ICC) implements its institutional mandate is dependent on the cooperation of the states. This is primarily because the court lacks a mechanism for enforcing the arrest warrants it issues. While it is not in contention that Jordan violated its responsibility under article 86 of the ICC Statute, the interpretation of the immunity of Omar al-Bashir taken by the court is problematic in many respects.

1039. Q: What is the implication of the court relying on customary law?

A: Firstly, the court relied on the customary nature of international law regarding immunity as inapplicable in the situation where the state is interacting with the international community rather than in relation to each other. In relying on customary international law, the ICC Appeal chamber in the foregoing case created the implication that regardless of whether a state is a member state to the Rome Statute or not, there is no encumbrance to the court exercising its mandate. The problematic nature of this interpretation is that it renders article 98 inapplicable.

1040. Q: What is the problem could involve inerplitation of Articles?

A: The second area that renders the court's interpretation problematic is the fact that it binds all states to the provisions of article 86 *et seq.*, and consequently the provisions of article 98. In effect, with regards to cooperation, the Jordan ruling elevated the third-party states to the level states parties, which might be interpreted as a violation of the provisions of article 34 and article 35 of the VCLT. To that end, while the conclusion reached by the ICC Appeal chamber was legally potent, the process taken by the court in reaching the decision was marred by questionable approaches to the interpretation of the existing legal provisions.

1041. Q: Can a judgement be use as case law for another case?

A: Another implication of this decision is to the effect that it is highly unlikely that another state might successfully use immunity as a defense against an arrest warrant issued by the court (Mudukuti, 2020).

1042. Q; Can individual be protected from international crime?

A: No, when it comes to the prosecution of international crimes, as has been demonstrated there is no protection under the ambit of immunity. However, there still exists immunity as the different states interact among themselves (Mettraux, Dugard and du Plessis, 2018). This therefore means that as a result of this case, third parties will not have the leeway of dodging the jurisdiction of the ICC. For this reason, the standpoint taken in the ruling on immunity poses several benefits in terms of the ICC gaining access to the individuals whose arrest warrant has been issued. Consequently, this might improve the achievement of the institutional mission of the International Criminal Court (ICC).

1043. Q; How far is head of state protected?

A; The notion of immunity, by definition, protects sitting Heads of State from being prosecuted in criminal cases or being sued in civil cases in the foreign jurisdictions.

1044. Q; Can head of state escape ICC

A: No, The protection does not extend to criminal prosecution in the International Criminal Court (ICC). In the *Jordan's Appeal Decision [2019],* the court correctly applied and interpreted the law to confirm the above assertion. However, while arriving at the accurate finding relating to the role that article 98 played in the case, the Appeal chamber applied an erroneous interpretation of the law. Nonetheless, in response to the discussion question, as a matter of principle, sitting presidents do not have immunity.

Chapter 38

International terrorism

1045. Q:Why is it difficult to define terrorism?

A: Terrorism is a disputed perception and there is no universally agreed definition. Can be express in different spheres, for example, political, legal, social science, media, popular usage, etc.

1046. Q: Why is it important to have international definition of terrorism?

A: According to Ganor (2002) To enable the formulation of international agreement to create laws against terrorism and to enable prosecution.

To enable punishment.

To limit public legitimacy or terrorist actions

To ensure coherent strategies to combat terrorism in both national and international.

1047. Q: What did Newman E. view on terrorism definition?

A In Newman E(2006) " Exploring the root cause of terrorism.

Newman highlights that a lack of definition of 'terrorism' leads to a lack of clarity regarding the root causes but also that certain types of terrorism lend themselves more easily to defining the root cause(s).

He highlights that the existence of these is not sufficient to give rise to terrorism: further contributing factors are necessary.

1048. Q: How is terrorism interpreted by people?

A; It is interpreted in different ways depending on each person's standpoint, example, in Northern Ireland some people view those in the Irish Republican Army (IRA) as freedom fighters fighting to liberate Northern Ireland from British rule, whereas others view them as terrorists who have committed serious crimes.

1049. Q; Which area is lack of terrorism definition useful?

A: Politics and media as they can create different viewpoint, of who can commit terrorism

1050. Q: Can state commit terrorism and give

example?

A; Yes, example state officials (militaries), acting against other states or within their own state against their own citizens.

1051. Q; Name few examples of how nations can sponsor terrorism group?

A; mercenaries or other such groups employed by the state to carry out terrorist acts under the control of the state

independent terrorist groups supplied with finance or weapons by the state

independent terrorist groups supplied with logistical support (such as training and information) by the state

1052. Q: How can one interpreted action being condoned by state?

A: terrorist actions disregarded by the state through not preventing or punishing such actions, can be view as providing a refuge for terrorist groups.

1053. Q: What other terrorist people?

A; independent terrorist groups or networks

Individuals

1054. Q: How can terrorism be compared?

A; Terrorism often involves violence and can be compared to warfare. Merari (1994, cited in Schmid, 2004) provides a useful comparison between conventional warfare, guerrilla warfare.

1055. Q: What is the size of people or leaders in terrorism?

A; Usually less than 10 people as leaders.

1056. Q; What weapons do terrorist use?

A; Handguns, hand grenades, assault rifles and specialized weapons, e.g. car bombs, remote-control bombs, barometric pressure bombs.

1057. Q; What are the tactics of terrorist?

A: Specialized tactics: kidnapping, assassinations, car-bombing, hijacking, barricade-hostage, etc.

1058. Q: Who do terrorist target?

A; State symbols, political opponents, and the public at large.

1059. Q: what is the aim of terrorism?

A: Psychological coercion.

1060. Q: How can terrorism be comparing to?

A: Although terrorism does not fall within the concept of war under international humanitarian law but can be compared to, or even measured as, a common crime under domestic law such as murder..

1061. Q: Name some Terrorist organisation?

A: the Black Panthers in the USA and the Kosovo Liberation Army in Kosovo, and those that have operated for decades, for example the IRA in the UK and Republic of Ireland, Hezbollah in Lebanon and the African National Congress (ANC) in South Africa.

1062. Q: What reason the IRA gave for their action?

A: The IRA argued that they were acting to liberate Northern Ireland.

1063. Q: What reason ANC gave for their action?

A: The ANC argued that they were challenging apartheid.

1064. Q What strategy did the ANC used?

A: The ANC used violence, including bombings, assassination and armed assault against facilities in South Africa, as part of their strategy to challenge the apartheid regime,

1065. Q: Who were ETA and what was their motivation?

A: ETA (known as Basque Fatherland and Freedom) was a terrorist group operating mainly in Spain, Its motivation was to cause the Basque country to secede from the rest of Spain.

1066. Q: What was the duration of ETA?

A: From 1970 to March 2017

1067. Q; What did the ETA action?

A: It predominantly carried out bombings, but also made extensive use of assassinations, armed assaults and, to a lesser extent, hostage-taking and disruption of infrastructure. Targets included the government, police, transportation, businesses and private civilians.

1068. Q: What is one of reasons for terrorism?

A: ‘propaganda by the deed’ is central to terrorism’.

1069. Q: What was used in the French revolution?

A: hijackings, truck bombs and suicide bombers.

1070. Q; What do some terrorism claim reason of their action?

A: Some organisation claim motivations such as liberation, democracy or freedom.

1071. Q: In United Kingdom, how is criminals assessed?.

A: it is only necessary to have the mens rea (‘the guilty mind’) as well as the actus Reus (‘the guilty act’).

1072. Q: How do terrorism create terror?

A: Terrorism differentiates as it addresses different audiences concurrently: while trying to immobilize one, it tries to mobilize the others by making them stiff with fear.

1073. Q: In terrorism targets those who already identify positively with the terrorist group what is their aim?

A: the aim is to increase their support.

1074. Q: In terrorism targets those who are their declared opponents, what is their aim?

A: Their goal is to demoralize, intimidate or blackmail them);

1075. Q: What is the aim of terrorist in targeting non- committed bystanders?

A; to impress them)

1076. Q; what is the aim of the terrorist own organization?

A: To keep it united through planning 'the big one'.

1077. Q; What is the terrorism aim in reference to rival groups?

A: goal: to show them who is more powerful

1078. Q: According to Schmid, A. P (2005a) " Root cause of terrorism" name some causes of terrorism?

A: The cause of terrorism include; lack of education, Failed States, lack of democracy, lower life expectation, lower standard of living,

Poorer health, lower standard of living, ideology, inequality, injustice, corruption, governance weakness\ failure or breakdown in the rule of law.

1079. Q: Name some organisation who have provided definition of terrorism?

A: Organisation of American States Convention to Prevent and Punish Acts of Terrorism Taking the Form of Crimes against Persons and Related Extortion that are of International Significance 1971

European Convention on the Suppression of Terrorism 1977

South Asian Association for Regional Cooperation Regional Convention on Suppression of Terrorism

1987

Arab Convention for the Suppression of Terrorism 1998

Convention of the Organisation of the Islamic Conference on Combating International Terrorism 1999

Organization of African Unity Convention on the Prevention and Combating of Terrorism 1999

Treaty on Cooperation among the States Members of the Commonwealth of Independent States in Combating Terrorism 1999

1080. Q: In general, what does terrorism refers?.

A: According to Schmid 2011a p 158,

Terrorism refers, on the one hand, to a doctrine about the presumed effectiveness of a special form or tactic of fear-generating, coercive political violence and, on the other hand, to a conspiratorial practice of calculated, demonstrative, direct violent action without legal or moral restraints, targeting mainly civilians and non-combatants, performed for its propagandistic and psychological effects on various audiences and conflict parties.

(Schmid, 2011a, p. 158) Schmid, A. P. (2011a) 'The Revised Academic Consensus Definition of Terrorism', Perspectives on Terrorism, vol. 6, no. 2, pp. 158–9

1081. Q: Which book contains about 260 definitions of terrorism?

A: the Routledge Handbook of Terrorism Research (Schmid, 2011b),

1082. Q: From academic viewpoints, what is considered in arriving the definition of terrorism?

A: the definition usually has an element of violence or action intended to cause terror or fear, usually with no regard to morals or law, relate to ideology, do have direct and indirect victims.

1083. Q: What law is used to punish terrorism?

A: Terrorism is punished under domestic rather than international law. This means that definitions of terrorism and punishments for those actions vary.

1084. Q: What is the UK definition of terrorism?.

A: In the UK terrorism is defined as the use or threat of

action which is designed to influence the government or an international governmental organisation or to intimidate the public or a section of the public, where that action or threat is made for the purpose of advancing a political, religious, racial or ideological cause (section 1 of the Terrorism Act 2000).

1085. Q: How does Spain define terrorism?

A: Spain defines terrorism as a type of crime further aggravated by its political intention (Spanish Criminal Code 571–9), for example arson aggravated by terrorism or murder aggravated by terrorism.

1086. Q: Where can one find Canada definition of terrorism?

A: Defined under the Criminal Code and also under the Anti-terrorism Act 2001.

1087. Q: where do one find France definition of terrorism.?.

A: Defined under the Criminal Code ss 421–2, 434

1088. Q: where in USA can one find definition of terrorism?

A: In USA, there is no single agreed definition; definitions created by FBI, State Department, individual state definitions under federal penal codes, as well as national law

1089. Q: Can terrorism be enforced under international law.

A; lack of enforcement mechanisms under the universal and regional instruments and therefore the reliance on political approbation to hold states to account in relation to the instruments and domestic application of the concepts.

1090. Q: why is it difficult to punish terrorist?

A: the matter of legal certainty (a fundamental principle of the rule of law), as what is prohibited in one country may not be forbidden in another due to the variation in definition and legislation at domestic level and the lack of an internationally agreed legal definition of 'terrorism'.

1091. Q: Which bodies do the United Nation use on terrorism.

A; global response to terrorism the UN has two key bodies, the UN Counter-Terrorism Committee (CTC) and the UN Counter-Terrorism Implementation Task Force (CTITF);

1092. Q: What does the international Bill f human Right consist of?

A: the International Bill of Human Rights, comprising the Universal Declaration of Human Rights, the International Covenant on Civil and Political Rights (ICCPR), and the International Covenant on Economic, Social and Cultural Rights (ICESCR)

1093. Q: Briefly describe the Lockerbie bombing?

A: the Lockerbie disaster occurred when Flight PA103 from London to New York exploded over the Scottish town of Lockerbie on 21 December 1988 killing 270 people (Figure 10). On investigation it was found that the explosion was caused by an explosive device.

1094. Q: What are the Islamic state?

A: the so-called Islamic State (IS) – also known as the Islamic State of Iraq and Syria (ISIS) and the Islamic State of Iraq and the Levant (ISIL).

1095. Q: When and where was the greatest terrorist attack in the western countries?

A: The terrorist attacks on 11 September 2001, in USA was the greatest terrorist threat to the West appeared to come from Osama bin Laden and al-Qaeda. Al-Qaeda, like many self-proclaimed 'jihadist' groups, seeks to re-shape the Muslim world, replacing secular states with a single Islamic state based on a fundamentalist view of Islam.

Chapter 39

International criminal laws

International criminal court

1096. Q: When was the United Nations created?

A; 1945

1097. Q: Who is currently the UN Secretary General?

Antonio Guterres

1098. Q: Who are the five permanent members of the UN Security Council?

France, UK, USA, China, Russia

1099. Q: Is Eu court of Human Right base in

Hague?

A:No. European Court of Human Rights is based in France

1100. Q: As of 2017, there is only one country in the world which failed to ratify the UN Convention of the Rights of the Child 1989. Which one?

A: USA

1101. Q: On which day of the year is International Human Rights Day?

A: 10 December

1102. Q: Where are the headquarters of the UN based?

A: New York

1103. Q: Who was the first person convicted by the International Criminal Court?

A; Thomas Lubanga Dvilo

1104. Q: Which of the following is not a member of the United Nations?

A: Kosovo

1105. Q: How do state states consent to international law?

A: State must not only sign the agreement, but they must

also ratify the treaty.

1106. Q: Why do states choose to be part of international treaties?.

A: There are various reasons include;, protection in case of war, international trade, financial arrangement, Human Right, extradition treaties.

International criminal law

1107. Q: What is ICL (international Criminal Law) function?

A; ICL is a branch of international law. Its function is to provide the legal basis for the prosecution and punishment of criminals of international crimes in accordance with the rules and procedures of international as opposed to national criminal law.

1108. Q: What condition can person be tried in foreign country?

A: person who has committed a breach of international

law could be tried in a national court of a foreign state subject to the satisfaction of certain conditions, example the jurisdiction over the crime committed and only if a clear link could be established between the crime and the prosecuting state

1109. Q: What must the prosecutor established?

A: if the breach of international rules must have been committed on the territory of the prosecuting state or by a national of that state or against a national of that state.

1110. Q: What difficulty exit in such prosecution?

A: The person immunity from prosecution to which some individuals (e.g. diplomats or heads of state) are entitled under international law.

Also, the rules of international law which were allegedly breached must have been implemented by the prosecuting state and form part of the state's national legislation.

1111. Q; What is the function of the Treaty of Versailles (1919).

A: The Treaty of Versailles (1919), which provided for the punishment of individuals who played the core role in committing war crimes during World War I.

1112. Q: What article was used against German emperor?

A; Article 227 of the Treaty explicitly stated that German Emperor, Wilhelm II, was responsible for 'a supreme offence against international morality and the sanctity of treaties'.

1113. Q: when was creation of modern international criminal justice?

A: the modern system of international criminal justice occurred after the end of the Second World War.

1114. Q: What are the two-military tribunal?

A: he establishment of the two international military tribunals (IMT): the International Military Tribunal at Nuremberg (IMTN) in 1945 and the International Military Tribunal for the Far East (IMTFE) in Tokyo in 1946.

1115. Q: why were the military tribunal created?

A: The tribunals were created to prosecute and punish major war criminals who were responsible for crimes perpetrated during the war in Europe and Asia. included acts of genocide and war crimes committed by the Nazis in Europe, but also crimes committed in the Far East,

1116. Q: What and when did the Rape of Nanking?

A: The Rape of Nanking known as the Nanjing massacre happened during the Second Sino-Japanese War (1937–45).

1117. Q Give brief account of Nanjing massacre?

A: In December 1937 the Japanese army invaded Nanking, at that time the capital of China, and soon took over the city, Japanese soldiers brutally and methodically tortured, killed and raped about 300,000 Chinese civilians. Some of the victims been buried alive.

1118. Q: What is the Rape of Nanking now refer to?

A: The Rape of Nanking, is referred to as 'the forgotten holocaust of WW II' (Chang, 1998), and regarded as one of the most brutal massacres in modern wartime history.

1119. Q: name one prominent army general prosecuted after the second world war?.

A: the trial of Adolf Eichmann (Attorney-General of the Government of Israel v Eichmann (1961) 36 ILR 5). Eichmann was a former SS-Obersturmbannführer (lieutenant colonel), who was directly responsible for the organisation of mass deportations of Jews to concentration camps and their extermination.

1120. Q: Name the two-tribunal established by UN?.

A; the UN Security Council established two ad hoc international criminal tribunals: the International Criminal Tribunal for the former Yugoslavia (ICTY) and the International Criminal Tribunal for Rwanda (ICTR).

1121. Q: who adopted the Rome statute in

1998?

A: On 17 July 1998, the Rome Statute of the International Criminal Court (the Rome Statute or the ICC Statute) was adopted by 120 states at a diplomatic conference in Rome.

1122. Q: What is the main reason for international law to act?

A:the first and the most apparent rationale is to end the liberty of the perpetrators by subjecting them to a fair trial, prosecution and (if convicted) punishment in accordance with the rule of law.

1123. Q: Where can we find retribution aspect of law?

A: the importance of the retributive aspect of international justice is explain ICTY in Prosecutor v Aleksovski, IT-95-14/1-A, Appeal Judgment, 24 March 2000:

1124. Q: Is retribution use as revenge?

A: No as duly expressing the outrage of the international community at these crimes. especially in the cases of Trial Chambers of this International Tribunal as well as Trial Chambers of the International Criminal Tribunal for Rwanda.

1125. Q How does prosecution affect the victims of crime?

A; The prosecution of international crimes gives a sense of justice to the victims, primarily by public (and global) recognition of the harms they suffered. The victims Seeing their perpetrator on trial and being sentenced may serve as case close

1126. Q: What is Principle of legality known in Latin?

A: The principle of legality (nullum crime sine leg)

1127. Q: What does the principal of legality states?

A: establishes that a person cannot be charged with a crime, which, at the time when the relevant act was committed, was not punishable by law. This includes provisions of the law in written (e.g. treaty) and unwritten forms (customary law).

1128. Q: What is Latin meaning of punishment in the Act?

A: (nullum poena sine lege)

1129. Q: What does nullum poena sine lege mean?

A: This principle extends to the issue of punishment but there can be no sanctions unless the law at the time foresees a certain type of punishment for a criminal act.

1130. Q: What is Principle of non-retroactivity

A: In accordance with this principle, a person cannot be punished for acts, which were not criminalized in law at the time they were committed.

1131. Q: What is Presumption of innocence

A: The accused is presumed innocent until proven guilty. The defendant does not need to prove his/her innocence before the court; instead, the burden of proof rests on the prosecutor, who needs to produce enough reliable evidence for the judges to find the accused 'guilty beyond reasonable doubt'.

1132. Q: What can lead to individual to be prosecuted?

A:

cover acts and omissions other than the actual physical commission of that crime by the accused,

planning the commission of a crime

incitement to commit a crime

aiding and abetting a criminal act
attempting to commit a crime
conspiracy to commit a crime
ordering a crime.

1133. Q: What is command responsibility as per ICL recognition?

A; entailing responsibility of military commanders for the actions of their forces

1134. Q; What is the doctrine of Command responsibility?

A: Under the doctrine of command responsibility, a superior may incur two types of liability:

if he/she orders, instigates or plans criminal acts carried out by his/her subordinates (direct criminal responsibility),

secondly, if he/she fails to prevent the crimes or punish their perpetrators (responsibility for omission, where there exist a legal duty to act) (Prosecutor v Delalić et al. (Čelebići), IT-96-21-T, Trial Judgment, 16 November 1998, 333–5).

1135. Q:What is the doctrine of Universal jurisdiction on crime?

A: Under the principle of universal jurisdiction, every country in the world has the authority to prosecute individuals accused of committing international crimes.

1136. Q: What is the reason why nations prosecuting criminals?

A: universal interest to international community of states in prosecuting crimes, primarily to maintain international peace and to avoid violations of human rights

1137. Q; Name one case dealt with under universal jurisdiction?

A: the core issues under consideration of the ICJ in Arrest Warrant of 11 April 2000 (Democratic Republic of Congo v Belgium) (the Yerodia case) ICJ Rep 2002

1138. Q; Summaries the main issue in the Congo v Belgium case?

A: The case concerned the issue of an international arrest warrant for a Congolese Minister of Foreign Affairs at that time, Abdulaye Yerodia Ndombasi, by Belgium.

1139. Q: Why was Belgium involvement?

A: Belgium wanted to extradite Yerodia to Belgium to be tried for alleged serious violations of international humanitarian law.

1140. Q: what grounds did Belgium sought extradition

A: In pursuing the issue of a warrant, Belgium claimed universal jurisdiction over crimes allegedly committed by the accused. Which include the question of the ability to rely on and exercise universal jurisdiction by Belgium, and the issue of diplomatic immunity from prosecution, to which Yerodia was entitled to as a governmental official (but he did not benefit from it at the time he allegedly committed the crimes).

1141. Q: Give example of how a state fails to prosecute an alleged criminal?

A: Hissène Habré (Belgium v Senegal, 2012)

1142. Q: Give brief description of Belgium v Senegal, 2012)

A; Habré is a former leader of Chad, who is accused of torture, war crimes and crimes against humanity of over 400.000 victims during his eight-year rule (1982–90). He sought political asylum in Senegal but was not prosecuted and Belgium refused to extradite him.

1143. Q: what does ICTs stand for?

A: International courts and tribunals

1144. Q: What is Ad hoc international tribunal?.

A: These courts and tribunals have been created by an agreement between the UN and the state hence the nation name attached.

1145. Q: give example of Ad hoc tribunal?

A; Special Court for Sierra Leone (SCSL) 2002

Extraordinary Chambers in the Courts of Cambodia (ECCC) 2003

War Crimes Chamber of Bosnia and Herzegovina (WCC) 2005

Special Tribunal for Lebanon (STL) 2007.

1146. Q; What is the principle of Primacy in international law?.

A: The Statutes of the ICTY and the ICTR provide that

both Tribunals have primacy over the national courts of all states in relation to the prosecution of violations of IHL (Article 9 ICTY, Article 8 ICTR).

1147. Q: why are some nations hesitant to act against criminals in their own state?

A: prosecutions of crimes in domestic courts might expose a significant degree of bias. Or some wrongdoers might become their own judges by bribery and corruption

1148. Q; name few circumstances that the ICC might asserts its jurisdiction?

A: the ICC may assert its jurisdiction over the crime only in particular circumstances, when:

the state is unable (Article 17(3) ICC Statute) or unwilling (Article 17(2) ICC Statute) to prosecute the accused,

.the case is of a sufficient gravity for the Court to exercise its jurisdiction.

1149. Q: What other reason that a state might be unable to prosecute individual?.

A: The domestic court might not be able to prosecute due to statutes of limitations, amnesty laws or other legislative obstacles.

1150. Q: What is expected of state by ICC or international tribunal?

A: states are under a duty to cooperate with an international court or tribunal (although the regimes of cooperation differ between the tribunals and the ICC).

Chapter 40

War Crimes

Definition

1151. Q: How will you define war crimes?

A: War crimes are violations of rules of international humanitarian law (IHL), committed during international armed conflict (IAC) or non-international armed conflict (NIAC). Might relate to customary or treaty-based nature,

1152. Q; Which article can you find definition. of war crime in The Charter of the International Military Tribunal at Nurnberg (IMTN Charter) 1945?

A: Article 6 IMTN Charter

1153. Q:Which article can you find definition of war crime Statute of the International Criminal

Tribunal for the Former Yugoslavia (ICTY Statute) 2009 ?

A: Articles 2 and 3 ICTY Statute

1154. Q: Which article can you find definition of war crime Statute of the International Criminal Tribunal for Rwanda (ICTR Statute) 2010 ?

A: Article 4 ICTR Statute

1155. Q:Which article can you find definition of war crime The Rome Statute of the International Criminal Court (ICC Statute) 1998.?

A: Article 8 ICC Statute.

1156. Q: what is the core doctrine of Geneva Conventions?

A: States must abide by the four Geneva Conventions of 1949) undertake responsibility for enacting domestic laws, which would criminalize and punish grave breaches of IHL(international humanitarian law)

(and virtually every state in the world is a party

1157. Q; what are state require doing under the Geneva convention?

A: all states are obligatory to pursue out, prosecute and punish or to extradite any person who allegedly committed act(s) amounting to a serious breach of IHL, regardless of that person's nationality or the place where the alleged crime was committed (Article 49, 50, 129 and 126 of the Geneva Conventions I–IV 1949 respectively).

1158. Q: What constitute war crimes?

A: These include

- pillage of public or private property
- unlawful deportation or transfer of civilian population
- using prohibited weapons and methods of warfare
- making improper use of the Red Cross emblem and other protective signs.

willful killing of a protected person

torture or inhuman treatment of a protected person

willfully causing great suffering to, or a serious injury to the body or health of, protected person.

1159. Q: where do one find the essential elements to prosecute war crimes?

A: the Appeal Chamber of the ICTY in Prosecutor v Tadic Decision on the Defiance Motion for the Interlocutory Appeal on Jurisdiction 2 October 1995.

1160. Q: Before a state brings prosecution against individual or group what must be establish first.

A; The answer to this question can be found in (the Appeal Chamber of the ICTY in Prosecutor v Tadic Decision on the Defiance Motion for the Interlocutory Appeal on Jurisdiction 2 October 1995,) para 94 which are

- The violation must constitute an infringement of a rule of international humanitarian law;
- ii. The rule must be customary in nature or, if it belongs to treaty law, the required conditions must be met;

iii. The violation must be 'serious', that is to say, it must constitute a breach of a rule protecting important values, and the breach must involve grave consequences for the victim. Thus, for instance, the fact of a combatant simply appropriating a loaf of bread in an occupied village would not amount to a 'serious violation of international humanitarian law'

although it may be regarded as falling foul of the basic principle laid down in Article 46, paragraph 1, of the Hague Regulations (and the corresponding rule of customary international law) whereby 'private property must be respected' by any army occupying an enemy territory;

- iv. The violation of the rule must entail, under customary or conventional law, the individual criminal responsibility of the person breaching the rule.

1161. Q: What factors must be considered to determine NIAC rule?

A: This can be found in paras (128-129) which states

- whether there exists a clear and unequivocal recognition of the rule, • whether there exists a state practice indicating intention to criminalise the prohibition,
- the gravity of the committed acts,
- the interest of international community in prohibiting these acts.

1162. Q; How does Article 8(1) of ICC says?

A: Article 8(1) establishes jurisdiction of the ICC over war crimes 'in particular when committed as part of a plan or policy or as part of a large-scale commission of such crimes'.

1163. Q: how can CAH (crime against humanity) view on crime?

A; 'widespread or systematic attack' for crimes against humanity (CAH

1164. Q: give an example of prosecution under article 8(2) of ICC(international criminal court?

A: Referring to Prosecutor v Thomas Lubanga Dyilo, ICC-01/04-01/06, Trial Judgment, 14 March 2012, was the first judgment pronounced by the ICC in March 2012. Thomas Lubanga was prosecuted for committing war crimes on the basis of Article 8(2)(e)(vii) (recruitment of children under 15 years of age into armed forces or groups and using them to participate in hostilities)

1165. Q: Reference to CAH (crime against human) Which Article can definition of CAH be found? The Charter of the International Military Tribunal at Nuremberg (IMTN Charter)?

A: .Article 6(c) IMTN Charter

1166. Q: Reference to CAH (crime against human) Which Article can definition of CAH be found? Statute of the International Criminal Tribunal for the Former Yugoslavia (ICTY Statute)?

A; Article 5 ICTY Statute

1167. Q: Reference to CAH (crime against human) Which Article can definition of CAH be found? Statute of the International Criminal Tribunal for Rwanda (ICTR Statute)?

A: Article 3 ICTR Statute

1168. Q: Reference to CAH (crime against human) Which Article can definition of CAH be found?. The Rome Statute of the International Criminal Court (ICC Statute).

A: Article 7 ICC Statute.

1169. Q: In what circumstance can CAH be committed?

A: Crime against human can be committed both during

armed conflict and in peacetime as define " 'widespread or systematic attack directed against any civilian population' that is determinative in establishing that particular acts amount to CAH.

1170. Q: Explain the term systematics in the definition of CAH?

A: The term 'systematic' has been defined by the ICTR and the ICTY in different ways (two examples that can be compared are: Prosecutor v Blaškić, IT-95-14-T, Trial Judgment, 3 March 2000, 203 and Akayesu, 580).

1171. Q: What does definition of systematic focus on?

A; Definition appear to focus on

- multiple commission of criminal acts
- high level of organisation
- an element of a plan, common objective or policy
- the use of resources (private or public).

1172. Q: What are the main element in CAH?

A: In order to prosecute under CAH the following element must be established;

- an inhumane act must be committed
- b. a criminal act must form a part of a widespread or systematic attack (not be a sporadic or isolated event)
- c.an attack must be directed against any civilian population

- d. the perpetrator must have the knowledge of a broader context in which the crime is committed

- (such as systemic policy or widespread large-scale abuses).

1173. Q: What is Mens rea element in CAH?

A: to prosecute an offence as CAH, the accused must be proven to have had:

- committed an offence listed in the relevant CAH provision (actus Reus)
- a mental element required for a particular offence (e.g. murder, rape, torture, etc.) and must be aware of the offence is committed, i.e. the existence of a 'widespread or systematic attack against any civilian population'.

Chapter 41

Genocide

1174. Q; Where does the word genocide originate and what does it mean?

A: 'Genocide' originate from (Greek: genos = 'race' and Latin: caedere to

mean 'to kill') was created in early 1940s by a Polish lawyer, Raphael Lemkin

1175. Q: How did United Nation acknowledged genocide?

A: United Nation declared genocide as "denial of the right of existence of entire human groups, as homicide is the denial of the right to live of individual human beings; [which] shocks the conscience of mankind"

1176. Q: When was Genocide convention and name the main architect?

the Convention on the Prevention and Punishment of the Crime of Genocide (Genocide Convention) was established in 1948. Led by Raphael Lemkin a Polish lawyer.

1177. Q: When did United Nation first dealt with Genocide?

A: It was in In 1946, when UN General Assembly

mentioned for the first time to the crime of genocide in Resolution 96(1) of 11 December 1946,

1178. Q: What happen in the Armenian genocide?

A: The Armenian genocide 1915–18, in Turkey under Ottoman rule. Armenians were deported, tortured and executed in massive numbers, forcibly transferred from their homes, deprived of basic human needs, leading to malnutrition, illness and eventual death about !.5 million died.

1179. Q: When did the convention adopted?

A: The Convention on the Prevention and Punishment of the Crime of Genocide was adopted by the UN General Assembly on 9 December 1948 and was the first international instrument to codify genocide as a crime

1180. Q: What were the main reason for

Genocide convention in 1948?

A: the massacre of Armenians during the First World War and the Holocaust in the Second World War, resulted the creation of an international legal instrument which would prohibit genocide as the 'ultimate crime' became an obvious priority.

1181. Q: Give the United Nation definition of genocide?.

A: Article 2 of the Convention defines genocide as:

Any of the following acts committed with intent to destroy, in whole or in part, a national, ethnical, racial or religious group, as such:

Killing members of the group;

Causing serious bodily or mental harm to members of the group;

Deliberately inflicting on the group conditions of life calculated to bring about its physical destruction in whole or in part;

Imposing measures intended to prevent births within the group;

Forcibly transferring children of the group to another group.

1182. Q:What does Article 1 state?

A: Article 1 of the Convention creates an obligation on confirms that genocide is prohibited irrespectively of whether it is committed in armed conflict or in peacetime.

1183. Q: What did the weakness identify in the convention?

A: Its definition of genocide is strictly limited to four groups only: national, ethnical, racial or religious, which are not defined in the instrument.

the enforcement of the Genocide Convention appears to be ineffective.

1184. Q: What are some of the reason a person can be guilty of genocide?

A: A person can be prosecuted of genocide even if they were not a direct wrongdoer of a genocidal act. Article 3 but involved in

Conspiracy to commit genocide

Direct and public incitement to commit genocide, attempt to commit genocide

Complicity in genocide.

1185. Q: What is the Mens rea of genocide?

A: The Mens rea is “ Intent to destroy” (dolus specialis)

1186. Q: Give a case of genocide?

A: The Media case In Prosecutor v Nahimana, Barayagwiza & Ngeze, ICTR-99-52-T, Trial Judgment, 3 December 2003 (The Media Case),

1187. Q: Briefly explain the media case?

A; The media consist of newspaper and radio station where three Rwandan media directors were found guilty of genocide and incitement to commit genocide. The three men were found to have played a major role in the process of both direct and public incitement to commit genocide and were accordingly convicted on these grounds.

1188. Q: Why can one describe ICC to begin to disintegrate and end?

A: absence of some of the world’s major powers from the ICC – China, Russia and the United States plus proposed plan for a mass exodus from the ICC by

African states poses a fundamental risk to its existence.

Burundi, South Africa and the Gambia have withdrawn from the ICC, following criticism, dating back a number of years, that it has a bias towards prosecuting crimes committed in Africa.

In 2016 Russia decided to remove their signature from

the ICC Burundi, South Africa and the Gambia to withdraw from the ICC, following criticism, dating back a number of years, that it has a bias towards prosecuting crimes committed in Africa.

Chapter 42

The Biggest Challenge facing the enforcement of International Law.

1189. Q: What is The Biggest Challenges Facing the Enforcement of International Law.?

A: One of the most significant issues facing the international community is the failure to comply with international law. While virtually every state is bound by the international law, each country chooses that laws which it can enforce while being adamant not to be bound by others.

1190. Q: How does politics affect enforcement of international law?

A: There lacks political consensus regarding international law, and this hinders its enforcement. Due to a lack of political resolve, it is difficult to subject new areas to international law or to expand its scope since it is currently limited as it is.

1191. Q: How is the 21st century activities affect enforcement of international law?

A: While the 21st century is marked by social, political, economic, and even technological conflicts, these conflicts are hard to resolve due to the unenforceability of international law. It is, therefore, essential to establish the challenges associated with international law enforcement.

1192. Q: Why is international law crucial?

A: International law is becoming crucial in the current era owing to modernization, globalization, and a range of advancements in different nations, which result in conflicts among nations. It is thus essential for international law to be implemented; however, there are challenges related to its enforcement, which need to be analyzed and resolved.

1193. Q: What evidence of effort to enforce international law?

A: The enforceability of international law has

been examined since the conclusion of World War 2. Studies reveal that the international community has tried various means to enforce international law. According to Johns (2019, p. 550), certain occasions may call for powerful economic sanctions.

1194. Q; Give example of when international law was enforced?

A: The best example to elaborate on this dates back in the early 1990s (1990-1991) to be precise when Kuwait was attacked by Iraq. The international laws had to be enforced through the armed forces of the UN Security Council to restore peace.

1195. Q: What other ways that enforcement can be implemented?

A: Other ways through which the international law can be enforced is through diplomatic dialogue and mediation, for example, in Kenya during the Post-Election Violence in 2008, reinstating domestic tribunals, and even using any other means to bring the dispute to a stand-still without indulging the agreement.

1196. Q: Why do some nations only adhere to enforcement of international laws?

A: Many studies focus on the realist argument

that asserts that nations only adhere to international law when it serves their interests is undoubtedly true.

1197. Q: Give example and case why nations self-interest lead to agreement?

A: The reason for this is attributed to the commitment that they show towards compliance with international laws (Shany 2017, p. 34). Various reasons justify this supposition. In the Democratic Republic of Congo (DRC), the ICC issued a warrant of arrest in May 2009, to bring to record to three leaders of DRC for the crimes against humanity (Shany 2017, p. 42).

1198. Q:Give an example of warrant of arrest issued in 2005?

A: In 2005, the same court issued a warrant of arrest for five Lord's Resistance Army leaders of Uganda to be accused of criminal offenses against humankind and the crimes on war and other evil, inhuman practices. In Darfur (Sudan), the violations of human rights were unmentionable. Again, the ICC has accused the Sudanese Prime Minister Johns (2019, p. 562).

1199. Q: In 2010, who was warrant issue against and what happened?

A: Later in 2010, a warrant of arrest was issued against President Omar El Bashir. It must be noted in all these circumstances. The accused never surrendered voluntarily to ICC since such orders were against their self-gain.

1200. Q: How does domestic politics affect international law enforcement support with case?

A: It is from these facts that prompt many scholars to shift to the side of realists when it comes to enforcement. There is a significant influence, especially on international policies. Betz (2018, 640) asserts that the role that the domestic politics play towards adherence with international policies in most cases serves to favor the actors themselves. For example, if an international law or policy is dismissed within a domestic set up, the likelihood of that particular policy to succeed internationally is not guaranteed.

1201. Q: has research been carried out regarding influence of sectarianism?

A: Studies also focus on sectarianism as a challenge to the enforcement of international law. Sectarianism is prevalent in the Middle East and North Africa. According to Lynch (2011, p. 5), sectarianism is such an ambiguous ideology.

1202. Q: what does the term sectarianism mean ?

A: The term can be used to denote different types of bigotry, discrimination, and historic commonalities related to either ethnic or religious groups or systems through which unfair social, political, and economic claims are made in both multiethnic and multireligious societies.

1203. Q: What else can sectarianism signify support the answer with case?

A: Alternatively, sectarianism can also denote a colonial method of an administration used mainly by colonial masters such as Britain, the United States, and France to distort the cultural, ethnic, and religious diversity of a given area to attain their imperial objectives (Lynch 2011, p. 7).

1204. Q: Considering the two definitions of sectarianism how can compliance of international law come to play.

A: Using the mentioned definitions of sectarianism, it can be deduced that both forms of sectarianism make countries reluctant to comply with international law. Whereas attempts have been made to achieve democracy in the Arab world, various reform efforts have been futile. As a matter of fact, the inputs of the U.S. in reinforcing reforms to set the citizens who are under the authoritative regimes were never successful.

1205. Q: How does authoritative countries influence law enforcement?

A; Additionally, the legitimacy of the

authoritative regimes in the Middle East and North Africa had been challenged in the past, and the indications are clear that eventually, democracy will prevail in countries that, for a long time, have had authoritative presidents. However, until this happens, the scope of international law will be limited in these regions.

1206. Q; Explain the weakness in international law?

A: With war raging in Syria, and the spill-over effects turning out to be more ostensible especially in Lebanon, the increased violence in Iraq, and the mounting tension in Bahrain, it is undoubtable that sectarianism is becoming the lens through which people are viewing the weakness of international law (Hashemi 2015, p. 68).

1207. Q: How has Sectarianism influence in some nations?

A: Sectarianism has become a substantial factor in some Arabic region's political landscape. Still, most importantly, it is needful to discern the political context in which sectarianism becomes eminent in a nation's politics and come to the realization that both sectarian conflict and sectarian political formations are too rigid to change (Gause 2013, par. 13).

1208. Q: Do religious doctrines affect enforcement of international law?

A: religious identities are proving to be quite significant, and they are never dominant. Instead, the current political context is proving to be more vital for comprehending how sectarianism contributes to modern conflicts in the Arab world and lack of adherence to international law.

1209. Q; Which countries might lack democracy due to sectarianism?

A: Concerning sectarianism, it is possible to establish that the modern Middle East and North African countries are deficient in the prerequisites of democratization; hence it is unlikely that such countries would comply with international law. They do not have powerful civil societies, substantial income, proper literacy levels, market-driven economies, or democratic cultures and neighbors (Hashemi 2016, p. 66). The factors listed above clearly explain why the Arab world countries spectacularly fail to comply with international law.

1210. Q: Give examples of some states activities that hinder law enforcement?

A: Taking the Arab-dominated countries in North Africa as an example, it is quite evident that the existing civil societies are fragile. Despite the social and economic inequalities, geographic remoteness, and poverty that are quite common in Sub-Saharan Africa in countries such as Botswana and Mauritius, they have managed to make a dramatic leap in embracing democracy (Hashemi 2016, p.

68).

1211. Q: How does sub-Saharan countries compare with other states?

A: world countries, which are better off when compared to these Sub-Saharan countries are yet to taste the fruits of democracy; this is a significant hindrance to the execution of international law in these regions where it is mainly required to solve conflicts.

1212. Q: How does Western countries policies affect international law enforcement give example?

A:Compliance with international law is also limited by the perceived effect of Western hegemony on developing nations. Taking the example of Libya, the participation of the U.S. and other western powers such as France and Russia in the civil war topped up an additional layer of external power intervention. Practically, the involvement of these powerful Western countries complicated a peaceful resolution to end the conflict. Due to such events, many countries are hesitant to comply with international law

1213. Q: What method can be used for such research of enforcement?

A: The study applies a qualitative methodology. In particular, it uses a case study approach since it enables an in-depth consideration of the challenges that face international law.

1214. Q: What does review consider?

A:The review involved a meta-analysis of past studies on the issue. The primary technique applied in highlighting and selecting the relevant and suitable sources involved an electronic search on trustworthy databases like peer-reviewed journal articles, books, and publications from reputable magazines.

1215. Q: Where do I get the sources to support my argument of international law enforcement

A: My search was confined to material published from 2010 onwards to ensure the sources are current. Another search structure entailed scanning the credentials of an author to ensure scholarly authority for the papers selected.

1216. Q: what were the terms I used for the research?

A: The search terms used included; international law; enforcement of international law; and challenges in enforcing international law.

1217. Q: Are there obligatory law international law enforcement?

A: The examination of past studies reveals that there is no mandatory enforcement of respect to the rule of law internationally; neither does it require the application of force to settle the disputes amongst different states.

1218. Q: How are national interest known?

A: Within the jurisdiction of the international legal systems like pacts, courts, or tribunals, matters of national interest are well addressed (Stephan 2017, p. 465). For example, the International Criminal Court (ICC) is a well-known international court where justice is done to all. The court tends to summon perpetrators who engaged in the violation of human rights to account for their actions.

1219. Q: What other laws highlight problems of international law enforcement?

A: In highlighting the difficulties about the enforcement of international law, it is vital to refer to the international human rights law due to the vagueness that surrounds its implementation.

1220. Q: Has there been any change in enforcing international laws since human right in1998

A; There is a pragmatic gainsay as far as international human rights law is concerned. The mode of the timing of its application has proved to be a quandary since the severe enactment arises during the sudden occurrences of crisis (Criddle and Fox-Decent 2012, p. 39).

1221. Q: How can sovereignty of state influence international laws?

A: According to Hall (2010), sovereignty gives the states the ability to settle their domestic matters without seeking for international intervention. This approach is entirely in conflict International Human Rights Law (IHRL), in which the responsibilities of the latter are perceived to be reducing the sovereignty of a nation (Jinks, 2019, p. 305).

1222. Q: What is global agreement amongst state with regard to international laws. Human Right?

A: The universal agreements amongst the states are based on the foundation of derogation clauses in which the states are allowed to pose restrictions on some rights, especially during threatening scenarios of human life. Therefore, using the derogation-centered approach within different states capacitates the IHRL to accept the interests of salvaging particular states during emergencies.

1223. Q: In emergency what happened to Human Right laws?

A: The only question that Criddle and Fox-

Decent tried to ask is all about situations in which human rights are belittled during emergencies, that is to say, the quantifiable and verifiable occasions that pertain to derogations in emergency periods. The idea of considering the violation of human rights came to its conception in the aftermath of the holocaust period.

1224. Q: Q: How can absolute power make head of state?

A: Having absolute power over territorial dominion makes the state's leader in bringing under total control, the state which he or she heads (Stephan 2017, p. 465). Stephan supports this claim by drawing an ex from the Treaty of Versailles in 1919, in which a commission was established to investigate the perpetrators of World War.

1225. Q: Why did the head of state of the in the world war denounce treaty of Versailles

A: The terms of the treaty was widely opposed by the victorious allies, claiming that any attempt to subject the head of state under trial in international criminal court was an act of abusing the sovereignty of a state. As Hall (2010, p. 16) could put it, these victorious allies were worried about the impending consequences that will meet them at some future time should they consent with the proposals of the Treaty of Versailles commission. It confirms that there exists incompatibility between state sovereignty and the International Human Rights Law.

1226. Q: What effect to have international obligation?

A: The recognition of international obligations facilitated the awareness of international rights. As contained in the "Article 2, Universal Declaration of Human Rights, of 1948", the United Nations general assembly agreed to meet the obligations on the very rights of an individual, intertwined with accountability by the violators. Any act of prejudice based on gender, religion, language, political, race, among others were not to be condoned.

1227. Q: When and what reason did human right started to take effect?

A: The realization of these matters of international interest came into existence in 1948, after a severe violation of Jews rights was practiced in Germany during the Second World War, in what may people identify as the Holocaust period (Hall 2010, p.29).

1228. Q: What did universal declaration of human right demanded

A: This declaration purported that all the nations were to fully meet the requirements of the standards that have been established in the document. It should be noted that the declaration was to be a "binding doctrine" within a state and did not give room for facultative principles. The incompatibility issue in this scenario is that not every state welcomed this idea as being mandatory towards enforcement of a working framework that is within their authority.

1229. Q: What other way can enforcement of international law be achieved?

A: The absolute concern highlighted in the question enforcement of international laws being tacked about undermining human rights in various states is met with a reality that the creation of awareness of human rights across the globe has not out rightly disputed the right of a sovereign state, but the current progression in human rights awareness is delimitating the perception of the whole world about the benefits of non-violation of the rights.

1230. Q: Q: What must nations do to avoid violation of human rights?

A: According to Criddle and Fox-Decent (2012, p. 39), the nations must initiate the antiphonal measures to put to an end the severe results from the serious violation of human rights even within the range of derogation notification of the state.

1231. Q: Give some norms of human rights that support law enforcement to prevent abuse?

A: Certain norms of human rights like "jus cogens" forbid against the acts of slavery, torture among others cannot be derogated at all, but other rights like freedom of expression, association and movement can be belittled by a state only if the situation demands so cost (Criddle and Fox-Decent 2012, p. 39).

1232. Q: What has encouraged people to protect each other against abuse?

A: The world widespread about the adoption of duties as contained in the international norm has made many nations to develop a strong desire to protect the state's individuals from being deprived of their rights (Hall 2010, p.14). As Jinks, (2019, p. 312) reports, the state will ultimately win the international recognition upon the fulfillment of its obligation to protect the rights of its citizen without any violation since without upholding of this concern, the citizens are bound to be at risk of losing their rights. It may be costly to reclaim them once they are violated.

1233. Q: Name some countries who violate human right and avoid enforcement of international law?

A: The gross misconduct of human rights violations which happened in Zimbabwe North Korea, Sudan, China, and even Russia in the recent past, have placed dubiousness about the responsiveness member states in responding to the human rights concerns within their states. Many people have questioned the inability and integrity of the IHRL in bringing the matter to an end.

1234. Q: Is it easy to resolve implementation of international laws?

A; The enforcement of international law faces various challenges that are not easy to resolve. The responsiveness of different states on how they find a blend between domestic and international laws have not affected fully.

1235. Q; Why do some state refuse to enforce international laws

A: The leaders of given states may

intentionally undermine the application and implementation of international laws, especially if the policies are out of their favor. On the other hand, domestic political influence could force the leaders to settle on international policy.

1236. Q: How should international law be applied?

A: International law should be applied in various states across the globe. On International Human Rights Law, while it is believed to be the core concern of every state to some degree, it has shown leniency in its application across some globe. However, it is within the capacity of every state to enact these laws and save innocent citizens whose rights are on the verge of being violated. Besides, the international human rights law will continue to increase in value and challenge the sovereignty of states directly in addressing the great concerns of citizens.

Chapter 43

Miscellaneous

Modern crime.

1237. Q: Which area of the dating agency do exhibit dishonesty which means theft and crime.?

A: some appear to use computer to generate text to men or women looking for love or it could be human sending text and demanding payment in a form of buying credit at a cost of sometimes $2 USD for reply to bogus text

1238. Q: What about men using female photos/video/punster to trick men on internet for money?.

A; This is false representation and it happens when amateurs send pictures copied from the internet to opposite gender and asking for money to buy food or phone credit etc. they target people who are sympathetic.

1239. Q: People pretending to be diplomat to defraud the public?

A: Example of this is someone pretend to be in the army and have secured large sum of millions USD dollars and want to send outside the unsafe country. They will then ask you to pay large sum of money for the money to go through customs

1240. Q: Can crime enforcement officer be charged with crime?.

A: Yes, in democracy countries no one is above the law?

1241. Q; Can members of parliament claim immunity to crime?

A: Not in their country. They could claim immunity if the go to another country as a diploma.

1242. Q: Do some government policies encourage crime?

A: Yes, a lot of government policies might have loopholes to allow people to exploit to their advantage. Example victim support payment; a drug addict or alcoholic who needs money just have to lie about sexual or violence assault and she get payment.

1243. Q: Do you think historic crime allegation is fair?.

Crime committed say over 30 years where there is no evidence for the accuse to proof their innocent is not fair. There are thousands of people in prison due to historic allege offence?.

1244. Q: Do you think women should be paid to make force or true allegation.?

A: No as it promote dishonest women as this has become big business in England. They should report genuine crime but not to be paid for it

1245. Q: Due to equality law and human right, must men be paid for reporting sexual or violence offence by women?

A: Yes

1246. Q; How must abuse of power and position be punished?.

A: This is criminal offence to use one position to commit crime of any sort include conspiracy.

1247. Q: What should happen to doctors who breach duty of care?

This could be civil claim under tort law but where there is evidence of conspiracy, then it became criminal and must be charged

Chapter 44

key legal terms in Criminology

It is essential, as someone interested in criminology understands the terminology used in the court system. More terminology can be seen at crown publication copy right

1248. Q: What is the function of the UK house of Lords?

A: The judicial function of the UK House of Lords is entirely separate from its role in government; the judicial work is done by a number of senior judges colloquially called Law Lords'. They hear appeals from the High Court and the Court of Appeal and until 1999, were in effect, the final resort for appeal in the UK legal system, at which time the Supreme Court of the United Kingdom became the final resort for appeal. House of Lords rulings are binding on all other courts

1249. Q: What does Advocate mean?

A: A barrister or solicitor representing a party in a hearing before a Court.

1250. Q: What does accused mean?

A: The person charged. The person who has allegedly committed the offence.

1251. Q: What does acknowledgement in law mean?

A: Form of reply to, or confirmation of, service of process

1252. Q: What does Acquittals of a person mean?

Discharge of defendant following verdict or direction of not guilty.

1253. Q: What does the case is adjourned mean?

A: Temporary suspension of the hearing of a case by order of the Court (maybe

for a short period, e.g. to next day or sine die).

1254. Q: What does Adoption mean?

An act by which the rights and duties of the natural parents of a child are extinguished and equivalent rights and duties become vested in the adopter or adopters, to whom the child then stands in all respects as if born to them in marriage

1255. Q: What does adultery mean?

Voluntary sexual intercourse between a married person and another person

who is not the spouse, while the marriage is still valid. This is a common fact relied on for divorce

1256. Q; What does Affidavit mean?

A: A written statement of evidence confirmed on oath or by affirmation to be true and taken before someone who has authority to administer it.

1257. Q; What is Affirmation?

A: Declaration by a witness who has no religious belief, or has religious beliefs, that prevent him/her taking the oath, that the evidence he/she is giving is the truth.

1258. Q: What is appeal?

A: Application to a higher Court or authority for review of a decision of a lower " Court or authority

1259. Q: What is attachment of earnings

A: An order that directs an employer of a debtor to deduct regularly an amount, fixed by the Court, from the debtor's earnings and pay that sum into Court

1260. Q: What is award mean?

A:Result of an arbitration hearing or the amount of damages assessed by a Court

1261. Q: What is bail?

A: Release of a defendant from custody, until his/her next appearance in Court, subject sometimes to security being given and/or compliance with certain conditions.

1262. Q; Who is regarded as bailiff?

Officer of the County Court empowered to serve Court documents and execute warrants

1263. Q: What does bankrupt mean?

A: Insolvent - unable to pay creditors and having all goods/effects administered by a liquidator or trustee and sold for the benefit of those creditors; as a result of an order under the Insolvency Act 1986

1264. Q: Who is barrister or counsel?

A member of the bar: the branch of the legal profession
which has rights of audience before all Courts

1265. Q: What is Bench warrant?

A warrant issued by the judge for an absent defendant to be arrested and brought before a Court

1266. Q: what is Indictment?

A written statement of the charges against a defendant sent for trial to the Crown Court, and signed by an officer of the Court.

1267. Q: What is Bind over?

A: In the Crown Court or (more usually) the Magistrates Court, and signed by an officer of the Court

1268. Q: What is Bind over for sentence?

A: An order which requires the defendant to return to Court on an unspecified date for sentence. Failure to observe this order may result in a forfeit or penalty to be enforced.

1269. Q: What is Brief?

A; Written instructions to counsel to appear at a hearing on behalf of a party prepared by the solicitor and setting out the facts of the case and any case law-relied upon

1270. Q: What is case conference?

A: Usually the first hearing in a Multi-track claim and an opportunity to take stock and consider the way forward

1271. Q: what is Caution?

A: Notice given to the Land Registry' by any person with an interest in particular

or

land to ensure that no action is taken in respect of the land without the person's knowledge

or

Warning, given by a Police Officer, to a person charged with an offence

Warning, given by a Police Officer, instead of a charge

1272. Q: What is Caveat?

A: A notice given to the registrar that effectively prevents action by another party
without first notifying the party entering the caveat

1273. Q: what is Cessate Chambers

Private room, or Court from which the public are excluded in which a District Judge or Judge may conduct certain sorts of hearings or Offices used by a barrister

1274. Q: Who is Circuit Judge Civil?

A: A judge who sits in the County Court and/or Crown Court Matters concerning private rights and not offences against the state.

1275. Q: What is Civil Justice Reform?

A: The result of the Access to Justice report by Lord Woolf The aim is to provide more effective access to Justice through quicker, cheaper and more proportionate justice for defended cases It introduced a unified set of Rules and Practice Directions for the County and High Courts, and Judicial Case Management The reforms came into effect on 26 April 1999

1276. Q: what is commissioner of oath

A; An addendum signed and executed which amends or adds something to a will Solicitors authorised by the Lord Chancellor to administer oaths and affirmations to a statement of evidence

1277. Q; What does Committal means

A: Committal for trial: Following examination by the Magistrates of a case involving and indictable or either way offence, the procedure of directing the case to the Crown Court to be dealt with

or

Committal for Sentence: Where the Magistrates consider that the offence justifies a sentence greater than they are empowered to impose they may commit the defendant to the Crown Court for sentence to be passed by a judge

or

Committal Order: An order of the Court committing someone to prison

or

Committal Warrant (see WARRANT OF COMMITTAL)

1278. Q: Concurrent sentence?

A: A direction by a Court that a number of sentences of imprisonment should run at the same time.

1279. Q: What is Consecutive sentence?

A: An order for a subsequent sentence of imprisonment to commence as soon as a previous sentence expires. Can apply to more than two sentences

1280. Q: What is Contempt of court?

A: Disobedience or wilful disregard to the judicial process

1281. Q: what is Corroboration?

A; Evidence by one person confirming that of another or supporting evidence, for example forensic evidence (bloodstain, fibres etc) in murder cases

1282. Q; Describe county court?

A; Sometimes inaccurately referred to as the Small Claims Court, County Courts deal with civil matters including all monetary claims up to £15,000. Many County Courts have extra powers which enable them to deal with divorce and other family proceedings, bankruptcy actions, matters relating to children and cases involving ships and boats known as admiralty actions. Some County Courts are also branch offices of the High Court known as District registries

1283. Q: Describe court of appeal

A: Divided into civil and criminal divisions and hears appeals:

from decision in the High Court and County Courts and

against convictions or sentences passed by the Crown Court,

1284. Q: what is Court of protection?

A; The branch of the High Court with jurisdiction over

the estates of people mentally incapable of handling their own financial affairs

1285. Q; Describe Crown court?

A; The Crown Court deals with all crime committed for trial by Magistrates Courts. Cases for trial are heard before a judge and jury. The Crown Court also

acts as an appeal Court for cases heard and dealt with by the Magistrates. The Crown Court can also deal with some civil and family matters.

1286. Q; how is Crown court divided?

A; The Crown Court is divided into tiers, depending on the type of work dealt with.

1287. Q: Describe first Tier?

A;

- Defended High Court Civil work.
- All classes of offence in criminal proceedings.

- Committals for sentence from the Magistrates' Court.

  Appeals against convictions and sentences imposed at Magistrates' Court.

1288. Q: Describe second tier

All classes of offence in criminal proceedings.

Committals for sentence from Magistrates' Court.

Appeals against convictions and sentences imposed at Magistrates' Court.

1289. Q: Describe Third tier?

A:

Class 4 offences only in criminal proceedings.

Committals for sentence from Magistrates' Court.

Appeals against convictions and sentences

1290. Q: What is decree Nisi

A: Order for divorce unless cause to contrary is shown within a set period

1291. Q: What is decree absolute?

A: A final certificate, resulting from an application, dissolving a marriage

1292. Q: Explain divisional Court?

A; As well as having an original jurisdiction of their own, all three divisions of the High Court have appellate jurisdiction to hear appeals from lower Courts and tribunals. The Divisional Court

of the Chancery Division deals with appeals in bankruptcy matters from the County Court. The Divisional Court of the Queen's Bench Division deals largely with certain appeals on points of law from many Courts. The Divisional Court of the Family Division deals largely
with appeals from Magistrates Courts in matrimonial matters a 'next friend' or 'guardian ad litem'

1293. Q: what is expert witness?

A; Person employed to give evidence on a subject in which they are qualified or have expertise

1294. Q: What is Garnishee?

A: A summons issued by a plaintiff, against a third party, for seizure of money or
other assets in their keeping, but belonging to the defendant

1295. Q: Name some branches of High court?

A:

A civil Court which consists of three divisions:

Queen's Bench (can be known as King's Bench Division if a King is assuming the throne) - civil disputes for recovery of money, including breach of contract, personal injuries, libel/slander;

Family - concerned with matrimonial maters and proceedings relating to children, e.g. wardship;

Chancery - property matters including fraud and bankruptcy

1296. Q: What is Indictable offence?

A; A criminal offence triable only by the Crown Court. The different types of offence are classified 1, 2, 3 or 4. Murder is a class 1 offence

1297. Q:What is justice of the peace?

A: A lay magistrate - person appointed to administer judicial business in a Magistrates Court. Also sits in the Crown Court with a judge or recorder to hear appeals and committals for sentence

1298. Q: who are Law lords?

A: Describes the judges of the House of Lords who are known as the Lords of Appeal in ordinary

1299. Q: Who is the Lord Chancellor?

A; The cabinet minister who acts as speaker of the House of Lords and oversees the hearings of the Law Lords. Additional responsibilities include supervising the procedure of Courts other than Magistrates or Coroners Courts and selection of judges, magistrates, queens counsel and members of tribunals Senior judge of the Court of Appeal (Criminal Division) who also heads the Queen's Bench

1300. Q: Who is Public trustee?

A: Person who prosecutes

A person (usually a barrister or solicitor) appointed by the Lord Chancellor as

i) trustee for trusts managed by the Public trust Office;
ii) Accountant General for Court Funds;
iii) Receiver (of last resort) for Court of Protection patients

(Pronounced Puny) High Court judge. Any judge of the High Court other than the heads of each division.

1301. Q: Who is regarded as Queens counsel QC?

A: Barristers of at least ten years standing may apply to become queen's counsel. QCs undertake work of an important nature and are referred to as 'silks' which is derived from the Courts gown that is worn. Will be known as king's counsel if a king assumes the throne

1302. Q: What is trial window?

A: A period of time within which the case must be listed for trial

1303. Q: Explain tribunal and give example?

A group of people consisting of a chairman (normally solicitor/barrister) and others who exercise a judicial function to determine matters related to specific interests, e.g. VAT tribunal - appeals against the amount of duty levied by Customs and Excise Lands tribunal - appeals against the valuation of land

1304. Q: What is restitution?

A: A remedy available following illegal re-entry of premises by persons evicted
under a warrant of possession. The bailiff is authorised to evict all occupants

1305. Q: What is Winding up?

A: The voluntary or compulsory closure of a company and the subsequent realisation of assets and payment to creditors

1. BA (Hons), Law: include Criminal, Tort, damages, Contract, Property, Equity and Trust, European law, Public, Constitutional, Judicial Review, Agency.
2. (LLM)Master of Law; which is on -going (2020), but I have passed the module " legal research", and "business, CSR Corporate social responsibility and human Right law" Institutional development and management, International Law.
3. Advance Dip. Business Law, Level 4: include Employment, Agency, Damages, Tort, Contract, employment tribunal etc.
4. Dip. Criminology
5. BA (Hons)op. Account: Financial Accountant and Management Accountant
6. Cert. Acct; Professional Certificate in Financial and Management Accounting
7. Dip. Book-keeping, Level 3
8. Nursing: RMN (Psychiatry trained nurse)
9. General Trained Nurse
10. Cert. in Education (Lecturer)
11. Business Certificate in Advanced Management
12. Cert. Business Enterprise
13. Advanced Food Hygiene
14. Intermediate Health and Safety

15. Dip. Safety Management
16. International Entrepreneur for over 25 years
17. Computers: Cert. Cisco Level 2 Technician, (build, repair, networking)
18. Dip. Clait Plus (in all software)
19. New Clait Dip. Level 2
20. Microsoft Specialist
21. ECDL Level 2
22. Script writing: Dip. TV, radio, stage and film
23. Non-fiction writing: Dip. Autobiography, Biography and Family History
24. Cert. in Counselling
25. Author/Self-Publisher: Over 30 books published (2020)
26. Plumbing: Level 3 City and Guild
27. Theology: Cert. Bible studies; researched

Theology for my PhD (most faiths)

28. Psychology and Social Science (university level certificate)
29. Photographer: Portrait, Glamour and Figure Photographer (PGFP).Dip.
30. Dip. Hypnotherapy
31. National Vocation Qualification (NVQ); Internal Verifier, (V1)
32. Trainer and Assessor A1 (NVQ)
33. RMA Registered Management award

List of my published Books in 2019/20

In June 2019, I published the following books plus other books translated into Arabic, Spanish, French and Chinese, plus different formats such as eBooks,

Faith Books - in English Language

1. *Love All Faiths*
2. *Faith Unity*
3. *Messengers*
4. *Islam v. Christianity*
5. *Allah Loves Islam*
6. *God Loves Christianity*
7. *God Enlighten Buddhism*
8. *Parama Nandra Loves Hindus*
9. *In Search of Wisdom in Freemasonry*
10. *Jesus Christ is Coming Soon*
11. *Psychology of Religion, Politics & Marriage*

Non-Faith Books- in English Languages

1. The One - Over 130 Poems "DCF"

2. Mood Disorder

3. Sweet and Sour women (plus over 500 love letters from women)

4. The Law (Over 1,160 Questions and Answers)

5. set up and manage a business

6. How to set up a care home and care agency

7. How to manage a care Home and care agency

8. Care Home; Staff training

The following are Translated completed and published books in June 2019.

The following translated in Spanish

1) Dios ama el Cristianismo (God loves Christianity)

2) V. Islamites Cristianismo (Islam v Christianity)

3)) De la Sabiduria En la Masoneri

(In search of Wisdom in freemasonry)

4) Ame todas Las creencias (love all faiths)

5) Mensageros De Dios (God's Messengers)

6)) Allah ama elIslam (allah loves Islam)

The following translated in French

1) Messagers de Dieu (god messengers)

2) Islamisme. v. Christianisme (Islam v Christianity)

3) A la recherche de la sagesse dans la franc-maçonnerie (In search of wisdom in freemasonry)

4) Aime Toutes les Fois (Love All faiths)

5) Dieu Aime Le Christianisme (God loves Christianity)

6) Allah aime l'Islam (Allah loves islam)

The following translated in Chines

上帝爱伊斯兰教 (Allah loves Islam)

伊斯蘭教訴基督教(Islam v Christianity)

The following translated in Arabic

الاسلام يحب الله. (Allah loves Islam)

حب جميع الأديان Love All Fait

REFERENCE AND FURTHER READING

These are group according to some of the specific topics covered in this publication

Miscellaneous

Andreopoulos, George. "Genocide, War Crimes, and Crimes against Humanity." *International and Transnational Crime and Justice*, 2019, pp. 321-326.

De Andrade, Dominique. "The "Drugs-Crime Nexus"." *Oxford Medicine Online*, 2018, pp. 10-426.

Diniz Pucci, Rafael. "Transnational crime in South America." *Research Handbook on Transnational Crime*, 2019, pp. 494-504.

DoCarmo, Tania E. "Major International Counter-Trafficking Organizations: Addressing Human Trafficking from Multiple Directions." *The Palgrave International Handbook of Human Trafficking*, 2019, pp. 1429-1444.

Lemkin, Raphael. "Genocide as a Crime Under International Law." *Genocide and Human Rights*, 2017, pp. 3-9.

Neto, Joana. "Social Network Analysis and Organized Crime Investigation: Adequacy to Networks, Organized Cybercrime, Portuguese Framework." *Cybercrime Organized Crime, and Societal Responses*, 2016, pp. 179-199.

O'Doano, Matthew D. "Gang Injunctions and Abatement." 2011, pp. 127-658.

Price, Jeffrey C., and Jeffrey S. Forrest. "Crime and terrorism in aviation." *Practical Aviation Security*, 2016, pp. 45-100.

Schoultz, Isabel, and Janne Flyghed. "Denials and confessions. An analysis of the temporalization of neutralizations of corporate crime." *International Journal of Law, Crime and Justice*, 2020, p. 100389.

Stancu, Ioana G. "Defining the Crime of Aggression or Redefining Aggression?" *The International Criminal Court and the Crime of Aggression*, 2017, pp. 87-91.

Sources of international law

THIRLWAY, H. W. A. (2014). *The source of international law*. Oxford [etc.], Oxford University Press.

D'ASPREMONT, J., BESSON, S., & KNUCHEL, S. (2017). *The Oxford handbook on the sources of international law*.

Tan, Y., 2018. The Identification of Customary Rules in International Criminal Law. Utrecht Journal of International and European Law, 34(2), pp.92–110.

Goldsmith. J & Posner. E, 2005. The Limits of International Law. Oxford University Press, Inc. 198 Madison Avenue, New York, New York 10016

Daniel M. Bodansky, The Concept of Customary International Law, 16 MICH. J. INT'L L. 667 (1995). Available at: https://repository.law.umich.edu/mjil/vol16/iss3/3

Panezi, M. 2007. Sources of Law in Transition Re-visiting General Principles of International Law. ANCILLA IURIS (anci.ch) 2007: 66

Elllis, J. 2011. General Principles and Comparative Law. The European Journal of International Law Vol. 22 no. 4 © EJIL 2011

Schreuer, C. 2010.Sources of International Law: Scope and Application. The Emirates Center for Strategic Studies and Research.

Reference

The Legal Implications of the Use of Force by the Military

Bethlehem, D., 2013. Principles of Self-Defense—A Brief Response. *American Journal of International Law, 107*(3), pp.579-585.

Brunnée, J. and Toope, S.J., 2019. Norm Robustness and Contestation in International Law: Self-Defense against Nonstate Actors. *Journal of Global Security Studies*, *4*(1), pp.73-87.

Conte, A., 2017. *Security in the 21st century: the United Nations, Afghanistan and Iraq*. Routledge.

Democratic Republic of the Congo v. Uganda, 2005 I.C.J. Rep 168 (2005).

ec.europa.eu, 2011.*Fines For Breaking EU Competition Law. Ec.Europa.Eu*, https://ec.europa.eu/competition/cartels/overview/factsheet_fines_en.pdf.

Etzioni, A., 2010. Terrorists: a distinct species. *Terrorism and Political Violence*, *23*(1), pp.1-12.

Gunaratne, R., 2011. *Lesson 5.3. First exception to the Prohibition on the Use of Force: Security Council Authorization to Use Force* [online], Public

International Law;

https://ruwanthikagunaratne.wordpress.com/2011/04/12/lesson-5-3-first-exception-to-the-prohibition-on-the-use-of-force-security-council-authorization-to-use-force

Islamic Republic of Iran v. United States of America, 2003 I.C.J. Rep 161 (2003).

Ker-Lindsay, J., 2011. Not such a 'sui generis' case after all: assessing the ICJ opinion on Kosovo. *Nationalities Papers*, *39*(1), pp.1-11.

Nicaragua v. United States of America, 1984 I.C.J. Rep 392 (1984).

Upeniece, V., 2018. Conditions for the lawful exercise of the right of self-defence in international law. In *SHS Web of Conferences* (Vol. 40, p. 01008). EDP Sciences.

Vidmar, J., 2014. Excusing Unlawful Use of Force Under the Law of State Responsibility. *Available at SSRN 2482741*.

von Einsiedel, S. and Fong, A.P., 2017. The Rise of High-Level Panels: Implications for the New UN Secretary-General.

Wood, M., 2013. International Law and the Use of Force: What Happens in Practice?. *Indian journal of international law*, *53*, pp.345-367.

www.un.org, 2020. *United Nations Office On Genocide Prevention And The Responsibility To Protect*. [online] Un.org. Available at: <https://www.un.org/en/genocideprevention/about-responsibility-to-protect.shtml>

Reference

IMMUNITY for head of state

Akande, D. and Shah, S., 2010. Immunities of State Officials, International Crimes, and Foreign Domestic Courts. *European Journal of International Law*, 21(4), pp.815-852.

Akande, D., 2004. International Law Immunities and the International Criminal Court. *The American Journal of International Law*, 98(3), p.407.

Baker, R., 2010. Customary International Law in the 21st Century: Old Challenges and New Debates. *European Journal of International Law*, 21(1), pp.173-204.

BESSON, S., 2016. State Consent and Disagreement in International Law-Making. Dissolving the

Paradox. *Leiden Journal of International Law*, 29(2), pp.289-316.

Chigara, B. and Nwankwo, C., 2015. 'To be or not to be?' The African Union and its Member States Parties' Participation as High Contracting States Parties to the Rome Statute of the International Criminal Court (1998). *Nordic Journal of Human Rights*, 33(3), pp.243-268.

Arrest Warrant of 11 April 2000 (Democratic Republic of the Congo v. Belgium), Judgment, I.C.J. Reports 2002.

Reinisch A., 2006. European Court Practice Concerning State Immunity from Enforcement Measures *Eur J Int Law,*17 p.803.

Iverson, J., 2012. The Continuing Functions of Article 98 of the Rome Statute. *Goettingen Journal of International Law*, 4(1), pp.131-151.

Mettraux, G., Dugard, J. and du Plessis, M., 2018. Heads of State Immunities, International Crimes and President Bashir's Visit to South Africa. *International Criminal Law Review*, 18(4), pp.577-622.

Mudukuti, A., 2020. Prosecutor v. Omar Hassan Ahmad Al-Bashir, Judgment in the Jordan Referral re Al-Bashir Appeal. *American Journal of International Law*, 114(1), pp.103-109.

Murphy, S., 2014. ImmunityRatione Personaeof Foreign Government Officials and Other Topics: The Sixty-Fifth Session of the International Law

Commission. *The American Journal of International Law*, 108(1), pp.41-57.

Nouwen, S., 2019. return to sender: let the international court of justice justify or qualify international-criminal-court exceptionalism regarding personal immunities. *The Cambridge Law Journal*, 78(3), pp.596-611.

Sadushaj, M., Shatku, S., Pustina, F., Kuka, E. and Taraj, G., 2017. Interpretation and Application of Article 98 of the Rome Statute. *Academic Journal of Interdisciplinary Studies*, 6(1), pp.141-147.

Scheffer, D., 2005. Article 98(2) of the Rome Statute: America's Original Intent. *Journal of International Criminal Justice*, 3(2), pp.333-353.

Schneider, É., Iglesias, J., Hallberg, K. and Kuperman, M., 2014. Crimes against Humanity: The Role of International Courts. *PLoS ONE*, 9(6), p.e99064.

Shi, X., 2019. Official Acts and Beyond: Towards an Accurate Interpretation of Diplomatic Immunity

Ratione Materiae under the Vienna Convention on Diplomatic Relations. *Chinese Journal of International Law*, 18(3), pp.669-694.

Zappala, S., 2001. Do Heads of State in Office Enjoy Immunity from Jurisdiction for international Crimes? The Ghaddafi case before the French Cour de Cessation. *EJIL*, 12(3), pp.595-612.

Judgment in the Jordan Referral re Al-Bashir Appeal, Case No. ICC-02/05-01/09 OA2.

Corrigendum to the Decision Pursuant to Article 87(7) of the Rome Statute on the Failure by the Republic of Malawi to Comply with the Cooperation Requests Issued by the Court with Respect to the Arrest and Surrender of Omar Hassan Ahmad Al Bashir No: ICC-02/05-01/09-139.

Decision pursuant to article 87(7) of the Rome Statute on the refusal of the Republic of Chad to comply with the cooperation requests issued by the Court with respect to the arrest and surrender of Omar Hassan Ahmad Al Bashir No.: ICC-02/05-01/09-140.

Decision on the Cooperation of the Federal Republic of Nigeria Regarding Omar Al-Bashir's Arrest and Surrender to the Court No. ICC-02/05-01/09-159.

Decision on the Cooperation of the Democratic Republic of the Congo Regarding Omar Al Bashir's Arrest and Surrender to the Court No. ICC-02/05-01/09-195.

Decision under article 87(7) of the Rome Statute on the non-compliance by South Africa with the request by the Court for the arrest and surrender of Omar Al-Bashir No. ICC-02/05-01/09-302.

Decision on the non-compliance by the Republic of Djibouti with the request to arrest and surrender Omar Al-Bashir to the Court and referring the matter to the United Nations Security Council and the Assembly of the State Parties to the Rome Statute No. ICC-02/05-01/09-266.

United Nations, 23 May 1969. Vienna Convention on the Law of Treaties, United Nations, Treaty Series, vol. 1155

United Nations 17 July 1998. General Assembly, Rome Statute of the International Criminal Court (last amended 2010)

United Nations 1961. Vienna Convention on Diplomatic Relations 500 UNTS 95, 23 UST 3227, 55 AJIL 1064

United Nations, 24 April 1963. Vienna Convention on Consular Relations.

Fox H., and Webb P., 2013, *The Law of State Immunity,* Oxford, Oxford University Press.

ICC (International criminal court)

Reference

Boister, N. (2003) 'Transnational Criminal Law?', Journal of International Law, vol.14, no. 5, pp. 953–76.

Cassese, A. (1998) 'Reflections on International Criminal Justice' , Modern Law Review, vol. 61, no. 1, pp. 1–10.

Cassese, A. (2008) International Criminal Law, 2nd edn, New York, Oxford University Press.

Chang, I. (1998) The Rape of Nanking: The Forgotten Holocaust of World War II, New York, Penguin Books.

Cryer, R., Friman, H. Robinson, D. and Wilmshurst, E. (2007) An Introduction to International Criminal Law and Procedure, Cambridge, Cambridge University Press.

Degan, V.D. (2005) 'On the Sources of International Criminal Law', Chinese Journal of International Law, vol. 4, no. 1, pp. 45–83.

Murray, J. (2002–3) 'Who will police the peace-builders? The failure to establish accountability for the participation of United Nations civilian police in the trafficking of women in post-conflict Bosnia and Herzegovina', Columbia Human Rights Law Review, vol. 34, no. 2, pp. 475–527.

Ndulo, M. (2009) 'The United Nations responses to the Sexual Abuse and Exploitation of Women and Girls by Peacekeepers during Peacekeeping Missions', Berkeley Journal of International Law, vol. 27, p. 127–61.

O'Brien, M. (2012) 'Prosecutorial Discretion as an Obstacle to Prosecution of United Nations Peacekeepers by the International Criminal Court. The Big Fish/Small Fish Debate and the Gravity Threshold', Journal of International Criminal Justice, vol. 10, no. 3, pp. 525–45.

Odello, M. (2010) 'Tackling Criminal Acts in Peacekeeping Operations: the Accountability of Peacekeepers', Journal of Conflict & Security Law, vol. 15, no. 2, pp. 347–91.

Schabas, W. (2009) 'International crimes' in Armstrong, D. (ed.) (2009) Routledge Handbook of International Law, Abingdon, Routledge.

Reference

War Crime/ Genocide

Boister, N. (2003) 'Transnational Criminal Law?', Journal of International Law, vol.14, no. 5, pp. 953–76.

Cassese, A. (1998) 'Reflections on International Criminal Justice' , Modern Law Review, vol. 61, no. 1, pp. 1–10.

Cassese, A. (2008) International Criminal Law, 2nd edn, New York, Oxford University Press.

Chang, I. (1998) The Rape of Nanking: The Forgotten Holocaust of World War II, New York, Penguin Books.

Cryer, R., Friman, H. Robinson, D. and Wilmshurst, E. (2007) An Introduction to International Criminal Law and Procedure, Cambridge, Cambridge University Press.

Degan, V.D. (2005) 'On the Sources of International Criminal Law', Chinese Journal of International Law, vol. 4, no. 1, pp. 45–83.

Murray, J. (2002–3) 'Who will police the peace-builders? The failure to establish accountability for the participation of United Nations civilian police in the trafficking of women in post-conflict Bosnia and Herzegovina', Columbia Human Rights Law Review, vol. 34, no. 2, pp. 475–527.

Ndulo, M. (2009) 'The United Nations responses to the Sexual Abuse and Exploitation of Women and Girls by
Peacekeepers during Peacekeeping Missions', Berkeley Journal of International Law, vol. 27, p. 127–61.

O'Brien, M. (2012) 'Prosecutorial Discretion as an Obstacle to Prosecution of United Nations Peacekeepers by the International Criminal Court. The Big Fish/Small Fish Debate and the Gravity Threshold', Journal of International Criminal Justice, vol. 10, no. 3, pp. 525–45.

Odello, M. (2010) 'Tackling Criminal Acts in Peacekeeping Operations: the Accountability of Peacekeepers', Journal of Conflict & Security Law, vol. 15, no. 2, pp. 347–91.

Schabas, W. (2009) 'International crimes' in Armstrong, D. (ed.) (2009) Routledge Handbook of International Law,
Abingdon, Routledge.

Reference

Baines, E.K. (2009) 'Complex political perpetrators: reflections on Dominic Ongwen', Journal of Modern African Studies, vol. 47, no. 2, pp. 163–91.

BBC (2012) 'Transitional Justice', Unreliable Evidence, Radio 4, 25 April.

Cassese, A. (2008) International Criminal Law, 2nd edn, New York, Oxford University Press.

Commission on the Responsibility of the Authors of the War and on Enforcement of Penalties (1919) Report presented to the preliminary peace conference, Paris, 29 March.

Cryer, R., Friman, H., Robinson, D. and Wilmshurst, E. (2007) An Introduction to International Criminal Law and Procedure, New York, Cambridge University Press.

ICC (2011) Elements of Crimes, The Hague, Netherlands, International Criminal Court.

Dugard, J. (2013) 'Palestine and the International Criminal Court: institutional failure or bias', Journal of International Criminal Justice, vol. 11, no. 3, pp. 563–70.

UN (1994) Report of the International Tribunal for the Prosecution of Persons Responsible for Serious Violations of International Humanitarian Law Committed in the Territory of the Former Yugoslavia Since 1991, Doc A/489/342&S/1994/1007 [online],

available at
www.icty.org/x/file/About/Reports%20and%20Publications/AnnualReports/annual_report_1994_en.pdf (accessed 10 April 2013).

UN News Centre (2010) 'Tackling sexual violence must include prevention, ending impunity – UN official', 27 April [online], available at www.un.org/apps/news/story.asp?NewsID=34502#.UW1RyaK0LTo (accessed 24 April 2013).

Vilmer, J-B.J. (2016) 'The African Union and the International Criminal Court:
counteracting the crisis', International Affairs, vol. 92, no. 6, pp. 1319–42.

Enforcement of international Law

References

Betz, T., 2018. Domestic Institutions, Trade Disputes, and the Monitoring and Enforcement of International Law. International Interactions, 44(4), pp.631-660.

Cassel, M and Al-Zubaidi, L.2013. Diaries of an Unfinished Revolution: Voices from Tunis to Damascus. London: Penguin Books, 2013.
Criddle, E.J. and Fox-Decent, E., 2012. Human rights, emergencies, and the rule of law. Hum. Rts. Q., 34, p.39.
Gause, Gregory. 2013. "Sectarianism and the Politics of the New Middle East". Brookings, Accessed at: www.brookings.edu/blog/up-front/2013/06/08/sectarianism-and-the-politics-of-the-new-middle-east/ [Accessed May 25, 2020].
Hall, A., 2010. The Challenges to State Sovereignty from the Promotion of Human Rights. University of Reading.
Hashemi, N. 2015. "Sectarianism in the Middle East: The Salience of Authoritarianism over Theology". Middle East Institute,
Hashemi, N. 2016. "Toward a Political Theory of Sectarianism in the Middle East: The Salience of Authoritarianism over Theology". Journal of Islamic and Muslim Studies, vol. 1, no. 1, pp. 65-76.
Jinks, D., 2019. The Geneva Conventions and Enforcement of International Humanitarian Law. In Revisiting the Geneva Conventions: 1949-2019 (pp. 300-326). Brill Nijhoff.
Johns, L., 2019. The design of enforcement: Collective action and the enforcement of international law. Journal of Theoretical Politics, 31(4), pp.543-567.

Lynch, M. 2011."The Big Think behind the Arab Spring". Foreign Policy, Accessed at: foreignpolicy.com/2011/11/28/the-big-think-behind-the-arab-spring/# [Accessed May 25, 2020]

Shany, Y., 2017. Sources and the Enforcement of International Law. In The Oxford Handbook of the Sources of International Law.

Stephan, P.B., 2017. Enforcement of International Law. The Oxford Handbook of Law and Economics: Volume 3: Public Law and Legal Institutions, p.465.

INDEX

www.ingramcontent.com/pod-product-compliance
Lightning Source LLC
LaVergne TN
LVHW100246210926
848480LV00003B/836
* 9 7 8 1 9 1 3 1 8 8 0 0 9 *